PEDAGOGY OF A BELOVED COMMONS

POLIS: *Fordham Series in Urban Studies*
Edited by Daniel J. Monti, Saint Louis University

POLIS will address the questions of what makes a good community and how urban dwellers succeed and fail to live up to the idea that people from various backgrounds and levels of society can live together effectively, if not always congenially. The series is the province of no single discipline; we are searching for authors in fields as diverse as American studies, anthropology, history, political science, sociology, and urban studies who can write for both academic and informed lay audiences. Our objective is to celebrate and critically assess the customary ways in which urbanites make the world corrigible for themselves and the other kinds of people with whom they come into contact every day.

To this end, we will publish both book-length manuscripts and a series of "digital shorts" (e-books) focusing on case studies of groups, locales, and events that provide clues as to how urban people accomplish this delicate and exciting task. We expect to publish one or two books every year but a larger number of "digital shorts." The digital shorts will be 20,000 words or fewer and have a strong narrative voice.

# Pedagogy of a Beloved Commons

PURSUING DEMOCRACY'S PROMISE
THROUGH PLACE-BASED ACTIVISM

*Sharon Egretta Sutton*

FORDHAM UNIVERSITY PRESS    NEW YORK    2023

Fordham University Press has no responsibility for the persistence or accuracy of URLs for external or third-party Internet websites referred to in this publication and does not guarantee that any content on such websites is, or will remain, accurate or appropriate.

Fordham University Press also publishes its books in a variety of electronic formats. Some content that appears in print may not be available in electronic books.

Visit us online at www.fordhampress.com.

Library of Congress Cataloging-in-Publication Data available online at https://catalog.loc.gov.

Printed in the United States of America

25  24  23    5  4  3  2  1

First edition

# Contents

# Prologue

During the spring of 2003, I was on a mission to recoup my sense of self after being thoroughly smacked down by the dean of my college during the preceding year. You see, as the only female full professor in the architecture department and the only African American among the college's eighty faculty members, I had applied for the position of department chair, feeling confident that I was the most qualified and the most "it's-about-time" person for the job. But the dean not only picked a barely tenured man, he told me—with a straight face—that he had not picked me because I was an activist and not a scholar. After spending almost an entire year in a blue funk that George W. Bush's declaration of war in Iraq made even bluer, I contacted a colleague about attending one of her writing workshops in Tepoztián, Mexico. As I wrote to her in an email: "One of the reasons I want to do this consultation/workshop is that I have been wandering around in circles a bit lost since my great defeat last spring in trying to get the chair position. This summer is my time to MOVE ON!"

In this state of suspended animation, I answered my telephone on July 29 to hear a voice on the other end explain that he was a program officer at the Ford Foundation (correct, a program officer from the Ford Foundation called me!). At first, I thought that perhaps I had suffered brain damage during the dean's smackdown, but as the conversation proceeded, I realized that this person was quite familiar with my youth and community development work and wanted to know whether I would be interested in conducting research on this topic for the foundation. As he explained: "The foundation needs considerably more knowledge development on how to make service opportunities available to marginalized youth. This topic is particularly challenging because of cutbacks to Americorp. There will be fewer dollars but, should we regain federal support, what might programs look like that would be attractive to poor youth?" Barely able to contain myself, I said, calmly, that I would have a conference call with my colleagues and get back to him with a proposal outline.

Subsequent to that call (and a restorative sojourn at the Tepoztián writing workshop), I organized a leadership team of six activist scholars (yes, you can be both!) and community practitioners representing the fields of architecture, environmental psychology, landscape architecture, and social work. In what we envisioned as a multistage process that would eventually involve youth, we proposed to create a social justice framework for a transformative community service experience targeting low-income youth and to test it on a small selection of case studies. Agreeing to limit our research to justice-oriented, community-based organizations that were at least one year old, we drew upon our national networks to develop a list of 134 referrals to organizations that fit our criteria. With this selective list in hand and an extensive literature review underway, we planned three studies, to include two focus groups that would help us scope out the boundaries of our work and a survey that would allow us to be systematic in selecting a set of case studies, which we initially envisioned as the centerpiece of the research. However, as a result of monthly debates about our emerging social justice framework among ourselves and seven members of a reflection team, the survey became the centerpiece.

Ultimately, we administered a seven-page protocol containing sixty-six open- and closed-ended questions to the directors of eighty-eight organizations, which generated rich ideas that did not appear in the literature, especially related to the involvement of youth organizations in economic development. In 2005, as Bush was sworn in for his second term, we received additional funding to expand the survey analysis and facilitate a web-based discussion of our findings with a peer review group consisting of members of five of the participating organizations (including youth), four of their grant makers, and four activist scholars. In this analysis, the case studies were merely illustrative of the social justice framework that we developed empirically from the survey. Yet, as I approved each case study interview—a total of eighty-two with staff, youth, parents, volunteers, and board members—I marveled at the incredible work that young people were doing in their communities. In the wake of the racism revealed by Hurricane Katrina, each one renewed my faith in humanity and roused my interest in mining these data at some future point.

Meanwhile, our team anticipated getting additional funding to organize a paid youth advisory board that would guide us in convening about twenty of the most outstanding organizations to devise the next phase of the research. However, by the time we delivered our peer-reviewed monograph to the Ford Foundation, its funding priorities had shifted to align with the conservatism of the times, and Harris's social justice program area had vanished. With two dissertations and several scholarly publications underway, one of the co-investigators and I began searching for another foundation to pick up the project. By then it was 2007, and the fiftieth anniversary of that turbulent, black-is-beautiful year of 1968 was approaching. Among other revolutionary events that year was my recruitment from the orchestra pit of the Broadway musical, *Man of La Mancha*, to the Columbia University School of Architecture as one of the first members of a large cohort of ethnic minority students who would attend the school in the aftermath of a university-wide student rebellion. As the anniversary approached, I became obsessed with the circumstances of my recruitment—and with the many privileges I enjoy because of having received a free Ivy League education.

As the urge to uncover the story of my recruitment to Columbia grew, my interest in the rich case study data took a back seat. Besides, I told myself, I could uncover the recruitment story expeditiously and return to the data in a year or so. Hah! Uncovering the story and then learning how to tell it so any-one would want to read it took ten years, until 2017. Ironically, as I brought that work to fruition, Donald J. Trump moved into the White House and the prospects for achieving a just America were at an all-time low. Not only had the challenges to low-income communities intensified since the Ford study because of failing schools, high unemployment, over-policing and incarcera-tion, poverty, and housing and food insecurity, but climate crises that were un-imaginable in that era were ever present. As Black Lives Matter activists faced off against white supremacists determined to "save" their race, that old data began to call out to me from the innards of my computer. Remembering the hopefulness that the case study interviews had given me during earlier dark days, I became convinced that the incredible youth work they described could be reframed as a solutions-oriented approach to addressing the nation's snow-balling descent into chaos. So, I resolved to present the old interviews in a new and exciting way in order to contextualize ideas that are resurgent today.

After several false starts, I picked three organizations and decided to present them not as case studies, but as illustrative of a constellation of approaches to helping young people contribute to the revitalization of their deteriorating communities and also equipping them with the skills and habits of mind to work toward justice in America. I would take a critically conscious look at the intersection between youth development and community revitalization, hop-ing to attract a combination of people-oriented and place-oriented readers who were united in their commitment to realize the nation's democratic ideals. At the suggestion of one of the reviewers of my book proposal, I conducted a small number of follow-up interviews with persons who had been affiliated with the organizations at the time of the Ford study, which opened a rare opportunity to explore what it takes for an organization to become truly community embedded. As the nation and world remained locked down in the pandemic and Joe Biden prepared to reclaim the White House, I was privileged to learn, through the miracle of Zoom, about the remarkable trajectories that two of the three organizations had taken in the years following the Ford study. I was also gifted with the expertise of long-time staff members whose insights helped me refine the theoretical framework I had developed from the earlier interviews.

So you see, writing this book has been a long and arhythmic ride. It took me back to a time of extraordinary personal trauma that a program officer at the Ford Foundation unwittingly but mercifully repaired. Then, after an extended detour and just as Trump ascended to the presidency, I began a five-year odyssey to turn old and new data into a compelling manuscript. I continued my writing through his administration's untold assaults upon democracy, the callous murder of George Floyd and many others, worldwide protests against U.S. racism, a global pandemic, an attack upon the U.S. Capitol, devastating natural disasters, the declaration of Juneteenth as a national holiday, and the continuing assaults upon democracy despite a change in the presidency, each shockwave increasing my resolve to present the story of democracy's promise in a compelling way. The outcome—completed as I traverse my ninth decade on this planet—is my best shot at showing how community-based organizations can support marginalized youth in their continuing quest for justice.

Many people made the production of this book possible. Though I cannot name them due to the confidentiality agreements in my university contracts for conducting human subjects research, my first thanks go to the forty-nine interviewees whose insights form the narratives in this book, especially those who participated in lengthy interviews during the pandemic, when they were responding to crises in their communities. Thanks go to Fred Nachbaur, director at the Press, who stuck by me through all my false starts and unmet deadlines. Thanks go to Ben Kirshner and the anonymous reviewer whose thoughtful feedback on earlier drafts informed the final outcome. Thanks go to my former Parsons student, Aditi Nair, who conducted and transcribed the follow-up interviews during the pandemic, fitting the assignment into her regular work schedule. Thanks go to Layla White-Forrest for her lean and concise editorial services and to Lynne Elizabeth at New Village Press for recommending her. And thanks go to my former dean, Robert Kirkbride, who created a welcoming space for me at Parsons School of Constructed Environments, providing me with the structure and intellectual stimulation that I needed to undertake this work.

Thanks also go to the many people who made the Ford Foundation study possible, most notably Loren Harris, the program officer who provided intellectual guidance and financial support, not only for the original study but also for an expanded data analysis and web-based peer review. Thanks go to Susan P. Kemp, my long-time writing partner at the University of Washington, who authored a youth development matrix that served as the primary lens for assessing the organizations. Thanks go to co-investigators Lorraine Gutiérrez at the University of Michigan and Susan Saegert at the City University of New York, and to consultants Jeffrey Hou and Monica Oxford at the University of Washington and Michael Conn at Girl Scouts of the United States of America. Thanks go to the research associates and technical assistants who collected and analyzed data, the faculty, graduate students, and practitioners who participated on the reflection team, the youth-serving organizations and foundations that participated in the peer review, and the social justice scholars who recommended organizations and participated in the review.[1]

Finally, thanks go to all the research participants who generously contributed their time in completing lengthy surveys and interviews, and a special thanks to all the idealistic young people who engage in their communities and sustain hope that a better, more just world is possible.

## Note

1. For the names of everyone in this group, see Sharon E. Sutton et al., *Urban Youth Programs in America: A Study of Youth, Community, and Social Justice Conducted for the Ford Foundation* (Seattle: University of Washington Press, 2006), xii–xiii.

PEDAGOGY OF A BELOVED COMMONS

# Introduction

## The Need for a Place-Based Approach

In his 2017 farewell speech, President Barack Obama reminded Americans that:

> The work of democracy has always been hard, contentious, and sometimes bloody. For every two steps forward, it often feels we take one step back. But the long sweep of America has been defined by forward motion, a constant widening of our founding creed to embrace all, and not just some.[1]

Until now, the trajectory of American democracy has moved consistently toward greater enfranchisement and inclusion despite serious cracks in its corpus. Yet, many activist scholars, especially those who believe that education has veered away from its public mandate to create informed and compassionate citizens, warn of a serious disruption in this trajectory.[2] They worry about a system that prepares young people as productive workers in a global economy but does not help them discern the forces that have shaped their lives and will determine their futures.[3] They also worry that the nation's insidious concentration of wealth has elevated elite voices over everyone else's, making ludicrous the idea of rich and poor coming together around shared interests.[4] These scholars predict dire consequences for a divided nation that is unable to articulate and work toward a common good. In this book, I offer an approach to cultivating citizens who have the critical skills to challenge injustice, the courage to hold the rich and powerful accountable, and the compassion to advance, not just their own self-interest, but the health and well-being of their community and the planet.[5]

I propose—and have evidence—that such a citizenry develops by inhabiting and exercising agency in "the commons," a political and psychic space whose values are mapped out in physical space. I argue—and demonstrate—that the concreteness of three-dimensional public space provides a literal stage where young people can experiment with collective life, become more discerning about the forces that have shaped their community, and practice working toward just and inclusive futures. In short, this book offers a pathway for cultivating young people's citizenship through the sociospatial processes of making and remaking the public space of their neighborhoods.

I begin this introductory chapter with a brief synopsis of the challenges to democracy that low-income youth of color experience within their surroundings, including surging injustices related to the economy, housing, race, and the environment, along with a pervasive intolerance of difference—challenges that are worsened by a neoliberal education system. Then, to support my assertion that young people hold the hope for righting these challenges, I establish that they have always been, and still are, foot soldiers in the march toward justice. That is, I show that my contention is but a new take on the tried-and-true strategy of advancing democracy by engaging the chutzpah and idealism of youth. With this framing, I set forth a bold proposition about taking a local, place-based approach to strengthening young people's critical abilities to deliberate and take action to achieve a just world and explain the methods I used to investigate it. I add a footnote that, while the investigation focuses upon community-based organizations for marginalized youth, the proposition applies equally to privileged students who are being prepared as workers in the nation's increasingly corporatized colleges and universities—a footnote I will expand upon in the Epilogue. I end this Introduction with an overview of the book.

## Youth Experiencing Place-Based Injustices

Low-income youth of color have first-hand experience with the challenges to American democracy, especially its appalling levels of race-based economic inequality. The median household income of African American families hovers at about 60 percent of white families, their median household wealth is less than 10 percent of those families, and their poverty is multigenerational, which means that poor African American youth are unlikely to escape poverty as adults.[6] Economic inequality translates to housing inequality and the greater concentration of families of color in high-poverty neighborhoods in comparison to whites with similar incomes.[7] Covert and overt discriminatory practices by the government, industry, and individuals[8] have consigned impoverished youth of color to neighborhoods that lack adult models of educational and occupational success, access to libraries and bookstores, summer job opportunities, and above all, good-quality schools.[9] These youth attend under-resourced public schools and are at greater risk for dropping out even though their teachers tell them that they will need more than a high school education to meet today's employment requirement of at least some college exposure.[10]

While the wealthy use palatial abodes as safety deposit boxes for vast sums of investment income, the impoverished live in segregated, inferior, but costly housing and are under constant threat of displacement. For example, during the economic boom of the mid- and late-1990s, high-earning professionals began moving back to cities and driving up housing costs in some areas of the country that were beyond the wages that even two-worker, moderate-income families could earn.[11] Today, in most states, workers must earn fifteen to twenty dollars or more per hour to afford a modest two-bedroom apartment; consequently minimum-wage workers need to put in more than eighty hours per week in some states and 114 hours in California.[12] The gap in wages-to-housing costs means that low-wage workers, especially African Americans, experience high rates of housing poverty and homelessness. At 13 percent of the population, in 2020 they were 40 percent of the homeless and 52 percent of homeless families with children.[13] Further, one in nine underage youth were living on the street by themselves in order to escape domestic abuse, because they had been thrown out of their homes, or because they were unaccompanied immigrants. African American youth were much more likely than youth of other races to experience homelessness, mirroring racial disparities in school suspensions, incarceration, and foster care placement.[14]

Given that the world's largest prison system is disproportionately filled with young, male, Latino, and especially African American inmates,[15] low-income youth of color experienced the reality of racial disparities long before the public murder of George Floyd brought them into mainstream consciousness. For these youth, being targeted for the school-to-prison pipeline was but one liability of living in neighborhoods with unsafe streets, polluted air and water, inadequate health care facilities and green space, and a dearth of nutritious, affordable food.[16] The coronavirus pandemic has only accentuated these longstanding disparities, making apparent "the life-and-death difference between sheltering in commodious spaces and sheltering in crowded ones or in streets and other spaces unfit for human habitation."[17]

In addition to economic inequality and its associated effects, low-income youth of color experience the reality of environmental injustice. They are affected when the plentiful energy resources that sustain the nation's prosperity become "fragile, fleeting as well as deeply damaging and unequally distributed";[18] when the unfettered extraction of fossil fuels, minerals, and metal ores from the earth's surface combines with increasing growth and technological dependence to destroy more and more of the world's ecosystems; and when the overuse and misuse of resources by previous generations creates a world for them and their children of rolling blackouts, food and water shortages, oceans filled with plastic, denuded forests, and diminished biodiversity. Impoverished youth of color are especially affected when their communities across America and worldwide are excluded from decisions about the use of land, water, and other natural resources but are disproportionately affected by ill-conceived polluting projects that force their displacement or increase their exposure to natural disasters.

Finally, these youth bear the brunt of the intolerance that challenges American democracy. They suffer when well-to-do persons perceive them as an entirely different species that threatens the nation's values and prosperity; when teachers hold stereotypic notions of their criminal and disorderly behavior, low educational attainment, and reliance upon welfare;[19] when greater diversity as a result of immigration prompts greater racial segregation of their families and greater self-segregation of higher-status ones, who retreat into their guarded enclaves; when sociospatial stratification combined with economic injustice all but eliminates any possibility that people will encounter and learn to feel empathic toward them;[20] and when imposed and self-imposed segregation results in the "intense isolation of one group from another," fueling "misinformation and misunderstanding . . . [and the inability] to be tolerant, to work things through, to compromise."[21]

These serious challenges to young people's democratic existence are worsened by the warping of American culture to reflect neoliberal market rationale. An insidious corporate power has penetrated deep into the education system, supplanting "the goals of democratic citizenship with the preparation of human capital for industry."[22] All levels of the system have shifted from serving a public good to being a private investment in future earning capacity, a shift that devalues pedagogy "oriented toward developing capacities of reflection and insight, the acquisition of multiple literacies, and obtaining long, large views of the human and natural worlds."[23] Yet, this is precisely the pedagogy that impoverished youth of color need to combat the injustices and intolerance they face as democracy veers off course. Some youth development scholars have found that, while poverty can impede traditional forms of civic participation like campaigning for local politicians or volunteering at neighborhood clubs, it can also inspire resistance to injustice. They believe that such activism can build awareness of the public good as young people learn "to confront pressing community problems and shift from individual blame to a consciousness of root and systemic causes of personal problems."[24] These scholars believe that activism has the potential not only to ameliorate community problems but also to lighten the burdens wrought by injustice as young people develop a collective social imagination about what their world could be.[25]

In her analysis of current threats to democracy, the Chinese American activist Grace Lee Boggs foresaw the need for an altered means of cultivating citizenship. Having spent sixty-two of her one hundred years in Detroit advocating for civil rights, labor rights, women's rights, the environment, and other causes, she concluded that the depth of injustice arising from globalization required "new, more socially minded human beings and new, more participatory and place-based concepts of citizenship and democracy" than was previously the case.[26] Emboldened by Boggs's forward thinking, I propose that the participatory, place-based activism of disenfranchised youth can help refuel the nation's trajectory toward justice. Specifically, I propose that their engagement in place-based social change can cultivate compassionate citizenship and address the deepening injustices of the twenty-first century. After all, persons thirty years old and under have already made remarkable contributions to the work of democracy, sometimes paying with their lives. To support my reasoning, I offer an abstract of young people's activism in the following section.

## Youth as Democracy's Foot Soldiers

Activism among African American youth upsurged in the 1920s and 1930s when they revolted against conservative leaders at HBCUs and then lent their voices to campaigns against segregation, lynching, and job discrimination. Subsequently, in the late 1930s and 1940s, African American youth organized to support striking tobacco workers, establish youth labor clubs and citizenship schools, advocate for voting rights, and publicize racial violence, among many other efforts to achieve liberty and justice for all.[27] During the sit-in movement of the 1960s, African American youth and their white counterparts risked racial terrorism in the rural South to campaign for justice, going on freedom rides and setting up freedom schools, organizing communities to implement survival programs, buttressing high school and college protests, working with African American political parties, and building alliances with prisoners.[28] During the late 1960s, young men led bloody protests nationwide, setting draft cards afire and disrupting college campuses in a show of resistance to fighting an unjust war in Vietnam.[29] During the 1980s, multiracial groups of college students organized to demand an end to racial apartheid in South Africa and, during the 1990s, set up many more freedom schools and took a stand against violence and childhood hunger.

Youth activism continues today with demands for justice on several fronts. Three young women catalyzed the Black Lives Matter movement, the largest

African American–led protest campaign since the Civil Rights movement, so compelling that large corporations have adopted its hashtag. Young people have formed clubs in the nation's schools where heterosexual, gay, lesbian, and transgender youth collectively fight against homophobia and transphobia. And this generation has protested the siting of noxious materials in low-income communities of color and the construction of oil lines through sacred indigenous lands and waterways.

Since the 1920s, youth have wielded undisputed influence on countless issues from education and health care to the economy, environment, gender, guns, incarceration, and immigration.[30] And they typically espouse "the most progressive positions on education, criminal justice, environmental justice and the many other issues they confront."[31] Still, the climate justice movement stands out in the repertory of youth-led activism. Initially sparked by the 1992 Rio Earth Summit and recently galvanized by the sixteen-year-old Swedish climate activist, Greta Thunberg, this movement cuts across race/ethnicity, social class, and geography. To force political action on climate change, young people used the internet to organize coalitions in countries large and small, rich and poor, developed and developing.[32]

Evidence of the movement's effectiveness has been on display in massive global strikes in which unknown numbers of youth and their adult allies have mobilized in cities on every continent with "turnouts in the range of 100,000 and many more in the tens of thousands . . . tied together by a common if inchoate sense of rage."[33] The youth climate movement, which went digital during the Covid-19 lockdown, demonstrates the power of youth to bring worldwide attention to a global crisis that politicians have failed to confront or even denied. I joined their protest in New York City in September 2019, managing to maneuver through throngs of bodies between Foley Square and Battery Park by becoming the "caboose" on a train of African American girls linked by clutching the backpack of the person in front. It was exhilarating.

## A Place-Based Approach

Unquestionably, youth activists have been, and are, vital foot soldiers in the journey toward democracy, uniting with adult allies like myself to protest injustice,[34] sometimes peacefully, sometimes not. In recent years, they have demonstrated in support of legislation that moves America toward its creed of embracing all and not just some, including anti-racial-profiling legislation that protects people of color from unreasonable searches and seizures,[35] gun control legislation that curbs the access Floridians have to assault rifles,[36] and the proposed Development Relief and Education for Alien Minors (DREAM) Act that would allow undocumented youth and young adults who have attended U.S. schools to adjust their legal status.[37]

While I in no way want to diminish the importance of protest, I contend that the breakdown of American democracy calls for another kind of activism—a new, more engaged, and practical concept of activism that would help people adopt lifestyles that slow global warming and reverse runaway economic inequality and social alienation. Imagine if all the youth who took part in strikes to demand that politicians address global warming also began "maintaining neighborhood streets, planting community gardens, recycling waste, rehabbing houses, creating healthier school lunches, visiting and doing errands for the elderly, organizing neighborhood festivals, and painting public murals."[38] Imagine if tens of thousands of youth worked with their neighbors to set up cooperatively run aquaponic farms, bicycle repair shops, plastic recycling industries, solar energy installers, landscaping services, and other small business that would create meaningful work and help people attain more sustainable, less energy-consumptive lifestyles.

The place-based approach to activism that I envision has broad support in the writings of leading twentieth-century democracy proponents, including Dr. Martin Luther King Jr., who advocated turning ghetto neighborhoods into a "vast school" that combines education with collective action,[39] John Dewey, who advocated "practical engagement in the material world," which he believed would level class differences and help individuals cultivate a diversity of talents,[40] and especially Paolo Freire, who promoted critical dialogue and analysis as a means "to change inequitable social conditions" and whose work underlies the framing of this book.[41] To support my approach, I use historical and current data to demonstrate how participants in community-based, youth-serving organizations acquired an understanding of injustice and the sense of efficacy that allowed them to tackle problems in their surroundings.

The place-based approach I envision also adopts Dr. King's advocacy of unconditional love as "the unifying principle of life"—an affinity I have expressed through the book's title. In his final call for peaceful coexistence, he wrote: "Love is the key that unlocks the door" to becoming one world community.[42] As challenges deepen that will require consensus and even material sacrifice, the organizations I present in these pages take on an intriguing significance. They illustrate a hands-on engagement with the material world that can help youth negotiate across difference and unlock social connectedness within contexts of austerity. I do not offer a blueprint for developing such organizations but rather use participants' lived experiences to define the dimensions of an aspirational framework for place-based, youth-led transformation.

Though I illustrate the framework with three youth-serving organizations in low-income communities of color, I believe that it is applicable to any situation in which educators and mentors want to heighten young people's agency to bring about social change. Indeed, over the years, I have employed aspects of the framework in my classes with privileged, mostly white professional students despite criticism from colleagues who caution that my job is to prepare them for success in the "real" (and unjust) world. But I save this topic for the Epilogue.

## An Aspirational Framework

The ideal of democracy is that "the people" or their representatives participate in dispensing the wealth of a nation, but the "shameless reach for ever greater riches and power by the already very rich and powerful" means that the poor can no longer participate equally in decisions that affect their lives.[43] As the power of money and big business increasingly shape electoral politics,[44] the organizations that I present herein demonstrate how youth can learn to resist their loss of political agency through hands-on action in "the commons" of their neighborhoods. In pre-industrial times, the commons consisted of the pastures that lay beyond individual possessions and thresholds and that provided for the subsistence of households. They were necessary for a community's survival and, in particular, guaranteed poor people's access to life-sustaining environmental resources like fields, forests, and rivers.[45] In early-modern England, notions of the commons also encompassed the idea of a political community that formed to secure the public good. These early notions established the commons as both the collective resources of a community and their governance. Ideally, it was the space that allowed citizens "to find, constitute, and sustain themselves and contribute to societal and individual flourishing."[46] However, enclosure of the commons redefined these resources as scarce commodities, to be reserved for "optimal use in the production of goods and the provision of professional care."[47]

In the mid-thirties, Dewey argued that poor people's segregation in slums isolated them from the direct cultural exchange of ideas that coexistence requires, thereby compromising democracy and making culture "the private possession of a small number of individuals."[48] He identified economic justice and participatory parity as "the heart of public life and deliberative democracy."[49] More than a generation later, Dr. King went further, calling for "eternal opposition to poverty, racism, and militarism" and envisioning a "beloved community" where all persons are interconnected, respected, and bound by the transformative power of love.[50] He hoped that this interconnected community would somehow learn to share the resources of a global commons despite vast differences in ideas, culture, and interests.

Today, as the price tag for purchasing scarce commodities continues to climb into the stratosphere, the space for participating in public life likewise continues to disappear, leaving poor people not only lacking the resources themselves but also lacking the possibility for exercising their democratic right to have a voice in decisions that affect their lives. The approach to place-based citizenship that I am advocating seeks to help poor people regain a measure of self-determination and local control over the commons, conceptualized as the space where they simultaneously experience collective life and participate in self-determining its nature. Indeed, the public domain only becomes a commons when individuals and groups participate in its governance.[51]

In claiming that youth can resist their loss of political agency through hands-on actions, I have amplified Dewey's notion and defined the neighborhood commons both as a space of shared resources and as a space of democratic participation. I contend that the exercise of voice therein can help change the racial stereotypes that threaten the fundamental dignity of youth of color[52] and suggest that, paradoxically, the disinvested neighborhoods where youth "witness daily symbolic reminders of their abandonment and marginal status"[53] in fact can serve as a call to action.[54] Though I eventually refine this proposition by analyzing the activism of the youth who populate these pages, I begin by considering the commons of their neighborhoods as the space where they experienced tangible infrastructure (like housing, streets, and food) and intangible infrastructure (like culture, safety, and beauty), and as the space where these politically active citizens came together to imagine and create their collective life. I propose a pedagogy—in particular, the notion of "critical place-making" that I explain shortly—that can help them become active change agents in securing the actual infrastructure that their surroundings lack, while simultaneously elevating their right to participate in self-determining their own future and the future of their community and nation.

## Critical Pedagogy

I have anchored my approach to place-based activism in the work of Paolo Freire—work I first encountered in doctoral school and have used as a guide throughout my academic career. Advancing what educators now refer to as critical pedagogy, Freire rejected a "banking" concept of education that dehumanizes students as passive collectors of information. In his seminal *Pedagogy of the Oppressed*, first published in English in 1970, he reacted to education that indoctrinates students to adapt to oppression, asserting that "knowledge emerges only through invention and re-invention, through the restless, impatient, continuing, hopeful inquiry human beings pursue in the world, with the world, and with each other."[55] Freire identified critical consciousness (*conscientização*) as the key to teaching Brazilian peasants to read and write,[56] a revolutionary notion that landed him in prison and then in exile. He believed that all human beings, no matter their level of literacy, were capable of joining with others to look analytically at their world, thereby developing a new self-awareness and sense of dignity and hope. Though not all scholars theorize critical pedagogy as having three distinct dimensions, I do, considering respectively cognitive, attitudinal, and behavioral mechanisms for developing critical awareness, achieving a sense of collective agency, and taking collective action.

Drawing from the literature, I define the cognitive dimension of critical pedagogy, critical awareness, as young people engaging with peers in deeply co-investigative dialogue about their personal experiences in order to understand the interlocking societal systems that perpetuate the injustices in their lives.[57] A key concept in theories of critical consciousness, critical awareness involves thinking analytically, detecting hidden assumptions and beliefs, and identifying the historical roots of community problems.[58] It gives young people the mindset to join forces and transform oppressive social structures;[59] only when they understand that injustice is not an individual fault line but a systemic one can they begin to transform it.[60]

I define the attitudinal dimension, collective agency, as young people perceiving a common purpose and becoming confident that they can work together to change their circumstances. Omitted by some scholars of critical consciousness, it is about developing the wherewithal to effect change. When young people see that others share their individual experiences, both positive and negative, they are positioned to work as a group to build collective power.[61] To turn these societal critiques into creative action, they need safe spaces where they can "test new avenues of struggle and resistance" with their peers.[62] Collective agency results from increasing young people's access to information, resources, and skills while also connecting them to social capital within the surrounding community, thereby motivating and channeling their energy toward action.[63]

I define the behavioral dimension of critical pedagogy, collective action, as young people working together to change unjust conditions through sociopolitical activism. It results from a reiterative process of creating, revising, and acting upon knowledge together with others, a process that Freire referred to as "praxis: reflection and action upon the world in order to transform it."[64] Through praxis, young people learn to perceive injustice not as fixed, but as a constraint that they can transform.[65] The shift from victimization to action comes about when they identify with peers, recognize the injustices they have experienced, and then perceive their collective power to transform them.[66]

Though Freire believed that tangible change did not occur without action, he framed the idea broadly to encompass dialogue and even critical reflection.[67]

Freire's method, which educators have successfully transferred to many different struggles for justice worldwide, generates a collective understanding of inequality. It validates young people's experiential knowledge and encourages them to "name, critique, and create knowledge about reality in a continual process of reconsidering what they think based on what they learn and hear from each other and from other sources."[68] By sharing their lived experiences, young people develop unconventional ways of thinking and generate the collective capacity to take action. Critical pedagogy cultivates young people who can diagnose the injustices in their world and then turn their thoughts into transformative action. Figure 1 sums up the reiterative dimensions of critical pedagogy.

As suggested earlier, I have additionally anchored this book in ideas put forth by Grace Lee Boggs. Whereas Freire emphasized conscientization as the corrective for structural oppression, Boggs was all about action, which initially engaged her in nonviolent protests. However, as Detroit continued its devastating decline despite numerous top-down actions, she and her autoworker husband,

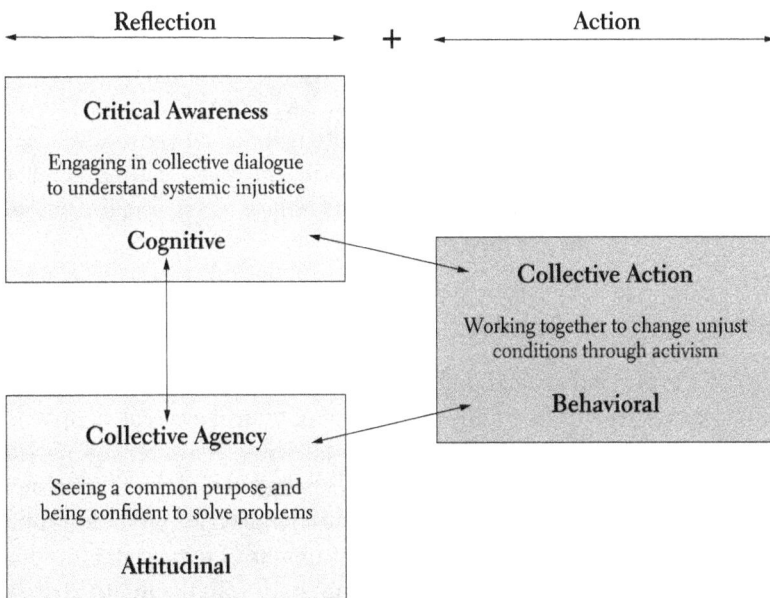

Figure 1. Dimensions of Critical Pedagogy
Image credit: Sharon Egretta Sutton, 2023

James, began to envision a new kind of involvement.[69] They imagined young people engaging in community building—planting gardens, recycling waste, organizing neighborhood festivals, rehabbing houses, painting murals—with the same fervor that they had engaged in protesting segregation during the Civil Rights movement. A year before Jimmie's death in 1993, the duo founded Detroit Summer, a multicultural, intergenerational youth program that I encountered back then as a University of Michigan professor of architecture and urban planning. The program combined hands-on work with intergenerational dialogue about how to rebuild a post-industrial Detroit, and it continues today, tapping the creative energies of Detroit teenagers who are joined by college students from all over the country. These youth are seeking to fashion a new city with new ways of contributing to it, which Boggs alternately referred to as "community activism" and "community-building activism."[70]

Boggs believed that hands-on activism within geographically bounded localities could provide a counterforce to global capitalism, which displaces people and destroys the localities that lie in its path of development. By uniting varied constituencies around their experiences of the immediate environment, she believed that they would be able to discover mutual concerns and situate race, gender, and class struggles within the specificity of place.[71] Borrowing from Boggs, I have grounded Freire's methodology in place—in locality—where youth experience the challenges that threaten democracy and where they can engage in small but persistent actions to transform them while also exercising their right to participate. Though global capitalism has turned place into a commodity to be sold to the highest bidder, it remains a dynamic backdrop to life, giving meaning to social relationships, reconnecting people with nature,[72] and providing a literal stage for rehearsing new societal structures. Borrowing from Dr. King, I contend that place is the locality of a beloved community where young people can somehow learn to coexist, despite their differences.

## Dimensions of Place-Based Activism

To create a grounded critical pedagogy that can enhance the commons of communities, I refocus its cognitive dimension, critical awareness, upon engaging youth in structured dialogue about the history, culture, and physical fabric of their neighborhoods so they can understand their strengths and shortcomings and the actions that others have undertaken to promote positive change; I refer to this dimension as "place awareness." I refocus its attitudinal dimension, collective agency, upon equipping youth with the information, resources, skills, and social capital they need to undertake their own actions, or what I refer to as "place agency." I refocus its behavioral dimension, collective

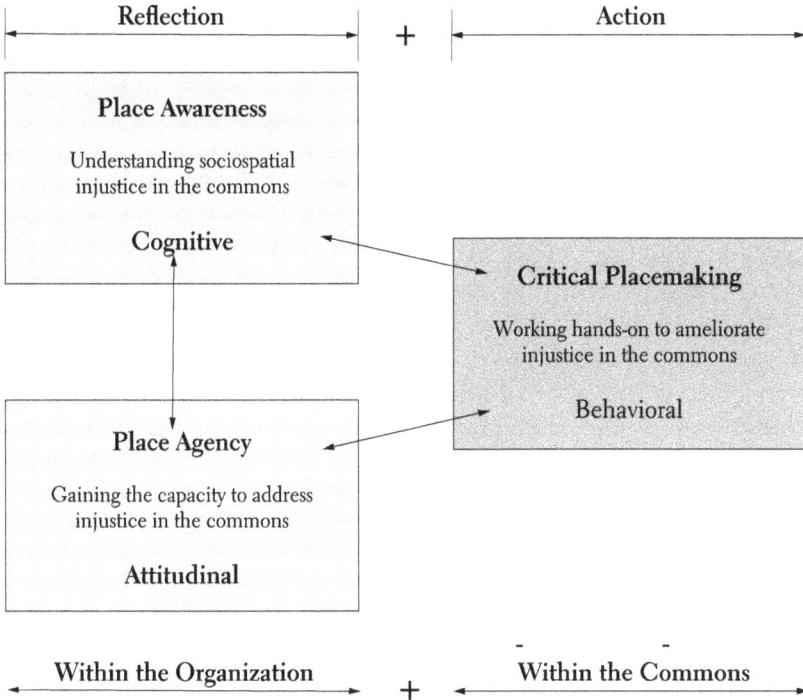

Figure 2. Dimensions of Place-Based Activism
Image credit: Sharon Egretta Sutton, 2023

action, upon working hands-on to ameliorate systemic injustice in the commons of their communities, or what I refer to as "critical placemaking," defined as the participatory process of transforming "racialized, under-resourced, and politically disenfranchised surroundings."[73] Because critical placemaking involves debate about living together and sharing resources, it "fosters civic competence and extends the idea of citizenship."[74]

Figure 2 sums up the dimensions of place-based activism, showing that, when young people develop place awareness and place agency within the safety of community-based organizations, they can engage in critical placemaking in the commons that helps transform the injustices they experience there, including disenfranchisement from decision-making processes.

## Realms of Place-Based Activism

Though activism takes myriad forms, place-based activism is the change-oriented activity that affects people/place relations within the commons, which I conceptualize as occurring within three distinct realms: emotional, physical, and intellectual. Within the emotional realm, youth explore how they feel about their neighborhoods and acquire the tools to turn their feelings into action. This form of activism engages them in reimagining their surroundings as places of abundance, not necessarily in material terms but in their cultural and social relationships. It strengthens those relationships, helping young people develop empathy and a sense of solidarity while shaping their identities and values as they recreate the meaning of the commons by "being within it, participating in its activities, and telling stories about it."[75] When teenagers engage in the emotional realm of activism, which likely involves the arts, their very presence in the commons—so often dissuaded both in terms of their use of its infrastructure and their participation in decisions that control it—injects an element of surprise and thus encourages creativity. The playfulness that this realm of activism engenders nudges adults out of sedimented, overly practical ways of thinking,[76] which can help community members build bridges not only across their many lines of difference, "but also between harsh realities and imagined possibilities."[77]

Within the physical realm of place-based activism, youth come together to make "tangible improvements in untenable sociospatial conditions."[78] This form of activism is what Ivan Illich referred to as the uniquely human act of "dwelling"—of making the world habitable by physically inhabiting it.[79] Young people inhabit their neighborhoods when they build small structures and playgrounds, cultivate fallow land and plant gardens, clean up rivers and school bathrooms, help the elderly and homeless, map neighborhood assets, and document neighborhood history.[80] Because of its concrete nature, the commons provides a literal stage where youth can work collaboratively with peers and community members to address such practical problems as trash-filled vacant lots, polluted rivers, unsafe streets, and lack of affordable housing, healthy food, and meaningful employment. By addressing pressing community problems hands-on, young people are able to enhance individual and community well-being while inserting their voices into the decision-making process.[81]

Within the intellectual realm of place-based activism, youth build the habits of mind they need to decide how they want to live, and then they work collectively to achieve that ideal. The thought processes that occur within this realm entail naming and analyzing problems, envisioning something better, and fashioning possibility out of the impossible; they entail experimentation and seeing connections; and they require planning, persistence, and improvisation. In addition to changing a young person's outlook on life, activism within the intellectual realm can change the appearance or functioning of space, or it can change the policies that govern the design and use of space, which requires a socially critical understanding of how systems work.[82] Young people bring about change through this form of activism by conducting research into a given system and then using it to plan actions and organize coalitions of individuals and organizations. Activism within this realm helps young people develop the place agency "to be in, act on, or exert control over a desired part of the built and natural environment,"[83] and it helps them develop the knowledge to advocate for change in that environment.

I do not define these realms as mutually exclusive but as primary arenas of endeavor. As you will soon see, they help me conceptualize the organizations that I present in this book in terms of their dominant approach to engaging young people in community change. In actuality, each organization blended realms, and I later argue that all three are needed for a fully animated commons.

## Research Methods

To support my proposition, I draw from a national study of community-based youth-serving organizations that I began the year Senator John Kerry ran for president of the United States and Senator Barack Obama delivered the keynote address at the Democratic National Convention, a time before a slew of crises, including runaway racism, devastating natural disasters, a pandemic, over-the-top political divisiveness, and desecration of the U.S. Capitol by white supremacists, upended America and made the book's exploration even more relevant. From the six case studies that were part of the historical research, I selected three organizations that were most involved in placemaking. I present them not as case studies but as exemplars, framing each as a distinct realm of the place-based activism I wish to advance. As you will see, the study has extraordinary currency today not only because all three organizations are grounded in the teachings of Freire, who died before the dawn of the twenty-first century but whose groundbreaking ideas continue to influence progressive educators and grassroots organizers worldwide,[84] but also because all three have stood the test of time for many years. To strengthen my framing, I add a follow-up study that I conducted of the three organizations at the height of the country's 2020 meltdown. You will learn about both studies and the three organizations in the next section.

### A 2004–2005 Study

The exemplar organizations were part of a Ford Foundation–funded study that I directed in 2004–2005 with a team of three co-investigators, two consultants, and twenty graduate research assistants (GRAs) from the University of

Washington, University of Michigan, City University of New York, and Girls Scouts of the United States of America. Our charge was to identify the characteristics of American out-of-school programs that successfully involved older low-income youth of color in community service. After an extensive scan of the literature and consultations with a wide-ranging network of academics and practitioners, we established selection criteria that allowed us to eliminate sports organizations and short-term activities such as summer camps. Instead, we identified eighty-eight community-based, justice-oriented organizations with proven longevity: most were over five years old, and some reached to over ten years. Subsequent to exploratory focus groups with two organizations, the GRAs administered a structured telephone survey of all eighty-eight directors to ascertain an organization's values, context, pedagogy, and self-reported outcomes, subjecting the data to both quantitative and qualitative analyses.[85]

Among the 237 variables that resulted from the survey analyses was a measure, "youth development philosophy," that reflected an organization's degree of "commitment to youth and community change through intergenerational collaboration," as reflected in its mission statement. "Not surprisingly, given the purposive nature of the sample, most organizations scored at the transformative end of this scale (an average of 4.08 out of 5.0)."[86] This measure, along with location, pedagogy, and availability, guided us in identifying (from among the first fifty organizations surveyed) six of the most transformative organizations for more in-depth study. The GRAs then administered eighty-two telephone and face-to-face interviews with the staff, youth, parents, volunteers, and board members of those organizations, using protocols that mirrored the survey but were totally opened-ended and adapted for each constituency. From those six organizations I selected three for this book that were the most involved in community-building, had high youth development philosophy scores, and (the deciding factor) illustrated a distinct realm of place-based activism, as I will explain shortly. They include Storyhouse Theatre Company in Southwest Detroit, Michigan, Hoʻoulu ʻŌpio Farms in Waiʻanae, Hawaiʻi, and Academe in Harlem, New York.

Though the book draws from the Ford study data set, the analysis I present here is entirely different, conducted for a different purpose than was originally intended. Whereas the initial analysis mapped out the parameters of beneficial community service experiences for underserved youth in order to target philanthropic support, this analysis views the organizations through the aspirational framework for place-based activism proposed herein. For this purpose, I created new transcripts, drawing from a total of forty interviews with constituents of the three selected organizations and including only those responses that related to the dimensions of the framework. These excerpted transcripts comprise what I refer to as the 2004–2005 study.

## A 2020–2021 Study

To strengthen the aspirational framework that I created from the 2004–2005 study, I worked with my research assistant (RA) at The New School in New York City to conduct a follow-up study. Our work, which took place at the end of 2020 and beginning of 2021, was greatly hampered by the ongoing racial, health, and political crises of that time. Nevertheless, she was able to conduct open-ended interviews via Zoom with a founding director at both Ho'oulu 'Ōpio and Academe and with three staff members at each organization who were familiar with its operations around 2004–2005. The resulting 2020–2021 transcripts for Ho'oulu 'Ōpio and Academe are roughly the same length as the ones I created for the 2004–2005 study. Because Storyhouse had a change in leadership, my RA was only able to do a single abbreviated interview with the new executive director, which yielded a much shorter transcript than the 2004–2005 study.

Whereas the interview protocol for the Ford study was unrelated to this book's aspirational framework, the protocol for the follow-up study addressed it head-on. In addition to questions about the interviewees, my RA asked five open-ended questions: four that called for a then/now comparison of strengths and shortcomings and the three dimensions of the framework, and a fifth about the future. I was honored to have the expert insights of people who have had a relationship with Ho'oulu 'Ōpio and Academe for many years—some for half their lives—and I was especially honored by their gift of time, given that both organizations were heavily involved in responding to the ongoing crises. In all, my RA administered nine interviews lasting a total of ten hours.[87] I use these data to strengthen my theorizing of the aspirational framework and to show the remarkable durability and contributions of these community-embedded organizations.

### Three Exemplar Organizations

As noted previously, the three exemplar organizations—presented using pseud-onyms as required by the participating institutional review boards—not only demonstrate the dimensions of critical pedagogy, but they also illuminate distinct realms of place-based activism. Accordingly, you learn about its emotional realm through Storyhouse, its physical realm through Ho'oulu 'Ōpio, and its intellectual realm through Academe. Please keep in mind that I am not pre-senting case studies of these organizations; rather I am using the lived experi-ences in each one to illustrate its unique contributions to a framework for place-based activism.

*Storyhouse Theatre Company as Illustrative of Activism's Emotional Realm*
Storyhouse Theatre Company, a community arts organization that began thirty-two years ago in Southwest Detroit, Michigan, introduces you to activism's emotional realm. The company used community problems as scripts for its performances, engaging company members and audiences in querying their values in an entertaining, artful manner; it incorporated talkbacks that involved the participants in reimagining the city's turbulence; and it developed empathy and tolerance as company members learned to trust one another enough to get out of scenes that went in unexpected directions. At the same time, Storyhouse developed competencies that the youth had been denied in heavily policed, under-resourced schools, thus helping them reshape the negative identities that had sapped their individual and collective confidence.

Storyhouse's dramatic enactments built bridges between Detroit's harsh realities and its possible futures, providing a public stage for company members and audiences to engage in a process of "social dreaming" and create a collective vision of their preferred future.[88] Performances allowed them to rehearse their sense of optimism and hope about attaining better tomorrows. They enhanced both the quality of the city's commons and the relationships of people to it, helping company members and audiences co-create joyful narratives that countered the city's negative stereotypes, celebrated its icons and natural resources, and even gave voice to its gang members. The 2020–2021 study revealed that Storyhouse's work was disrupted several years ago by a crisis of funding and leadership, but it has survived and remains true to its mission; it offers important lessons about the contradictions and tensions that exist within justice-oriented organizations and the choices they make to endure. The 2020–2021 interview affirmed that the expressiveness of drama can ignite young people's passions for making a difference in the commons. Though Storyhouse engaged in all three dimensions of critical pedagogy, it excelled in the attitudinal dimension, tapping into the imaginations of company members and audiences and helping them explore preferred futures for a city where cultural wealth and material poverty coincide. For the same reasons, it exemplifies place-based activism's emotional realm.

*Hoʻoulu ʻŌpio Farms as Illustrative of Activism's Physical Realm*
Hoʻoulu ʻŌpio Farms, an organic farming social enterprise that began twenty-two years ago in Waiʻanae, Hawaiʻi, introduces you to activism's physical realm. The organization was dedicated to reclaiming ancestral agricultural knowledge on an island where poverty restricted access to a nutritious diet for about one-third of the island's largest Native Hawaiian community. It organized local

advisers and partners to create an enterprise that offered interns a labor-intensive experience of "working in the mud" to grow crops without using pesticides or fertilizers; it taught them such soil-management techniques as growing cover crops, applying compost, and rotating crops and then charged them with teaching these techniques to middle and high school students; and it helped Wai'anae residents adopt healthier eating habits, modeled sustainable practices to local farmers, and increased the social bonds within families.

Ho'oulu 'Ōpio helped the interns reinhabit the lands that colonialism had stolen by drawing upon ancestral concepts that combined *aloha 'āina* (love of the land), *ohana* (devotion to family and community), and *kuleana* (responsibility). It used *malama 'āina* (care for the land) as a literal stage where the interns worked collaboratively with one another and with their families to recreate sustainable people-place relationships. The 2020–2021 study revealed a hugely expanded operation, both agriculturally and educationally. Ho'oulu 'Ōpio has liberated hundreds of acres of land; it is run by credentialed young leaders who have been involved with the organization since they were teenagers and are now brilliant spokespersons for activism's physical realm. The 2020–2021 interviewees affirmed that, by using their hands to care for place, young people can achieve their right to self-determine life-sustaining resources in the commons. Though Ho'oulu 'Ōpio engaged in all three dimensions of critical pedagogy, it excelled in the behavioral dimension, engaging the interns and apprentices in working hands-on in the mud to grow food, eat well, and reinhabit the land. As such, it is illustrative of place-based activism's physical realm.

### Academe as Illustrative of Activism's Intellectual Realm

Academe, an organization founded twenty-eight years ago in Harlem, New York, introduces you to activism's intellectual realm. To achieve its mission of developing African American and Latinx youth as critical thinkers and leaders, Academe featured a gender-specific program that created a space-apart for chapter members to articulate a vision of the life they wanted and then to work responsibly to achieve it. It also offered a mixed-gender program that was deeply grounded within the Harlem locality and that involved the members in carrying out hands-on actions and organizing or joining large coalitions to campaign for policy changes.

By conducting community research, mapping neighborhood assets, and writing reports to document the policies that produced housing inequity, the members seized control of the community narrative related to displacement and gentrification. Academe additionally organized intergenerational conversations with long-time residents, positioning them alternatively as teachers and students in order to advance a more participative, self-determining community. The 2020–2021 study revealed that Academe has expanded to become a nationally recognized leader in balancing individual youth development with community revitalization. The organization benefits from dedicated staff and alumni who grew up in Academe, went on to acquire academic or professional credentials, and are now brilliant spokespersons for activism's intellectual realm. The 2020–2021 interviews affirmed that, as part of a new intelligentsia, the young people at Academe are able to co-create a shared story within Harlem's storied history. Through their political activism and cultural expressiveness, they are creating a commons that disrupts negative narratives of themselves and their community. Though Academe engaged in all three dimensions of critical pedagogy, it excelled in the cognitive dimension, engaging young people as scholars who could name and analyze problems, articulate public policy, and teach and organize others to join their efforts. For the same reasons, it exemplifies place-based activism's intellectual realm.

Figure 3 illustrates the unique ways that Storyhouse, Hoʻoulu ʻŌpio, and Academe contributed to the three realms of place-based activism.

## Overview of the Book

In the Prologue, I described how this project began and why it is only now coming to fruition, serendipitously at a moment that calls out for social imagination. In this Introduction, I summarized the threats to democracy that marginalized youth experience, acknowledged their achievements as democracy's foot soldiers, and pointed to the need for a new, solutions-oriented approach to citizenship. I laid out an aspirational framework and described my research methods, including briefly introducing the three organizations that I will use to explore the framework. I have organized the main body of the book into three parts, one for each organization.

Additionally, I have divided each part into four comparable sections. In the first section, I combine archival sources with the interviews to provide the historical context of the organization and overview of its programs, staffing, and setting. In the second, I construct a narrative using the 2004–2005 interviews to present the organization's lived experience of critical pedagogy. In the third, I construct a similar narrative using the 2020–2021 interviews. In the fourth, I use the literature to theorize both narratives as they speak to a specific approach to critical pedagogy and to a given realm of place-based activism (except in the case of Storyhouse, where I reflect upon the crisis the organization encoun-

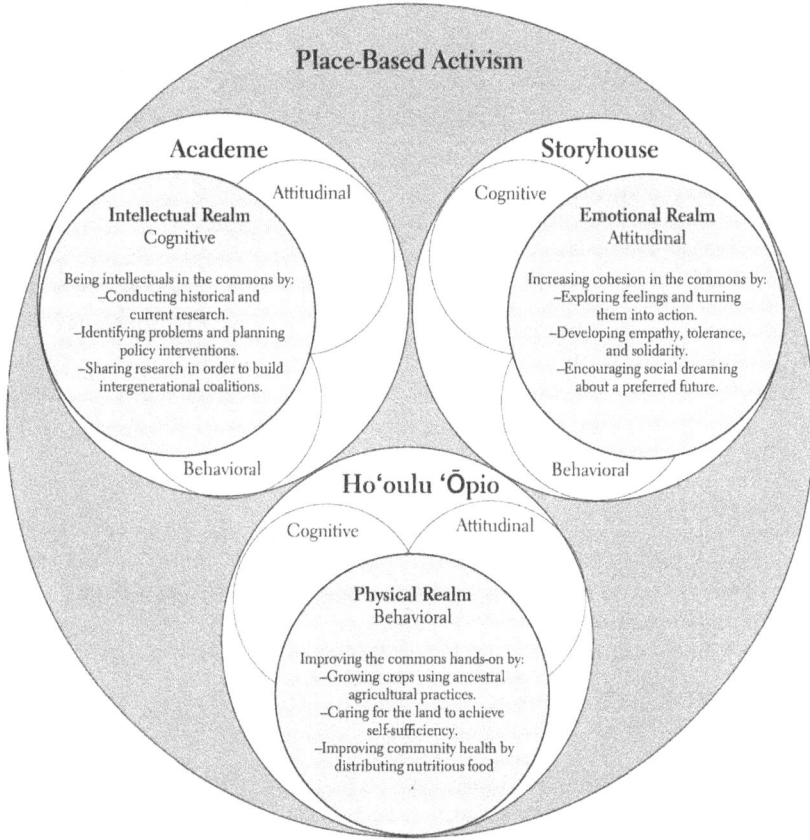

Figure 3. Realms of Place-Based Activism
Image credit: Sharon Egretta Sutton, 2023

tered), and I conclude with lessons learned from the organization about place-based activism.

I have bookended this Introduction with a Conclusions where I use my analysis of the three exemplars to set forth a refined theoretical framework; it considers the kind of organizations that can advance place-based activism, the commons that they can help reimagine, and the pedagogy that they can draw upon to call forth the full potential of young people. In addition, I consider how these organizations can sustain themselves, especially given their funding difficulties, and whether they have altered the challenges to American democracy that I expounded at the beginning of the Introduction. I end the Conclusions by synthesizing the critical placemaking strategies that can help reboot America's trajectory toward democracy. In the Epilogue, I shift my focus from youth and community-based organizations to universities where students and faculty in the community development fields have been organizing for change since George Floyd's murder, proposing that the pedagogy offered herein can help them create more community-engaged, non-racist institutions.

## How to Read This Book

Should you decide to read this book selectively, you should know that I have written each of the three parts to stand on its own as an independent whole, but you need to read (or assign) an entire part in order to understand each organization's story. Another option would be to combine this Introduction with any one of the parts or to combine it with the Conclusions. Of course, I hope that you will read the entire book cover to cover.

## Notes

1. "Read the Full Transcript of President Obama's Farewell Speech," *Los Angeles Times*, January 10, 2017, https://www.latimes.com/politics/la-pol-obama-farewell -speech-transcript-20170110-story.html.

2. Richard Neumann, "American Democracy at Risk," *Phi Delta Kappan* 89, no. 5 (January 2008): 331, https://www.jstor.org/stable/20442493.

3. Wendy Brown, "The End of Educated Democracy," *Representations* 116, no. 1 (Fall 2011): 19–41.

4. Brown, "End of Educated Democracy."

5. These dimensions of educating for critically informed citizenship blend two sources: Henry A. Giroux, "Introduction," in *On Critical Pedagogy* (New York: Bloomsbury, 2020), http://ebookcentral.proquest.com/lib/washington/detail.action ?docID=5997010; and Neumann, "American Democracy at Risk," 328–39.

6. Richard Rothstein, *The Color of Law: A Forgotten History of How Our Government Segregated America*, Kindle ed. (New York and London: Liveright, 2017).

7. Joint Center for Housing Studies of Harvard University, "The State of the Nation's Housing 2020" (Cambridge: Mass.: Harvard Graduate School of Design / Harvard Kennedy School, 2020), https://www.jchs.harvard.edu/sites/default /files/reports/files/Harvard_JCHS_The_State_of_the_Nations_Housing_2020 _Report_Revised_120720.pdf.

8. Ruby Mendenhall, "The Political Economy of Black Housing: From the Housing Crisis of the Great Migrations to the Subprime Mortgage Crisis," *Black Scholar* 40, no. 1 (Spring 2010): 20–37, https://www.jstor.org/stable/41163903.

9. Rothstein, *Color of Law*.

10. Ben Kirshner, "Introduction," in *Youth Activism in an Era of Education Inequality*, Kindle ed. (New York and London: New York University Press, 2015), 1–19.

11. Chris Benner and Manuel Pastor, *Equity, Growth, and Community: What the Nation Can Learn from America's Metro Areas* (Los Angeles: University of California Press, 2015).

12. "Out of Reach 2020," Washington, D.C.: National Low-Income Housing Coalition, 2020, https://reports.nlihc.org/oor.

13. Joint Center for Housing Studies of Harvard University, "State of the Nation's Housing 2020."

14. Matthew H. Morton et al., "Prevalence and Correlates of Youth Homelessness in the United States," *Journal of Adolescent Health* 62 (2018): 14–21, https://www.jahonline.org/action/showPdf?pii=S1054-139X%2817%2930503-7.

15. Michelle Alexander, *The New Jim Crow: Mass Incarceration in the Age of Colorblindness*, Kindle ed. (2010; repr. New York: New Press, 2012).

16. Linda Villarosa, "'A Terrible Price': The Deadly Racial Disparities of Covid-19 in America," *New York Times*, April 29, 2020, https://www.nytimes.com/2020/04/29/magazine/racial-disparities-covid-19.html.

17. Sharon Egretta Sutton, "Sharon Sutton: Envisioning a Communitarian World House," *Architect Magazine*, June 5, 2020, https://www.architectmagazine.com/practice/sharon-sutton-envisioning-a-communitarian-world-house_o.

18. Paul Chatterton, *Unlocking Sustainable Cities: A Manifesto for Real Change* (London: Pluto, 2019), 41.

19. Jon Bannister and Ade Kearns, "The Function and Foundations of Urban Tolerance: Encountering and Engaging with Difference in the City," *Urban Studies* 50, no. 13 (October 2013): 2,700–2,717, https://www.jstor.org/stable/10.2307/26145612.

20. Bannister and Kearns, "Function and Foundations of Urban Tolerance."

21. William W. Goldsmith, "From the Metropolis to Globalization: The Dialectics of Race and Urban Form," in *Globalizing Cities: A New Spatial Order*, ed. Peter Marcuse and Ronald van Kempen (Oxford: Blackwell, 2000), 41.

22. Neumann, "American Democracy at Risk," 331, referring to Henry A. Giroux, *America on the Edge: Henry Giroux on Politics, Culture, and Education*. (New York: Palgrave Macmillan, 2006).

23. Brown, "End of Educated Democracy," 24.

24. Shawn A. Ginwright, "Peace Out to Revolution! Activism among African American Youth: An Argument for Radical Healing," *Young* 18, no 1 (2010): 82.

25. Kris D. Gutiérrez et al., "Youth as Historical Actors in the Production of Possible Futures," *Mind, Culture, and Activity* 26, no. 4 (2019): 291–308, https://doi.org/10.1080/10749039.2019.1652327.

26. Grace Lee Boggs with Scott Kurashige, *The Next American Revolution: Sustainable Activism for the Twenty-First Century*, Foreword by Danny Glover, Afterword with Immanuel Wallerstein, Kindle ed. (Berkeley, Los Angeles, and London: University of California Press, 2011), Location 151.

27. Sekou Franklin, "Black Youth Activism and the Reconstruction of America: Leaders, Organizations, and Tactics in the Twentieth Century and Beyond," *Black*

*History Bulletin* 79, no. 1 (Spring 2016): 5–14, http://www.jstor.org/stable/10.5323 /blachistbull.79.1.0005.

28. Franklin, "Black Youth Activism."

29. Charles Kaiser, *1968 in America: Music, Politics, Chaos, Counterculture, and the Shaping of a Generation*, Kindle ed. (New York: Weidenfeld & Nicolson, 1988).

30. Kirshner, "Introduction."

31. Soo Ah Kwon, Chapter 2, "Youth Organizing and the Nonprofitization of Activism," in *Uncivil Youth: Race, Activism, and Affirmative Governmentality* (Durham, N.C.: Duke University Press, 2013), 45–72, citing Daniel HoSang's "Traditions and Innovations: Youth Organizing in the Southwest," an essay published in 2005 by a nonprofit organization in New York, the Funders' Collaborative on Youth Organizing. The organization no longer distributes the essay.

32. Somini Sengupta, "Climate Strike N.Y.C.: Young Crowds Demand Action, Welcome Greta Thunberg," *New York Times*, September 20, 2019, https://www .nytimes.com/2019/09/20/nyregion/climate-strike-nyc.html?action=click&module =RelatedLinks&pgtype=Article.

33. Sengupta, "Climate Strike N.Y.C."

34. Boggs with Kurashige, *Next American Revolution*.

35. Franklin, "Black Youth Activism."

36. Collin Binkley, "U.S. Students Stage Massive Walkout to Protest Gun Violence," *AP News*, March 14, 2018, https://apnews.com/c183323b5e6546419ae08b8c469b065a.

37. Kirshner, "Millennial Youth and the Fight for Opportunity," in *Youth Activism in an Era of Education Inequality*, 53–82.

38. Boggs with Kurashige, *Next American Revolution*, Location 2370.

39. Martin Luther King Jr., *Where Do We Go from Here: Chaos or Community?*, Kindle ed. (Boston, Mass.: Beacon Press, 1968), 165.

40. Christopher England, "John Dewey and Henry George: The Socialization of Land as a Prerequisite for a Democratic Public," *American Journal of Economics and Sociology* 77, no. 1 (January 2018): 178.

41. Matthew A. Diemer and Cheng-Hsien Li, "Critical Consciousness Development and Political Participation among Marginalized Youth," *Child Development* 82, no. 6 (November/December 2011): 1,816, https://www.jstor.org/stable/41289885.

42. King, *Where Do We Go from Here*, 201.

43. Brown, "End of Educated Democracy," 19.

44. Kwon, "Introduction," in *Uncivil Youth*, 1–25.

45. Ivan Illich, "The De-Linking of Peace and Development," in *In the Mirror of the Past* (New York: Marion Bayers, 1984), 24.

46. Robert J. Antonio, "Plundering the Commons: The Growth Imperative in Neoliberal Times," *Sociological Review* 61, S2 (2013): 20.

47. Illich, "De-Linking of Peace and Development," 24.

48. England, "John Dewey and Henry George," quoting John Dewey, "Politics and Culture," in *John Dewey, the Later Works, 1925–1953*, vol. 6, *1931–1932*, ed. Jo Ann Boydston (1932; repr. Carbondale: Southern Illinois University Press, 1985), 45.

49. Antonio, "Plundering the Commons," 36.

50. King, *Where Do We Go from Here*, 201.

51. David Harvey, Chapter 3, "The Creation of the Urban Commons," in *Rebel Cities: From the Right to the City to the Urban Revolution* (London and New York: Verso, 2013), 67–88.

52. Kirshner, "Conclusions," in *Youth Activism in an Era of Education Inequality*, 163–84.

53. Erin E. Toolis, "Theorizing Critical Placemaking as a Tool for Reclaiming Public Space," *American Journal of Community Psychology* 59 (2017): 192.

54. In his legendary 1968 essay "The Tragedy of the Commons" (*Science* 162, no. 3859 [December 13, 1968]: 1,243–1,248, https://www.jstor.org/stable/1724745). Garrett Hardin argued that over-exploitation of resources would lead to their eventual collapse and proposed either to convert them into a private good or to have an external authority (e.g., a government) regulate them. Elinor Ostrom thoroughly disproved Hardin's theory in *Governing the Commons: The Evolution of Institutions for Collective Action* (New York: Cambridge University Press, 1990), showing that communities can often regulate the use of resources more efficiently and sustainably than markets or states (for more information, see Dana D. Nelson, "The Enduring Appeal of the Commons," *Arizona Quarterly* 75, no. 2 [Summer 2019]: 1–21). However, my concern is not with how best to steward resources but with the deficits in low-income neighborhoods that can instigate the participation of youth who are critically conscious of injustice, a premise that I organized in a book I coedited with Susan P. Kemp: *The Paradox of Urban Space: Inequality and Transformation in Marginalized Communities* (New York: Palgrave Macmillan, 2011).

55. Alia R. Tyner-Mullings, "Central Park East Secondary School: Teaching and Learning through Freire," *Schools: Studies in Education* 9, no. 2 (Fall 2012): 227–45, https://www.jstor.org/stable/10.1086/667919, quoting Paulo Freire, *Pedagogy of the Oppressed*, 30th Anniversary ed. (1970; repr. New York: Continuum Press, 2003), 72.

56. Diemer and Li, "Critical Consciousness Development," 1,815–33.

57. Brian D. Christens, Lawrence T. Winn, and Adrienne M. Duke, "Empowerment and Critical Consciousness: A Conceptual Cross-Fertilization," *Adolescent Res Rev* 1 (2016): 15–27.

58. Alexis Jemal, "Critical Consciousness: A Critique and Critical Analysis of the Literature," *Urban Rev* 49 (2017): 602–26.

59. Paolo Freire, *Pedagogy of the Oppressed*, trans. Myra Bergman Ramos (New York: Seabury Press, 1970).

60. Gutiérrez et al., "Youth as Historical Actors in the Production of Possible Futures."

61. Kwon, "Youth Organizing," referring to Ditra Edwards, Nicole Johnson, and Kim McGillicuddy, *An Emerging Model for Working with Youth: Community Organizing + Youth Development = Youth Organizing*, a monograph published in 2003 by the Funders' Collaborative on Youth Organizing and no longer distributed.

62. Soo Ah Kwon, "Moving from Complaints to Action: Oppositional Consciousness and Collective Action in a Political Community," *Anthropology and Education Quarterly* 39, no. 1 (March 2008): 63, https://www.jstor.org/stable/25166648, quoting Daniel HoSang, "Beyond Policy: Ideology, Race, and the Reimagining of Youth," in *Beyond Resistance! Youth Activism and Community Change*, ed. Shawn Ginwright, Pedro Noguera, and Julio Cammarota (New York: Routledge, 2006), 16.

63. Marion Coddou, "An Institutional Approach to Collective Action: Evidence from Faith-Based Latino Mobilization in the 2006 Immigrant Rights Protests," *Social Problems* 63, no. 1 (February 2016): 127–50, https://www.jstor.org/stable/44014898.

64. Julio Cammarota, "A Map for Social Change: Latino Students Engage a Praxis of Ethnography," *Children, Youth, and Environments* 17, no. 2 (2007): 345, quoting Paolo Freire, *Pedagogy of the Oppressed* (New York: Continuum Press, 1993), 33, https://www.jstor.org/stable/10.7721/chilyoutenvi.17.2.0341.

65. Kwon, "Moving from Complaints to Action," referring to Freire, *Pedagogy of the Oppressed* (New York: Continuum Press, 1996).

66. Kwon, "Moving from Complaints to Action," referring to Jane Mansbridge, "The Making of Oppositional Consciousness," in *Oppositional Consciousness: The Subjective Roots of Social Protest*, ed. Jane Mansbridge and Aldon Morris (Chicago: University of Chicago Press, 2001).

67. Jemal, "Critical Consciousness," referring to Freire, *Pedagogy of the Oppressed* (New York: Continuum Press, 2000).

68. Michelle Billies, "PAR Method: Journey to a Participatory Conscientization," *International Review of Qualitative Research* 3, no. 3 (Fall 2010), https://www.jstor.org/stable/10.1525/irqr.2010.3.3.355, 363, referring to Freire, *Pedagogy of the Oppressed* (1970; repr. New York: Continuum Press, 1994).

69. Boggs with Kurashige, *Next American Revolution*.

70. Boggs with Kurashige, *Next American Revolution*, Locations 1796/2581.

71. Boggs with Kurashige, *Next American Revolution*.

72. Arif Dirlik, "Place-Based Imagination: Globalism and the Politics of Place," *Review* 22, no. 2 (1999): 151–87, https://www.jstor.org/stable/40241454.

73. Sharon E. Sutton and Susan P. Kemp, "Introduction: Place as Marginality and Possibility," in Sutton and Kemp, *Paradox of Urban Space*, 113.

74. David W. Orr, *Earth in Mind: On Education, Environment, and the Human Prospect* (Washington, D.C.: Island Press, 1994), 114.

75. Siobhan McEvoy-Levy, "Youth Spaces in Haunted Places: Placemaking for Peacebuilding in Theory and Practice," *International Journal of Peace Studies* 17, no. 2 (Winter 2012): 2, http://www.jstor.com/stable/41853033.

76. Sharon E. Sutton and Susan P. Kemp, "Children's Participation in Constructing a Socially Just Public Sphere," in *Children and Their Environments: Learning, Using, and Designing Spaces*, ed. Mark Blades and Christopher Spencer (Cambridge: Cambridge University Press, 2005), 256–76.

77. Sharon E. Sutton and Susan P. Kemp, "Place: A Site of Individual and Collective Transformation," in Sutton and Kemp, *Paradox of Urban Space*, 121–22.

78. Sutton and Kemp, "Introduction: Place as Marginality and Possibility," 2.

79. Illich, "Dwelling," in *In the Mirror of the Past*, 55–64.

80. Lynda H. Schneekloth and Robert G. Shibley, *Placemaking: The Art and Practice of Building Communities* (New York: Wiley, 1995).

81. Ginwright, "Peace Out to Revolution!"

82. McEvoy-Levy, "Youth Spaces in Haunted Places," referring to Maarja Saar and Hannes Palang, "The Dimensions of Place Meanings," *Living Review of Landscape Research* 3 (2009), http://www.livingreviews.org/lr1r-2009-3.

83. Alesia Montgomery, "Reappearance of the Public: Placemaking, Minoritization, and Resistance in Detroit," *International Journal of Urban and Regional Research* (2016): 93.

84. Boggs with Kurashige, *Next American Revolution*.

85. For a complete report, see Sharon E. Sutton et al., *Urban Youth Programs in America: A Study of Youth, Community, and Social Justice Conducted for the Ford Foundation* (Seattle: University of Washington, 2006), http://faculty.washington.edu/sesut/Sutton%20Website%20PDFs/UrbanYouthPrograms.pdf.

86. Susan P. Kemp, "Leaders of Today, Builders of Tomorrow," in Sutton and Kemp, *Paradox of Urban Space*, 137.

87. The 2004–2005 narrative for Storyhouse drew from a thirty-seven-page, 17,500-word transcript of ten interviews with staff, youth, parents, and a board member; the 2020–2021 narrative drew from an eight-page, 4,300-word transcript of a single interview with the executive director.

The 2004–2005 narrative for Hoʻoulu ʻŌpio drew from a seventy-two-page, 30,500-word transcript of seventeen interviews with staff, youth, mentors, parents, and board members; the 2020–2021 narrative drew from a sixty-four-page, 30,500-word transcript of four interviews with the associate director and three staff who were affiliated with the organization around 2004–2005.

The 2004–2005 narrative for Academe drew from a fifty-three-page, 25,000-word transcript of thirteen interviews with staff, youth, parents, and a volunteer; the 2020–21 narrative drew from a sixty-one-page, 29,000-word transcript of four interviews with the co-founder/program and organizational coordinator and three staff who were affiliated with the organization around 2004–2005.

88. Gutiérrez et al., "Youth as Historical Actors in the Production of Possible Futures."

# PART I

## Southwest Detroit, Michigan: Activism through Theatre

In this part of the book, I present an exemplar of how community-based organizations can cultivate citizens who contribute to the emotional realm of the commons, defined as the public space of democracy where youth simultaneously explore how they feel about their neighborhoods and then acquire the tools to turn their feelings into action. For this exemplar, I take you to Storyhouse Theatre Company, the pseudonym for a community arts organization in Southwest Detroit, Michigan, that a couple began in 1991.[1] Based within an area that had long been home to Mexican immigrants and was historically viewed as "the definitive heart and soul" of that part of the city, the company blended creativity with social consciousness in order to build community within a culturally rich but economically impoverished neighborhood and city . Unlike many small youth-serving organizations, Storyhouse drew from a broad geographic area, with most of its activities taking place outside its facility and beyond the immediate neighborhood. Using the ritualistic nature of theatre, Storyhouse engaged multiple generations in dramatizing social problems and reclaiming fragments of a disinvested urban landscape. Over the years, as Detroit slipped deeper into decline, the company used an expanded notion of "performance" to demonstrate how aesthetic engagement can contribute to community revitalization even within one of "the most negatively stereotyped cities in the nation."[2] My research team studied Storyhouse in 2004–2005, thirteen years into its tenure, and then I revisited it at the height of the Covid-19 pandemic in 2020–2021.

I have created a narrative from the 2004–2005 study using excerpts from a thirty-three-page, 15,500-word transcript of a survey and nine interviews that graduate research assistants at the University of Michigan School of Social

Work administered.[3] Study participants, consisting of one of the cofounders, staff, youth, parents, and a board member, responded to questions about the company, its setting, and its activities.[4] I have organized the narrative according to the dimensions of critical pedagogy (critical awareness, collective agency, and collective action), though the protocols did not ask about this educational philosophy.[5] I have also created a narrative from the 2020–2021 study using a six-page, 3,000-word transcript of a single interview with the new executive director that my graduate research assistant at The New School administered. She responded to questions intended to validate my framing of the organization's 2004–2005 curriculum as critical pedagogy. Her interview confirmed the soundness of my framing and revealed a shift in Storyhouse's administration but not its mission.[6]

This four-section part of the book presents Storyhouse as an exemplar of what I theorize as "heart-centric critical pedagogy" within the emotional realm of place-based activism because of its use of performance to increase social cohesion among company members and audiences. In the first section, I situate Southwest Detroit within a city that fell from greatness in the post–World War II era to "war zone" status in the years just prior to the 2004–2005 study. I describe the origins of the founders' commitment to community-based theatre, the pedagogy they evolved, and the challenges they encountered. In the second section, I present the 2004–2005 narrative, organized within a critical pedagogy framework, and in the third section, I describe current conditions in a city where revitalization is occurring but poverty remains. I use the 2020–2021 narrative to reveal Storyhouse's leadership crisis and the executive director's efforts to reorganize a leaner organization that can remain true to its original mission.

I begin the fourth section by using both narratives to conceptualize Storyhouse as an exemplar of heart-centric critical pedagogy. I then ground this pedagogy in the commons as the emotional realm of place-based activism, refocusing its dimensions as place awareness, place agency, and critical place-making.[7] I conclude with observations of Storyhouse's developmental trajectory and how the organization could help spark a more democratic, non-racist commons than the one that exists in Detroit today.

# Historical Context

So that you understand the real-life script for Storyhouse's plays and other ritualistic performances, I begin this chapter by portraying its economically impoverished but culturally rich surroundings. Then I explain how a newly minted Ph.D. in theatre stepped into an ongoing childcare predicament in the role of "in loco parentis" and, in turn, received resounding applause from Southwest Detroit's actual parents, thereby setting the stage for establishing Storyhouse as a much-needed out-of-school activity. I describe the intergenerational, community-engaged company that she and her actor husband co-founded and end by previewing operational shortcomings that would later become significant in the organization's evolution.

## Southwest Detroit, Michigan

Mexican families had clustered in an area of Southwest Detroit known as La Bagley since the 1920s, when the city introduced the world to the automobile age, assembly lines, and the modern blue-collar working class. In the 1940s, when Detroit was dubbed "the arsenal of democracy" because it had manufactured the weapons that helped win World War II,[8] La Bagley was a thriving neighborhood that boasted a movie theatre, supermarket, butcher shop, restaurants, and many other Mexican-owned businesses.[9] Its busy commercial district lay in the shadow of the Michigan Central Train Depot, a gem in the city's collection of art deco and Beaux Arts architecture, rivaled only by the early twentieth-century buildings in New York and Chicago and indicative of the city's extraordinary wealth.[10] With its abundant unionized manufacturing jobs, Detroit was one of the nation's most prosperous metropolises,[11] and La Bagley's hardworking Mexican immigrants fueled that prosperity. So did its other immigrants and migrants—Irish, Maltese, Puerto Rican, Appalachian whites, and Southern African Americans—who had easy access to the city's auto industry from this working-class locality. La Bagley was truly a good place to settle.[12]

Then, in the late 1950s, a federal freeway system enabled the relocation of Detroit's industry and white residents to the suburbs, resulting in a loss of 67 percent of its manufacturing jobs and 35 percent of its population by 1980, with 20 percent of the population departing in the 1970s alone.[13] The city's policy of clearing land in low-income residential areas—for freeway construction and to attract industries, major institutions, and well-to-do residents—furthered population loss and neighborhood decline.[14] In keeping with this policy, city officials condemned an area of Southwest Detroit in 1957, declaring it a slum in order to relocate downtown firms on bulldozed sites. Despite protests by homeowners, removal got underway, but redevelopment never materialized because most of the industries that were to move there had found other locations by the time properties were cleared.[15] Then in the late 1960s, another large portion of La Bagley was eaten up for the I-75 freeway, a massive project that bulldozed more properties and disconnected businesses on the east side of the neighborhood from residential areas to the west.[16]

By the late 1980s, General Motors had closed its three auto plants, leaving Detroit's impoverished, mostly African American residents jobless in neighborhoods that were "scarred by broken-down homes, vacant lots, dope, and too many break-ins, car thefts, and assaults." As city officials shut down police stations and recreation centers, warehoused fire rigs, reduced trash collection, and cut back on already sparse bus service, many of the city's neighborhoods became islands of poverty, lacking in essential services and entirely surrounded by overgrown, desolate landscapes.[17] Explaining how plant closings affected families, Storyhouse's founding youth director, Lamar, said:

> There were a couple of big, huge factories that closed down and left
> people without jobs who'd had paying jobs for a long time. There was a
> strange displacement of the fathers moving out of the home, leaving
> mothers with children. The mothers, being unskilled, in order to bring in
> money to get food on the table, would go get menial, McDonalds jobs,
> sometimes two of them, and the children were then unsupervised. And
> that's what caused the gang problem. The kids were just hanging out on
> the street and then the rough elements started taking over (Lamar).

Recognizing these conditions, the federal government designated much of Southwest Detroit as an empowerment zone in 1994, intending to improve enterprise and reduce unemployment and poverty.[18] The resulting tax breaks to businesses and increased social services to residents were perhaps why its commercial district, dubbed "Mexicantown" back in 1980, grew 7 percent in the 1990s, the only area of Detroit to do so. At the time of the 2004–2005 study, the neighborhood exhibited a multiethnic (but predominantly Hispanic) character; an array of human service, housing, economic development, and arts organizations; and a Mexican-derived appreciation for incorporating art into everyday life.[19] Study participants characterized it as "very ethnic" with "a bazillion Mexican restaurants," their comments reflecting the actual presence of about 1,000 Latinx-owned businesses within a three-mile radius of Mexicantown.[20] They portrayed an impoverished community with the usual car thefts, break-ins, drugs, and homelessness—an image that Kordell, a young white board member, elaborated by saying:

> It's an urban community with a lot of small businesses that are owned mostly by Mexican Americans. Or actually they are run by Mexican Americans; I have no idea who owns them. There are lots of trucks, like semi-trailers, that drive through the community often because we're right by the bridge that goes to Canada. The neighborhood's pretty run down. People own their houses, but there's not a lot of money to fix them up. There are also a lot of unoccupied houses and empty lots where houses used to be (Kordell).

Lamar depicted the area's changing demographics and resultant good fortunes, saying that:

> There is an interesting group, of all the various groups, of thirty-year-old mostly white but also Latinos who have just moved into this neighborhood within the last ten years. There's a large group of twenty-year-old Mexican men who came up for the jobs, and they're a dynamic group. They bring lots of skills up to the area and they are really good for the economy here. I think one of the reasons that Southwest Detroit is booming is because of this migration from Mexico (Lamar).

Jena, a youth participant, attributed the neighborhood's amicable social milieu to the fact that "many of the people who work there do live very nearby. It is very rooted in that certain common heritage. It is unique unto itself when compared to the city because there is a lot more personal exchange between the people." Storyhouse's only full-time staff member, Angie, agreed, adding that:

> The schools I've been into—walking into them breaks my heart with all the gates, but once inside, the people are great and care about the

kids. Detroit has a scary exterior, but once you're inside and learn about the city of Detroit, the reason why I've always come home is because there's a huge heart to Detroit that other cities don't have (Angie).

Still another youth participant, Rufus, who did not live in the area, at first made a pejorative comment about its ethnic makeup and then walked it back, attempting to cover over his stereotypes about the neighborhood's residents.

There's a lot of Mexicans there. No that's a joke. The Ambassador Bridge is around there. There's the Rosa Mexicano restaurant down the street. There's also a recreation center down the street. They have programs there. I know two people who live over there in that area. They're friendly. Two of the people used to be in Storyhouse. One still is. The people are nice and friendly, that's all. I don't know that much because I don't live in that area but from the vibe that they give when I go over there, it seems they're nice and friendly (Rufus).

Cultural conflicts existed for sure, but Storyhouse benefited from a Mexican immigrant population that worked hard to maintain its cultural traditions. Residents patronized many live musical and dramatic performances and, in the late 1990s, supported over twenty-five cultural organizations—more than in any of the city's other residential neighborhoods.[21]

## Storyhouse Theatre Company

Storyhouse Theatre Company was cofounded after what turned out to be a debut performance directed by Lillian Montgomery at a Southwest Detroit branch library. The performance came about when the head librarian solicited her assistance with a problem he was having shortly after she and her husband, Lamar, moved cross country to Detroit just when the city entered a steep downward spiral. The librarian explained that working parents were sending their middle-school children there because they could not afford childcare after the school day ended. He said that the middle-schoolers were hanging out and being very disruptive, but that he could hardly boot them out onto crime-ridden streets. Knowing that Lillian had recently earned a Ph.D. in theatre and was interested in community arts, he suggested that she attempt to turn their negative behavior into something positive.

Lillian began chatting with the mostly Latinx middle-schoolers and soon engaged them in reading *House on Mango Street*, a novel by Sandra Cisneros about a Mexican American girl named Esperanza who grew up in a Chicago ghetto. Lillian had the youngsters read aloud vignettes about Esperanza's transformation as she matured and began using writing to express herself and escape ghetto life. They got the message: *House on Mango Street* was about them growing up in Mexicantown, where they could use writing to imagine a positive future. Eventually, Lillian guided the youngsters in writing their own play, rehearsing it, building scenery, and ultimately staging a standing-room-only performance in the children's room of the library. As the librarian explained:

> On the day of the play, we had so many people in the library they were standing outside the door. Mothers, fathers, siblings, aunts, uncles, cousins—everybody came to see these kids perform. It was the largest crowd we ever had in that little branch library in Southwest Detroit— over one hundred.[22]

Having been directed toward a meaningful theme, the middle-schoolers and their significant-other audience were able to reimagine their lives through playwriting and performance. Seeing the power of theatre to engender hope and possibility, Lillian and Lamar conceived of Storyhouse during a year that poverty and crime peaked in Detroit, as did the need for keeping young people safe and "out of trouble."

## Combining an Aesthetic and Social Vision

Initially, the cofounders established Storyhouse as a touring company whose mission was to improve lives and foster social justice through the transformative power of theatre. After securing a permanent performance space in their tenth year of operations, the two launched a wide-ranging agenda that combined professional theatre with education for people of all ages, offering programs in playwriting, performance, puppetry, and urban gardening. At the time of the first study, Storyhouse had ten programs, including six education programs oriented to three age groups: eight- to fourteen year-olds, fifteen- to eighteen-year olds, and those over eighteen up to the elderly. It engaged more than 300 program participants year round in such activities as playwriting, directing, and acting; making and operating giant puppets; dancing and painting murals; and reclaiming vacant lots for community gardens.

The male, female, transgendered, and two-spirited youth who attended Storyhouse were African American (38 percent), Caucasian (35 percent), Latinx (20 percent), Asian (3 percent), mixed race (3 percent), and Native American (2 percent). Through an eclectic approach to performance, the company aspired to develop leadership, teamwork, problem solving, creativity, writing, literacy, job-readiness, and a positive sense of place. Adults, youth, and occasional parent and community volunteers staffed Storyhouse, its annual budget of about $175,000 coming from foundations (primarily), corporations, government agencies, individuals, fundraisers, and ticket sales.

## Being Rooted in the Community

Set apart from its surroundings by vacant lots and located within a tiny 1900s building that once housed a church behind its paneled wood doors, Storyhouse was a community landmark. According to Gloria, whose fifteen-year-old daughter attended its programs, the repurposed building afforded a good space.

> The way they got it set up, it's just like a real theatre. And they have, in the window, a display of old things, like part of the history of Detroit. And inside the benches come from, I think they said, something that was downtown—the YMCA that was downtown. And the lighting came from there, because they tore it down to make the stadium (Gloria).

In effect, Storyhouse had collaged together fragments of Detroit's storied history within its diminutive headquarters, the structure's unassuming artisanship preserving the memory of better times for working people. In a reciprocal relationship with Detroit, company members staged performances about life in the city, which in turn engendered the support of individuals and institutions. Jena clarified the give-and-take, stating that "a really big part of Storyhouse is that the theatre is rooted in the community and that it is responsive to the community. That is the foundation of the company, and they wouldn't exist without that foundation." Lillian agreed, noting that most youth bring "a strong connection to community" and that most parents and other community members bring "food and transportation. They also bring huge community networks of churches, family, peers, other organizations. . . . It's an active community."

Storyhouse's roots in the community were deepened when, by default, two problems became an asset. Because the city had almost no public transportation to bring company members to its miniature facility, and because the company had no resources for renting a larger one, Storyhouse did most of its work off-site in facilities provided by other entities, solving two problems at once. As Lamar explained:

> Almost all our programs are done in other buildings. For example, our elementary school program is done in the elementary schools, middle school program in the middle schools. Our high school programs are done at the studio, but the performances are done in other buildings.

One of the other programs I run is in conjunction with the blind and physically handicapped program. I have a radio playwriters program for elders, mostly blind, physically handicapped folks we meet with once a week to do radio dramas, so we meet over at the Frederick Douglass Library. We have programs scattered out and about. Every year, Lillian tries to get everybody together so we can look at each other to see what we've been doing (Lamar).

Having dispersed facilities meant that Storyhouse was omnipresent. Hazel, mother of fifth-grader Dayton, spoke with pride about having "the kids" all over the city, saying that "they performed the play four or five different times at different venues and each time they got a good response. They performed their main presentation at the Winter Festival. They also performed at the Detroit Public Library, at Storyhouse's theatre, another library, and the recreation center." Rufus bragged about his performance at Cobo Hall and his weekly tours to public schools and various social service facilities. Kordell was especially enthusiastic about the exchanges that occurred at outdoor performances, noting that "the interaction with random people passing by who wouldn't necessarily come to a performance fulfills more of the mission of trying to engage the community on a number of different levels. It's also more fun to be outside, and there is a lot more audience-performer interaction."

Asked how Storyhouse measured its level of community support, Angie responded that "success is based on the number of volunteers who come in, the amount of audience that is physically in the building, the amount of money that comes back, but money isn't the highest factor—we don't turn people away from seeing plays." In addition to providing free admission to those in need, Storyhouse distributed its meager financial resources among a thirty-eight-member staff that included eleven paid adults, with Angie being fulltime, and fifteen paid youth. In Lamar's words: "We're employing people—actually giving people jobs—and the bigger we grow, the more we employ." Lamar also admitted that, to keep the company afloat, sometimes "we will finance our own projects. I have actually done this—financed my own project with my salary from the high school. Lillian sometimes will do the same thing. She will take her salary and she will fund her own program."

## Operationalizing the Vision

Despite its many strengths, Storyhouse was unable to operationalize some aspects of its vision, especially in relation to how staff engaged the youth, which Lillian and Kordell assessed quite differently. As a director who managed staff, she saw a synergistic youth/adult partnership; as an outside observer, he saw an unrealized aspiration to include them as active company members.

> The director is actually pretty good at youth involvement, but she's not a good supervisor and therefore it's easy for there to be a big discrepancy in how the different program managers are doing their work and engaging the youth. I'm not sure everyone shares the same vision about youth involvement, and I think that's a supervising issue. There hasn't been a good melding of the vision and the actual practical stuff for program managers to implement good youth involvement (Kordell).

Kordell attributed the misalignment of intention and practice to insufficient funding, stating that "people aren't paid very well, so there's a lot of turn over, which is a problem." He said that grant-maker requirements also diminished Storyhouse's ability to realize its vision of intergenerational programming, explaining that "mostly it's segmented into specific age groups. I think that has to do with funding—that funding happens for certain age groups." Angie agreed that funding constraints compromised Storyhouse's ability to achieve its ideals, saying that:

> We have enough money to feed the kids after school, pay the teachers, schedule the tours. So technically enough [money] to function, but we're really getting hit and it's program-year to program-year to keep the programs running, or even by quarters. Programs are built so youth can join at six and never leave. And that's just the writing and acting; our oldest is eighty. We want to sustain that and bring more people in and grow, and it's hard to do with all the funding cuts (Angie).

Despite these operational misfires, Storyhouse was in the trenches carrying out uplifting creative work within a devastated urban context, as you will see.

# 2004–2005 Narrative

In this three-part narrative, I present the 2004–2005 study participants' perspectives on Storyhouse's curriculum. Though the protocols did not ask about critical pedagogy, I have conceptualized the narrative to illustrate its three dimensions, showing how the curriculum helped company members unpack injustice and generate positive images of themselves (critical awareness), prepared them to stage plays about social issues that were also entertaining (collective agency), and engaged them in ritualistic celebrations of their community's cultural and ecological resources (collective action).

## Encouraging Critical Awareness

### Exposing Structural Marginalization

Storyhouse company members suffered from the fallout of living in a disinvested ghetto, exposed to all of the pathologies and racial assaults that I detailed in the previous section. According to Kordell, the youth who attended its programs were dealing with extraordinary circumstances; for example, he said that they were literally locked down in their schools, surrounded by "a lot of police" who enforced "ridiculous rules" and (illegally) restricted their use of the fire stairs that insured unrestricted exit in an emergency. He said that they were further compromised at home, their impoverishment burdening them with adult responsibilities, "like they have to take care of younger siblings." Other staff claimed that the youth understood the dangers of living in Detroit. For example, Lamar said that the youth worried about being seduced by guns and gangs while navigating between home and school on abandoned, garbage-filled streets, and Lillian said that they were concerned about how their health would be affected by environmental degradation and pollution.

Kordell emphasized that the youth were keenly aware of the limitations in their lives, especially those caused by racism, explaining that they "are aware that they are part of a larger group and one that is often ignored. I think it differs by kid, too. I think they're aware that their educational facilities are different and with fewer resources than other communities, and they think that's unfair." At another point, Kordell mused: "Yeah, the youth are aware that army recruiters are in their schools a lot and that they might not be recruiting in non-poor schools. They're aware that the resources in their schools aren't as good as other people's."

Given the daily assaults that the youth faced, Storyhouse staff had become passionate about helping them understand that they were not responsible for what they were experiencing. As Jena put it, the company helped its members understand that "there are structural things that you can't overcome on your own. That is why things like Storyhouse are important to help counteract these forces in the system that are beyond an individual's control." The staff believed theatre was a potent means to engage the youth in dissecting their everyday experiences. For example, Josephine thought that writing and performing plays about social issues helped company members "put a name on what they are doing. They also get to act it out, which helps them express what they are feeling about these issues. It helps them see where the problems are by talking about them." Kordell concurred, explaining that theatre helped company members "learn to think about social problems as much bigger than the overt manifestation of the problem. They learn that problems have ecosystems or external factors. The company lets them see how they could fight for social justice."

### Exposing the Historical Roots of Problems

To produce socially critical plays, Storyhouse staff made company members aware of the historical underpinnings of the problems they were experiencing; for example, Josephine explained that "we go way back to before the white man came here. We talk about the land. They learn about the landscape and the land, before the white man came here. The youth are very fascinated by that because it looked totally different than it does now." The staff also instructed company members in the government policies that had ravaged the city; for example, Lamar decribed the research that accompanies collective playwriting, saying that:

We look up various aspects of the neighborhood, trying to explain to the youth the impact of having the freeway cut right through the neighborhood and how that affected it. The youth, of course, don't understand but the people who lived here before the freeway of course, they saw the impact and it was huge. I'm not sure when the freeway happened. I think it was late '60s early '70s when I-75 cut through this area. A big swath of land got cut through. They cut the main street of the neighborhood right in half. And there could have been an element of racism. If this had been an all-white neighborhood, that probably maybe wouldn't have happened, but because it was the Mexican neighborhood, they just decided that was okay (Lamar).

Only by providing the critically conscious instruction that was missing in the public schools could Lamar and the other Storyhouse staff equip company members with the grounding that they needed to produce critically informed plays on such topics as gangs, violence, and poverty.

## Creating Positive Images of Youth

Storyhouse company members had to rise above a plethora of stereotypes— for example, that they were the cause of problems, were self-involved and overly dramatic, and were into drugs. Both Jena and Hazel felt that theatre provided an antidote to prevailing conceptions of youth by generating positive images of their idealism and energy. For example, Jena believed that "the fact that the kids in this company are recognizing social issues and writing about them and giving creative expression to these issues is taking away those stereotypes and misconceptions. I think a lot of what the young directors do counteracts what the community thinks about them negatively." She said that Storyhouse's performances allowed audiences to see the youth "really being involved in something that they are passionate about and sticking to it."

Similarly, Hazel believed that "the company addresses negative stereotypes by letting people know that the kids are giving their time at Storyhouse and not doing whatever they could be doing in the streets. They are able to demonstrate that they have been contributing their time and . . . the end products that they are able to make in the company." Thinking about her ten-year-old son, she added that audiences "see the kids doing things that are selfless actions. People can see that, even though they are such a little person, the youth can have such a big impact. They see them as being involved in things other than gangs or just street violence."

## Fostering Collective Agency

### Developing Multiple Competencies

One of Storyhouse's primary activities, collective playwriting, required literacy skills—a daunting challenge, as some company members could neither read nor write, even though they were in high school. As Angie explained:

> There's a girl in one of our classes—I don't know her name or who she is—she cannot read or write—we do free-form writing in developing the plays where they write about their lives. We were talking about how can we accommodate this, and I don't know how the decision will be made but the last time we thought about it we were going to give her a tape deck and tell her the final has to be written. We haven't fully tackled it yet. There was another kid a couple of years ago with that issue who now is starting to read and write at a fifth- or sixth-grade level. Lots of cases that slip through the cracks in the big school system, and all of their school skills get better (Angie).

Josephine, who was convinced that Storyhouse's social mission motivated the youth to develop cognitive skills, said:

> We tie in literacy with puppetry. If they have problems reading, they become more interested in reading through these activities. We use the arts to strengthen those faculties. Some other organizations do this as well, but Storyhouse is unique, especially in this area. They are not just doing meaningless activities; they are doing projects with meaning and symbolism (Josephine).

Beyond developing the literacy skills that had slipped through the cracks of a dysfunctional school system, Kordell noted that company activities helped members "be articulate because they have to communicate with audience members" and in a strong, confident voice. Or as Rufus put it: "You've got to be loud in theatre." The youth became culturally literate as well, not only learning about the city's history but also discovering the community icons who were missing from their textbooks, taking field trips to museums and theatres, and conducting oral histories of their neighbors. In the process, according to Lillian, they learned "about why things are the way they are."

### Providing Supports for Producing Quality Work

The cofounders of Storyhouse were as committed to artistic innovation as they were to advancing social justice and, in fact, saw these aspirations as interdependent. To produce superior performances that would heighten company members' capacity for social change, they equipped the staff to advance this dual mission. Lillian said that "we require and provide training for learner-based strategies, curriculum development, collaborative learning and collective playwriting, and authentic assessment," explaining that artists-in-residence received instruction that prepared them as "mentors and supporters of youth." She emphasized that artists needed special preparation "so they don't do command and control teaching but youth-centered training. That's not taught in schools and definitely not in theatre departments, so we have to teach them to do that." Lamar added that Storyhouse's approach actually required its college-educated staff to unlearn practices.

> Sometimes there's quite a bit of training because we're a different kind of theatre and because it is all original. We don't take a pre-existing piece and do that, though occasionally we will do that, but for the most part, it's original theatre. So sometimes with people who are theatre majors whose whole experience is theatre, getting to let them know that we write our own plays and that we're social justice-oriented takes some training. But most of the time, once they get on board, most of the professionals really like it (Lamar).

Storyhouse had multiple checkpoints for excellence. Though older teens wrote the plays, Lamar emphasized that the professional staff insured the artistic integrity of their scripts because "you have to have someone who knows dramatic form and how to put people's stories in writing." Lillian and Angie stressed that the staff identified resources so the young people could realize their ideas, and Rufus noted that the youth conducted their own research, explaining that:

> For each play we do, we learn something about it because before we do a play, we have to do research about it. . . . Before we tried to take parts from the old script, we were told to look up on the Internet more stuff about it so we could add just a little more. During the summer program when we had to do the puppet thing, we had to do research on the animals, because it was Metamorphosis, and we had to learn about their habitats and the different animals that we were playing—dragonflies, frogs, bears, and all that (Rufus).

Lillian explained that once the youth had "determined the topic, it goes to the adults to contact community agencies who provide support on that topic and to bring in resources for the youth. Then the youth act as final judge and use their eye to determine how to proceed." In this way, Lillian said that Storyhouse provided the "structured spaces and experiences" that helped company members produce informed, high-quality plays. Recalling Kordell's earlier critique of adult/youth relationships, you can imagine how the complex back and forth of developing a professional-quality performances might, in some circumstances, result in less-than-ideal youth engagement.

## Providing Opportunities for Intergenerational Exchange

All the study participants agreed that Storyhouse was, as Josephine put it, "really good at interfacing all different ages." Its intergenerational focus meant that, despite extremely limited financial resources, the staff had to help company members with wide-ranging skill sets co-create performances, which required thoughtful scaffolding of staff and company member expertise. Lillian explained that:

> We have adult mentor artists who lead the company, who are supported by resource artists and volunteers who provide guidance and support. Parents have different roles in different programs, but largely they provide support around travel and touring around for special events like field trips, as chaperones, driving youth to places. We are beginning to explore using parents in terms of co-creation for programs. We have opportunities for young people to directly collaborate with adults in programs, both as crew and as performers. They work in a peer relationship, not in a power relationship (Lillian).

Through intergenerational programming, the company created relationships between teens and adults and between teens and young children and the elderly. Several study participants spoke to the benefits of this approach; for example, Josephine said that "it is good for youth to work with their peers, but they should really work with other age groups, because then they can get a sense of their community. When you are always with your same group, then you don't know about other community members." Josephine observed that working with seniors brought out another sensibility in the teens, explaining that while they sometimes had problems relating to the children, "when we went to the senior citizen center, I saw something different come out of them. They did admit that they liked working with the older people better than younger ones. I think that they respected them. They helped them. It was as if they viewed them as their grandparents."

As a parent, Hazel emphasized the need for mutual learning between the adults and the youth, explaining that "the adults are there to show the youth how to do things and to let them know what is to be done. The adults, on the other hand, are learning as well. They are learning about the different learning styles of each youth." She added: "For instance, one group of kids may get something right away, like doing art, while another group may take a while. That is what the adults must learn about and from the youth to work well with them. They basically just learn how to interact with one another." However, Lamar most succinctly summed up the benefits of Storyhouse's intergenerational pedagogy.

> I have found that when they get into one of these programs and associate with large numbers of people through our intergenerational programming, the youth get a sense of the larger community. I really like that because Southwest Story, for example, was a program where our oldest member was sixty-five and the youngest one was twelve years old, and everyone in between—a whole community of people, predominantly African Americans and Latinos. When you have a whole group of people who are in a close association as they're developing these programs a couple of times a week for six to seven months, they get the sense of the larger community. I think this is the same thing that used to happen in our society before television, when people would get together at town meetings or church. The whole community would gather once a week and get to know each other, and I think that's one of the good functions of church that fell off. And so, this is kind of taking the place of that. And the afterschool activities are also a place where students can meet and get a larger sense of being part of the larger community. So, it's just a matter of getting around a bunch of people and hanging out with them, and having fun, and working toward a common goal, and theatre is a perfect venue for this kind of thing (Lamar).

## Providing a Space for Invention and Action

Angie summed up what company members learned by being successful within a world that they themselves had invented, explaining that:

> When you walk into a space where you're looking for something to do after school and you create a whole world for yourself, a whole play and you're able to express yourself and you're able to write and you're able to act and you're able to do all of these many, many things that it takes to do one play, I think you don't have any choice but to feel good about yourself at the end. I think everything we do gives kids at least a sense of accomplishment, and helps them learn more, better, bigger. They're better writers, better emoters (Angie).

The invented space that Storyhouse enabled was therapeutic for those company members who were negotiating downright scary circumstances. According to Jena: "Some kids get to use it as an outlet for domestic abuse and other issues that they are facing at home, school, etc." Lamar also believed that Storyhouse's invented space was therapeutic because "when you identify something in the community that needs to be dealt with, it is a healing process." It undoubtedly helped build company members' confidence—for example, by letting Hazel's son "know that, although he is just a kid, he can do things and that he does have opinions that matter." Kordell said that theatre helped company members who were so ignored and tossed away that they felt like their lives were worthless—who believed "that there is nothing in them that is capable of creating change. Being in the company, I think they feel proud of themselves for having written and performed the play. I think they feel more confident in themselves. I sense more engagement in other parts of their lives."

Storyhouse provided a space for inventing a more confident, competent self, which Josephine believed was priceless. She said that the space gave company members "a sense of purpose and community. I think it also helps them discover things about themselves that they didn't know about before. It gives them hope. It lets them express themselves in a fun, creative way. It gives them an opportunity that is not there at school or at home." For Jena, the space showed company members "how effective the individual voice can be and how effective grassroots organizing can be. It opens an awareness of what ways you can be effective and active." But Rufus highlighted the space as one of action, boasting that "we go out and do things—volunteer for stuff, do plays for people, all sorts of stuff"—a topic that is the focus of the next section.

## Activating Collective Action

### Tackling Violence through Theatre

In the late 1980s and early 1990s, Southwest Detroit was plagued by domestic and teen dating violence, but gang violence, which Lamar's very first play tackled head on, dominated all other social problems. Explaining how middle and high school students became involved in scripting the play, he recalled:

> This area was going through a terrible gang violence episode, so . . .
> we contacted the schools and asked the counselors if they could
> recommend to us students who might be interested in writing and
> participating in a play about the nature of violence—where it comes
> from and how to deal with it. We got real good reception from one
> particular middle school, Earhardt Middle School, and interestingly

enough, the counselor there sent to us their kids who were particularly involved with counseling in the school, that is who were involved with violence. So, we sat down and met twice a week, and we discussed what the sources of violence were, and then we started crafting a play, which is called the collective playwriting process. It took us approximately three months to put the play together, and during the last three months of the school year we had the production. When the play was being written, I myself did not think it was a strong script, but audiences loved it. We had just incredible reception from it. It won an award that year from the Humanities Council, and it addressed those issues in the community. When we played it at social service agencies and schools and community centers, we were able to make a difference. People saw the source of violence and saw also possible solutions to that problem, and we also had a referral situation. We could refer families if they were having problems within their families. A lot of times people just didn't know where to go when they were having these problems (Lamar).

At the time of the 2004–2005 study, the city's crime rate had decreased considerably from its 1980s peak, but the homicide rate was still a significant 10 in 100,000,[23] and many of the teen victims were murdered by other teens. At first, Lamar said that he had proposed that company members investigate why handguns were proliferating in the area, but then the community's seeming denial of the deaths became an even more compelling subject. He explained that eventually, company members decided to write "memorials to the slain children, and that had a nice effect; it gave closure to these problems." Later, Lamar explained that "the parents in that project wanted to make sure the stories were told to their satisfaction, so they actually became part of the writing process themselves. When we got stories written down, we made sure that the parents read it, clarified it, made any changes." Then he said that company members recited their memorials to audiences that were experiencing loss.

## Sparking Collective Conversations

The conversations that Storyhouse facilitated between company members and audiences were entertaining and educational simply because, according to Lamar, that was what the community members wanted. "They like to be given points of view that they have never ever thought of before, and they want those views to be presented in an entertaining way." To increase engagement, Lamar explained that "we always have talkbacks after each show, and in those shows, the audience themselves can talk to company members and to us about what they've just seen. They sometimes will add their own solutions and will ask questions. I think that's where the change comes in the community."

Carrying on in-character dialogues with audiences not only resulted in shared understandings of issues, but audiences sometimes also became co-creators of Storyhouse's plays. Occasionally, audience solutions even became plays in themselves so that the initial scripts were only beginning points for conversations about what was happening in the lives of people in the audience.

## Developing Tolerance through Theatre

Storyhouse took advantage of its multicultural population to address the cultural divisiveness that existed not only in the city but also in the nation. As Angie put it: "We have an emotionally disabled country at the moment and [we need] to have kids more knowledgeable about being tolerant instead of afraid of something they don't know." Lillian explained how the staff helped company members rise above prevailing stereotypes.

> We work on transgender issues, multicultural issues, and cultural democracy, because it's a very diverse community, and they're dealing with latent or not so latent cultural divisions when they're present. Also, a big issue in the neighborhood is the homophobic bias which is really present. We don't know how to address that yet, but we're working on it (Lillian).

Angie described company members' evolution, saying that initially "we start out with a division between the Latino, African American, and white kids, and by the end they're friends. So, you're breaking down the racial barriers, which are huge." She also talked about how playwriting created a space for being different, noting that the youth "trust each other to talk about these hard issues that they're writing about. And I think they feel safe to discuss these issues with each other, which you know you don't in school." Later, Angie unequivocally said that company members learn "tolerance. They learn a lot of tolerance. They learn that it's okay to be different; that everybody is different, and that it's a good thing not a bad thing, which you don't learn at all in school." Jena added that the creative process helped eliminate stereotypes about her as a white person whose experience was unlike that of most company members.

> Even though I grew up in the city, I did have a much different life than the youth in the company. I am white and didn't go to a public

school. Since there are so many African Americans and Hispanics, there are these preconceptions about me and others that they realize aren't true. Being able to see talents and personalities about people helps change these misconceptions (Jena).

Through the creative process, Jena said that she was learning to be more courageous in expressing her opinions, explaining that "just seeing how much respect there is for everyone's voice at Storyhouse and how much everyone just respects one another in the grand scheme of what we are trying to do is great." Kordell specifically called out public performance as a means of promoting intergroup solidarity, noting that "over time there has been some cohesion that has happened, and I think it happened when they had to perform outside of their schools. I think it was a little scary to perform probably and they bonded over that experience and decided it was an important thing to do." Then Kordell added:

> From working with each other, I think they learn how to listen. I think all actors learn how to listen in a lot of ways. And over time, this has definitely not been easy, but one of the things is that if something happens in a scene that is unexpected, you have to do something other than just stop. And over time, they have started to trust each other enough to get out of a scene that has gone in an unexpected direction. I think they've learned to respect each other's time by arriving for rehearsals on time and stuff like that. In this particular play, they've learned that some of them have had abusive relationships, so they've learned personal things about each other's lives that influences what they do on stage and maybe helps them take the issue more seriously (Kordell).

The parents heartily agreed that Storyhouse had strengthened their children's cultural competence. Hazel noted that her "son works well together with the other youth. He has made some friends." Then she added that the youth "learn how to get along and that it is okay to have different opinions." And Gloria said flat out: "Oh definitely, the company has helped my child. She's learning how to deal with different kinds of people."

## Generating a Sense of Ownership

Storyhouse hired Francesca, who held a graduate degree in fine arts, as an artist-in-residence for a summer-long gardening project. During her interview, she seemed ambivalent about her assignment because it "didn't really involve art" but instead consisted of creating "organic gardens and a green space out of an empty lot." As she alternated between disappointment and pride, Francesca revealed the breadth of Storyhouse's approach to theatre in a way that other study participants had not. The project, which she said created "an awareness of the Detroit River and its value as a resource in the community," was done in partnership with a nonprofit housing association and engaged a work crew of Storyhouse staff, artists-in-residence, parents, and youth who "were there because they wanted a summer job."

According to Francesca, each morning, the parents would drop off their not-very-motivated children at a building near the gardening sites where the workers stored their tools and supplies. Then they set out for a day of cleaning up littered lots, planting, composting, watering, building rock sculptures, and whatever else needed doing. At the end of the week, the parents would join their children and the other workers for a parade to Detroit's tourism-oriented waterfront. Francesca laid out the choreography, explaining that:

> The overall project created a path to the river with five sites along the path. One of the sites was the garden I had started the previous summer with Bagley Housing. I was also involved with the other sites, and each week we would parade to one of the sites and the youth would be involved in performance and some kind of earth restoration ritual. It could be planting or something like that. And then it culminated with an event at the park on the riverfront, with a more lengthy performance by the youth. So I was involved and had a part at each of the sites along the path, but it was a small part at the other sites because my main focus was on the garden. Actually, of course I had my heart in the garden so I would have to say that my favorite activity involved the artmaking that went on in the garden (Francesca).

She also laid out the workday, explaining that the youth "would drag themselves in first thing in the morning. And mornings were the time when they were told what the events were going to be, so it was a time to sit and listen. But by lunchtime and after that, they were animated." She said that during lunch, the youth "would sing, they would dance, tell jokes, laugh, comb each other's hair, hang on their boyfriend." Francesca emphasized that gardening helped the youth experience their physicality in a new way, stating that:

> They learned their physical limitations as well as how far they can really push themselves—I am speaking physically now about the garden and some of the rock sculptures. I had to get help from some of the stronger teens to move some rocks and they pushed themselves

and got a big job done, and they were really proud of themselves. Prior to that, their exercise involved football and sports, not being outdoors and not art (Francesca).

She recalled how the parade lengthened over time, explaining that "each week we progressed farther along the path to the river. So, the first week we just visited the first site, and the second week we added the second site, and so on until we culminated with the parade passing through all sites on the way to the river." Because Storyhouse wanted the work to have meaning beyond simply cleaning up littered lots and planting gardens, the workers engaged with their tasks in a performative, ritualistic manner, but according to Francesca, this artful approach was initially lost on the teens.

These kids had no clue about gardening or what was important about organic gardening for health and for the environment. They had no clue, and they didn't care to know, either. We had them for a summer, so I'm not saying it changed their lives, but the program created an awareness, and it did raise their consciousness a bit because they didn't care at the beginning that they were not recycling their pizza boxes. They didn't care if there was litter in the garden. It didn't really affect them. But by the end of the summer, they understood more about the cycle of life, and it wasn't just because of the garden; it was cumulative. They were also working on a performance that they did at the Riverfront Park for the culminating event, and the story was really about the cycle of life. Because of their participation in that, along with everything else, I think they gained a greater respect for the environment and an awareness and understanding of it. . . . It was very touching at the end, because one of them wrote a poem and in her own words talked about the earth, the environment, and the importance of all creatures and how everyone is connected (Francesca).

The transformation that occurred among the teens also touched the home-less people who had been hanging out at these sites. Francesca described how they staked a claim to the site where she had begun working the year before with volunteer families and the housing association.

There's a sense of ownership with this particular plot that we turned into a green space. It was littered with debris and weeds and homeless people, and after we took it over—we didn't displace anybody because the homeless people are also part of the community. But now, instead of seeing broken booze bottles and litter all over, the homeless people who hang out on that corner where the park happens to be pick up and maintain it. They pick up their litter; they don't leave their bottles. There's a garden there and a sense of ownership. That's the most satisfying for me, to see how within the community there's a sense of pride in this small plot (Francesca).

## Staging Celebratory Community Rituals

To create Storyhouse's larger-than-life puppets, Josephine developed hands-on history lessons for the school-based programs. She explained that the youth made "large puppets of characters—hero puppets, Mother Jones, Martin Luther King. We learn about these people and what they did in the world. I learn about these things and relay it to the youth. They learn how they changed things and who these people are and what they have done." Then, the youth learned to work the puppets, which according to Jena required extensive collaboration among a team of puppeteers.

> I have been involved in two different kinds of activities. The first involves taking out the bigger puppets and holding them up during plays and at dinner. Holding these puppets takes about three people. I did the King March in January as well, where we also used the puppets. . . . I really do like doing the big puppets, because we get a good response, especially at the King demonstration. Again, this form of art is pretty unique, which I think is nice. They have about six puppets now. Some people work the hands, and someone then puts the head on. Everyone gets involved to work the puppets. We have, for instance, Martin Luther King Jr. and also other puppets that are people who are important to Detroit. It is something that you don't see all the time and it strikes a chord with the people who are there watching (Jena).

Rufus—in his most animated voice of the interview—conveyed the thrill of performing for people on city streets. He declared that his favorite activity was when "we were in downtown Detroit and I got a chance to be the MLK puppet, and I walked everywhere, and I didn't know there was a couple hundred people behind me. It scared me when I took the costume off because I couldn't see behind me!" Though Rufus said he was scared, his voice communicated exuberance about leading a couple hundred people through downtown streets, a charismatic pied piper helping his followers celebrate someone who had changed the world.

## Celebrating the Contributions of the Youth

Staff were effusive in describing the contributions that the youth made to tackling difficult social problems. Josephine pointed to their energy and different way of seeing the world, asserting that the youth "carry the future. . . . If they are healthy youth, they have the vitality to carry this to the future. They have a different perspective that's worth looking at and honoring." Pointing to their fearlessness, Angie declared that "kids can change the world more easily than adults; they're not afraid to. There's a lack of inhibitions; they're not afraid to test the water, to try. And a lot of adults won't say how they feel. Kids are braver than us." She observed that the youth had "the ability to imagine and create a whole other world, which opens your mind and makes you more able to express yourself, create things."

Hazel believed that combining the adventurousness of youth with the staidness of adults was beneficial, noting that "the older people, who are so stuck in their ways, can't see any other way of doing things. The children have fresh ideas and are more flexible at times. At the same time, we need good people to introduce their values to the young." And Lamar talked about the pluckiness of youth, noting that they had personal experiences that adults may not have had when they were young.

> Youth have creativity. They have a certain chutzpa in the sense that they've made the effort to join the company—a little sense of adventure. They bring in their own personal experience into the setting, and we can learn what they're all about, where they're coming from, what's going on with them. . . . I believe that youth can be part of any solution to a problem. What I have found is that the youth have anywhere from twelve to eighteen years' worth of experience, and as adults that's something we must recognize. But they also have that twelve to eighteen years of experience that adults often don't have (Lamar).

# 2020–2021 Context and Narrative

In this section, I bring the 2004–2005 narrative into the present, revealing Storyhouse's changing context in Southwest Detroit, where gentrification has progressed but where racially based inequities still plague this majority African American city. Because a crisis in management prevented me from conducting a follow-up study with long-time staff as I had intended, I draw upon a single interview with a recently hired executive director, Hattie Ahearn. As she explained, the company has "had a great deal of turnover in the last couple of years and no one is here who was here in 2004." Nevertheless, I reach back into the 2004–2005 study to piece together the crisis that Storyhouse faced and reveal how the study participants' identification of its shortcomings related to funding and management proved prescient. I explain how the company adapted to the crisis and characterize what aspects of its critical pedagogy have remained, despite a realignment.

## Southwest Detroit Today

Census data tell the unvarnished truth about Detroit's insidious legacy of racial injustice that Storyhouse's scripts drew upon. In 2019, the city's ever shrinking population of 670,031 was 77 percent African American in a state where that population was only 14 percent. Furthermore, 36 percent of its population was living in poverty—one of the nation's highest poverty rates—in comparison to 14 percent of the population statewide.[24] Though some areas of Detroit have seen significant investment, these data confirm the city's persistent deterioration. As one lifelong resident said: "We have downtown, Midtown, Corktown, East English Village, which seem to be highly resourced, lots of capital being poured into them, and new mostly white residents. . . . The rest of the city, as far as I can see, continues to languish."[25] Within this uneven terrain, the twenty-block Mexicantown neighborhood has witnessed rapid change as Hattie, who lives about six blocks from Storyhouse, explained:

> The demographic of our neighborhood is changing actually quite rapidly. We used to be all low income, but because of the resurgence of the city of Detroit becoming more resilient again and more vibrant and Ford Motor Company has purchased our train station and is creating a whole mobility campus there. So a lot of young people, young professionals are moving in. Our demographic is changing and so we have attorneys and architects and professionals along with people who are working in the local Mexican restaurants (Hattie).

Storyhouse sits between the long-abandoned Michigan Central Station Depot and downtown, where white investors have undertaken a massive rebranding of Detroit's public domain, creating privatized spaces that incorporate such capital-generating features as fountains with booming water jets, fruit trees, bioswales, urban gardens, bistros, yoga classes, and jazz festivals.[26] The campus that Hattie mentioned is the brainchild of William C. Ford Jr., chair of the Ford Company and a great-grandson of its founder, who envisions a facility that will attract people from all over the world.[27] To support this ambitious vision, the city approved a $5.4M plan to reconfigure two blocks in Mexicantown with flat shared streets "without raised sidewalks that's more flexible for festivals and markets, with foliage and overhead 'artistic' lighting."[28]

Plans to "green right-size" Detroit have attracted global capital for these types of amenities but made the city more unendurable for low-income residents who are being evicted to make room for high-end housing or finding themselves stranded in neighborhoods targeted for cutbacks in essential services. Scenes of large groups of alienated protesters from the neighborhoods and even from distant cities have marred the image of a newly radiant downtown with its white-collar jobs and revitalized cultural institutions. For example, in 2014, throngs of protesters rallied downtown against water shutoffs for thousands of low-income customers, demanding that the city, not the emergency manager, control the water department.[29] Similarly, parents, teachers, and community members vigorously protested conditions of "classroom overcrowding, mold in classrooms, collapsing ceilings, and dilapidated buildings" in Detroit's public schools under the emergency manager who "carried out the now-infamous decision to use the Flint River as a temporary source of drinking water for the city" when he was manager there.[30]

## An Organization in Crisis

As you will recall, during the 2004–2005 study, thirteen years after the company's founding, Kordell cautioned that Lillian's strong suit was in her artistic and social vision and not in her supervisory skills in implementing the vision, a weakness that he said was exacerbated by insufficient funding. Kordell noted that financial constraints restricted staff salaries and resulted in "a lot of turn over." Consequently, when Lillian departed in the twenty-fourth year of operations, disaster struck, as Hattie explained:

> I had been doing marketing consulting for them for about six years . . . and the founder retired very suddenly, and they brought in a consulting firm for a year [and] that really sort of drained the coffers, financially; didn't do much else. Then they hired an executive director who came in, really only stayed for about six months and she left. So the staff was really sort of shell-shocked, you know what I mean? They were just going through it. They just felt like everything was so tumultuous. So I offered to the board that I would take over the position while they were looking to find someone— another director. But when I came on, I realized that because of all this craziness that had gone on, the financial situation was somewhat tenuous. So we weren't able to hire someone to come in. I was working just part-time at a very reduced salary, just because I love the organization. So for the last four years, we really sort of got lean and mean and found new sources of income and created some fundraising activities and pulled the organization out of this horrible debt that it was in (Hattie).

In addition to identifying the lack of supervisory skills, both Kordell and Angie had complained that funding targeted to specific age groups compromised the company's ideal that the youth would "join at six and never leave." No one exists among Storyhouse's staff who can explain what happened to this ideal, and alumni are nonexistent. As Hattie lamented: "We're having our thirtieth anniversary and we're talking about an alumni event. And like, we don't have—when we became computerized, we do have those records, but before that, we don't have. We don't know where those pieces of paper are." Over the years, when someone graduated high school, the attitude of staff had apparently become one of "okay, fine, good luck, bye." Hattie recognized the limitations of this approach but, in envisioning a fix, reinvented the wheel, proposing anew Storyhouse's founding ambition to create an intergenerational community of change agents. As she explained:

We had a strategic kind of planning session and realized that we have the professional theater and then we have the school of theater. But when a youth reaches eighteen or graduates from high school, there's nothing for them unless they become a professional actor or director. So, we decided to create a space and bring back our Second Stage Theater, is what we're calling it, so that if you're eighteen and you still want to be a part of Storyhouse and the social justice focus of our theatre, you can do that now (Hattie).

## A Continued Mission

Despite radical change and persistent sameness within the city and a leadership crisis within the company, Hattie explained that Storyhouse continues to create award-winning performances that raise young people's critical awareness of social issues.

We have our kids come up with what their concerns are and what the issues are in their lives. And then we take that information, and we work with them to build a performance piece based on that issue. . . . We've done things on immigration and deportation and how it's torn families apart. We've done plays on the environment and the kids write their own plays and perform their own plays (Hattie).

As was true in 2004–2005, Hattie confirmed that struggles around the city's social inequities continue to provide source material for Storyhouse's scripts, explaining that "we've done some really incredible stuff and we've done shows on the education system and the inability of the education system to do a good job with our youth." Extending its earlier investment in raising awareness of urban wildlife through the play Metamorphosis, she said that Storyhouse recently turned its attention to Detroit's water heritage, creating performances and puppets to tell the story of the city's buried rivers, streams, and wetlands. According to Hattie, its well-attended public programming encourages water conservation and helps audiences understand "how important water is. It's a lifeline."

She said that the young children continue to participate in writing activities and acting games intended to instill collective agency in the real world. For example, Hattie affirmed that Storyhouse still offers activities that "really are centered on social justice" and helping the youth gain the confidence "to speak out and speak out in an informed way about their concerns or their beliefs." She explained how Storyhouse seeds company members' interest in the transformative potential of theatre, saying that it exposes them to social problems like homelessness and wrongful convictions, to ex-prisoners who have become civic leaders, and to local activist artists who share its visions for utilizing the arts to help Detroit become sustainable, affordable, and socially just. She emphasized that such experiences improve company members' attitudes about the city.

In addition, Hattie confirmed that the teens still receive professional mentoring for producing plays that catalyze collective action on problems they experience like bullying, gang violence, ethnic intimidation, and homophobia. As she recalled:

> The activity that stands out to me is the one that the teen group did about an undocumented family and the father was torn away from the family and sent back to Mexico and what that did to them, how that affected them. I believe the idea was from a youth who had a friend whose family was going through it (Hattie).

She noted that Storyhouse also continues to develop innovative collaborations with the many arts- and youth-focused organizations in Southwest Detroit and pointed to its "non-sports programming at the recreation center because they only have sports programming. So for those kids who aren't in sports, we're able to do arts programming." She said that this relationship led to a more ambitious "joint fundraiser for both organizations" than a singular effort would have afforded. Hattie added that Storyhouse had been working with other arts organizations that provide in-school enrichment activities "to put a pool of teaching artists together that we can all share so that's much better for the teaching artists, because they can make more money and have more work, but it also helps us as we create a database." She said that Storyhouse has additionally extended its reach beyond Detroit, partnering with schools, organizations, and agencies throughout Southeastern Michigan to propagate its justice-oriented workshops and puppetry experiences.

Despite its budget crisis, Hattie said that the company continues to share its wealth, offering scholarships to dedicated youth who are unable to pay. She envisions that, as a result of their experiences in the company, alumni will go on to join movements, work in socially oriented nonprofit organizations, run for political office, or even become performers. Hattie was adamant that, if the organization was "going to be committed to social justice, you, yourself, the staff should be also involved in it," and that meant sharing their passion for the arts and social justice with other non-arts organizations. Yet, Hattie's business expertise tells her that Storyhouse must find a way around the enormous roadblock that lack of funding poses. As she explained:

> There aren't a lot of organizations that give to the arts because I think people don't understand how important the arts are. Like it's been

shown over and over and over again. The research shows how much
the arts help children with their learning. Those children who
participate in the arts have higher math scores, higher reading scores,
higher English scores. But for some reason—it's like we have a foundation here that funds programs for youth, and they've just decided to
put all their money into the public school system (Hattie).

To get around this roadblock, Hattie said that you have to "let your mind
go crazy" and look for unconventional relationships that will allow the organization to remain unwavering in its use of theatre to transform lives, build
inclusive communities, and foster social justice. However, changing demographics means that the population Storyhouse serves is also changing. For
example, Hattie noted that among forty 2019 summer camp participants were
lower-income children from the neighborhood, and "some were Hispanic,
some were African American, some were white. And we also had the higher-
income parents sending their children. And it was just this mix of kids from
every walk of life. And they all were able to come together with common interests, common concerns, common issues." Hopefully, as the demographics
of Southwest Detroit and the youth attending Storyhouse shift, the plays "the
kids write" and perform will continue to give voice to longtime residents' struggle for place agency in the city. But more on that later.

# Theorizing the Narratives

In this section, I first theorize Storyhouse Theatre Company's curriculum as heart-centric critical pedagogy, and then I ground it as an emotional realm of place-based activism occurring within Southwest Detroit and beyond. To do that, I situate the company within the genealogy of community-based theatre in order to demonstrate how performers can use the expressiveness of drama to evoke feelings of hopefulness among actors and audiences alike. Figure 4 offers a visualization of the relationship between heart-centric critical pedagogy and the emotional realm of place-based activism.

## Community-Based Theatre as Heart-Centric Critical Pedagogy

Community-based theatre is a relatively old field that has many names, including grassroots theatre, community cultural development, applied theatre, theatre of the oppressed, and community arts among others.[31] Its traditions stretch back to early twentieth-century pageants that used themes rather than plots to encourage audience participation in community or civic life. It blossomed as a theatrical form during the 1960s' civil rights struggle and gained increasing currency during the rest of the century.[32] Community-based theatre brings forward the lived experiences and priorities of local communities, typically seeking to help deprived groups make sense of and improve their circumstances.[33] It combines social activism with emotional, therapeutic, and educational benefits that far exceed the aesthetic aspirations of traditional theatre.[34]

Featuring original scripts and aiming for social rather than individual change, this theatrical form has ranged from Americanizing immigrants to promoting women's suffrage, civil rights, and gay rights. Here I use scholarship

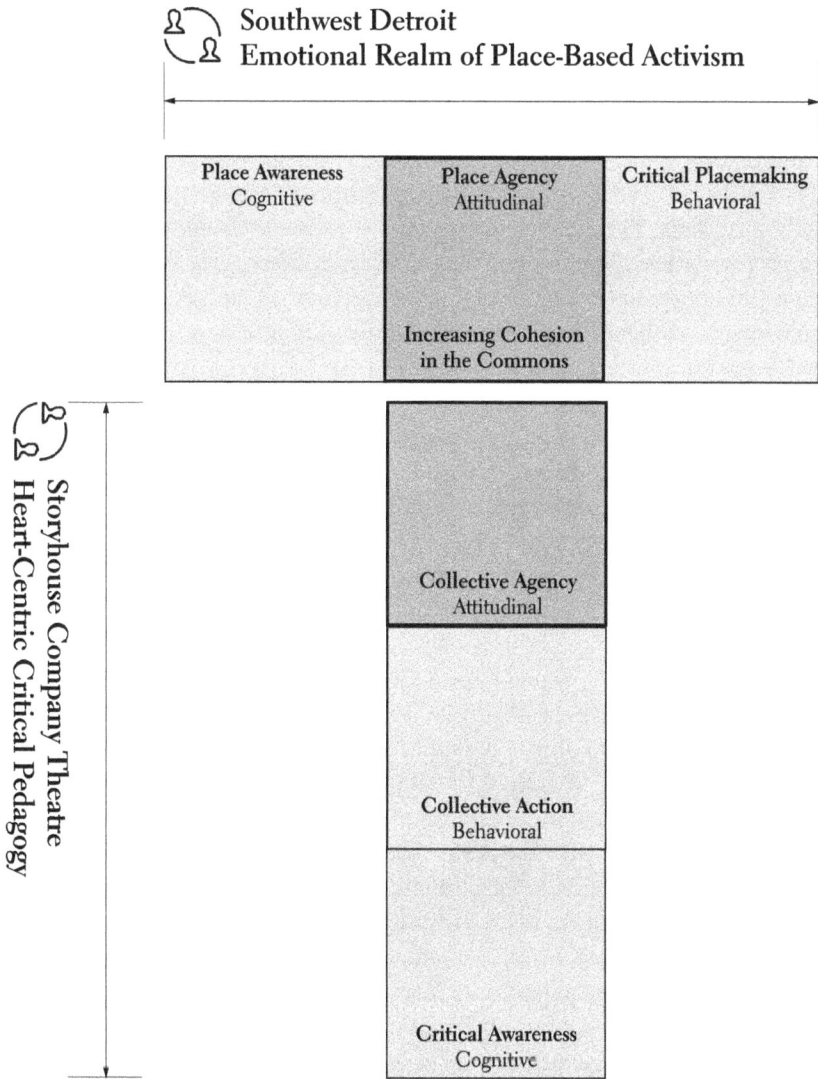

Figure 4. Heart-Centric Critical Pedagogy and the Emotional Realm of Place-Based Activism
Image credit: Sharon Egretta Sutton, 2023

on community-based theatre to theorize Storyhouse's curriculum as heart-centric critical pedagogy that helped company members make sense of, and reimagine, the city's desolate landscape.[35]

Using community-based theatre as pedagogy first occurred in Britain in the 1960s and drew from theories of active learning. Then, in the 1970s, Brazilian theatre director Augusto Boal adapted Freire's seminal work to envision a new theatrical form in his first book, *Theatre of the Oppressed*. Boal set out to revolutionize the idea of passive "spectators" and argued that citizens could struggle with real-life conflicts and be propelled into transgressive action by becoming emotionally involved in a dramatic "fiction," but at a safe distance.[36] Boal reasoned that audiences could be transformed through genuine dialogue with performers in the same manner that Freire envisioned students being transformed through genuine dialogue with teachers. As with critical pedagogy, this approach to community-based theatre uses experiential knowledge to unlock an audience's capacity for collective action.[37]

Observations by community-based theatre scholars and activist arts educators align with my contention that Storyhouse's hands-on dramatic experiences developed critical awareness, the cognitive dimension of heart-centric critical pedagogy. These experiences engaged company members in fictional situations where they mutually agreed to adopt perspectives other than their own. In this space-apart, they could safely examine complex and difficult emotions because they were doing so within an ambiguous space that lies "between the actual world and the dramatic one."[38] Storyhouse embraced Boal's theatrical fiction, engaging company members and audiences in co-creating scripts that aimed to help them make sense of Detroit's devastation. As a form of community-based theatre, its youth-scripted performances utilized local themes that blurred the real with the fictional, inviting company members to voice personal narratives of struggle and visions for possible futures.

In addition, observations by community-based theatre scholars and activist arts educators align with my claim that Storyhouse's dramatic experiences developed collective agency, the attitudinal dimension of heart-centric critical pedagogy. Indeed, Storyhouse excelled in this dimension. Advancing company members' passions for making a difference both on stage and in the community,[39] the company helped them develop the competencies they lacked, particularly in relation to literacy. To build the practical skills that company members needed to generate meaningful and innovative outcomes,[40] Storyhouse offered both out-front and behind-the-scenes opportunities that tapped into their varied strengths, goals, and personalities, which is one of theatre's greatest appeals as a social justice practice. The young children, teens, and adults who lacked the self-confidence or desire to be on stage could be involved in many of roles, building props, serving as stagehands, making masks and puppets, doing community clean-ups and gardening, or engaging vulnerable populations in the creative process. This array of roles appealed to varied personalities and offered company members multiple opportunities to develop the confidence that many lacked.[41]

Storyhouse additionally advanced collective agency among company members by increasing their access to information, resources, and skills—for example, by bringing in community agencies to provide the support that the teens needed to write their scripts and assigning artists to give them a compelling dramatic form, thus enabling teen authorship of award-winning plays. Community-based theatre offers a means of representing a place and the young people who reside there and for transcending societal stereotypes about them. It provides a "site of resistance" where they can directly challenge negative representations of themselves as dangerous and disorderly.[42] In a city that, for decades, had been flooded with images of young people engaging in antisocial behaviors, Storyhouse's performances not only supplanted negative stereotypes with positive ones, but they also transformed the negative attitudes that many of the youth had about themselves. Research suggests that being successful and staking claim to a positive identity in performances would have helped company members counteract stereotypes about themselves and their community,[43] allowing them to rise above societal labels and glimpse the possibility of excelling in school and other endeavors.[44]

Storyhouse further advanced company members' collective agency by connecting them to social capital, which scholars believe results when young people have a supportive social milieu in which to exercise creative authority and express their feelings about injustices.[45] Storyhouse generated synergistic relationships within a multi-age family, scaffolding collaborative effort in a way that allowed the teens to partner with adults as performers or crew, while also exercising leadership with young children and elders. Research suggests that by engaging company members in working together to transform social problems through their artistic creations, Storyhouse would have motivated and channeled their passions toward action.[46]

Finally, observations by community-based theatre scholars and activist arts educators support my contention that Storyhouse's dramatic experiences promoted collective action, the behavioral dimension of heart-centric critical pedagogy. Because community-based theatre by nature is interactive, grounded in local experiences, and entails the physicality of performance, it beckons audiences to delve into their feelings and asks them to connect with one another through their minds and hearts, and even their bodies.[47] As a form of collective action, community-based theatre offers "a powerful tactic for reaching broader audiences with narratives, experiences, and perspectives that contradict and complicate dominant ones."[48] Storyhouse's performances, whether in the theatre or on the city streets, situated company members as "civic actors" within a world that they themselves had invented, perhaps to escape domestic violence or other traumas in their lives. Scholars believe that the imaginary realm of theatre can help youth rehearse alternatives, "inaugurate new ways of seeing," and glimpse a transformed world, which can help them critique their circumstances and then try out "what might be."[49] Storyhouse used the imaginary realm of theatre in precisely this manner.

For example, company members gained insights into the problems that they were portraying, such as teen dating violence, and, in the process, they developed new positions on addressing these problems as individuals and as a community. Indeed, their recitations of memorials to slain youth provided a compelling example of theatre's potential "to produce a change of view, attitude, awareness, and understanding" of traumatic loss in a community.[50] Notably, the transformative power of Storyhouse's performances often resided in talkbacks that helped audiences grapple with such perplexing issues as gang violence and teen homicide and sometimes offered specific community resources that they could utilize. In this way, Storyhouse sought to promote both individual and social change through performances that helped company members understand and rise above the marginalization that they experienced—for example, because of racist planning policies. The performances not only helped the youth and their immediate families, but they also became problem-solving tools for the local community. As Boal envisioned, Storyhouse engaged company members in transgressive action, helping them reinvent the laborious tasks of cleaning up and beautifying garbage-filled lots while celebrating the city's icons with puppets so large they required teams of puppeteers. These ritualistic parades situated Storyhouse's intergenerational civic actors within the public domain, simultaneously contradicting Detroit's negative stereotype as a war zone and its positive equivalent as a neoliberal oasis by articulating a counternarrative of grassroots struggle and hope.

## Illustrating Place-Based Activism's Emotional Realm

In the previous section, I reviewed literature on community-based theatre to validate my characterization of Storyhouse's curriculum as heart-centric critical pedagogy. Here I ground that pedagogy in literature on place to validate my assertion that this form of theatre can help young people develop the place awareness and place agency to engage in critical placemaking in the commons of their communities. I conceptualize this reiterative process as the emotional realm of place-based activism, which helps young people explore their feelings about their localities and then turn those feelings into action, a process that likely involves the arts. The stereotype of a lone genius producing works of beauty and emotional intensity, "though valid and valuable in its own right, can obscure the more integrated roles that art, artists, and educators can have in community building, cultural affirmation, and articulating a need for change."[51] Rather than protesting in the streets or arguing in the courts to achieve Constitutional rights, activist artists facilitate conversations that frame alternative worldviews for young people, thereby heightening their social and political consciousness and enabling their inner readiness to change oppressive conditions or assert their cultural identity.[52]

Activist artists engage in social change as an ongoing, multilayered, and complex process that strives to transform young people's outlook "from hopeless submission to oppressive conditions to a readiness to change those conditions."[53] Their activism takes on special significance in community-based theatre because performances are both inspired by and dependent upon relationships with a particular place and group of people. This art form is the essence of place-based activism, and Storyhouse offered an exemplary model through its grounding in the distinctive culture of Southwest Detroit. Like other change-oriented art forms, the transformative power of community-based theatre derives not from exposing a community's marginality but rather by animating its promise of hope and possibility;[54] it helps young people move toward democracy by kindling their urge to belong, participate, connect, and contribute to society.[55] In a city that had been resistant to top-down intervention,[56] Storyhouse's activism engaged the emotional realm, generating hope and healing while giving young people the placemaking authority to transform trauma into resilience.

## Place Awareness: Nurturing Hope and Optimism

Social problems in Southwest Detroit threatened to obliterate its legacy as "a good place to settle." Investigations of how young people can help reclaim such neighborhoods suggest that they need to differentiate systemic problems from personal ones in order to build their capacity to imagine the kind of places where they can thrive.[57] Storyhouse built this capacity by co-creating scripts about the city's social problems. It nurtured company members' "hope, optimism, and vision to create justice," even though they were surrounded by social and environmental toxins. Its plays helped company members and audiences alike name what may have seemed to be personal misfortunes as systemic oppression, enabling them to see that their circumstances were not permanent, and then providing them with a public stage for acting out new possibilities.[58]

Increasingly, scholars have come to recognize the importance of hope in helping youth reimagine oppressive conditions. Their research lends support to Storyhouse's decision to stage plays about both the perpetrators and victims of teen violence. Company members' multi-year explorations of antisocial behavior and ways to increase tolerance among their peers helped them understand how they could "act on behalf of others with hope, joy, and a sense of possibility."[59] Scholars also believe that marginalized urban youth in particular benefit from having a "community of care" that connects them across age groups through creative social change.[60] Storyhouse provided just such a community, its dramatic enactments creating a public stage for company members and audiences to rehearse the cognitive abilities that result in a sense of optimism about being able to attain better tomorrows.[61] They encouraged company members to reimagine both the quality of the city's commons and the relationship of people to it.

## Place Agency: Encouraging Optimism about Civic Life

Places are not simply backdrops for social life; rather, they are the medium, along with time, through which social life occurs. Places are created through human activity and imagination even as they help shape those activities and imaginaries.[62] As geographic locales, they have personal, social, and cultural meanings that provide important mechanisms for shaping the identities of individuals and groups. Research in several fields suggests that these identities reflect "both the qualities of places and the characteristics and relations of people to places."[63] The performances that Storyhouse staged throughout Southwest and Downtown Detroit, particularly the exchanges that occurred during talkbacks, helped everyone understand the city as a medium for the turbulence that was creating a war zone of violence and disengagement. These were not static exchanges but rather offered company members an opportunity to reimagine the city's social life, thus helping them reshape the negative identities that had sapped their individual and collective confidence.

Some scholars argue that increasingly fractured news sources, especially cable television, talk radio, and social media, have eroded the spatially situated nature of behavior, contending that communities share geographic locales but occupy vastly different psychic ones. They assert that not having mutual experiences has contributed to the nation's increasing polarization since the 1970s.[64] Storyhouse resisted this trajectory, using dramatic form to bring company members and audiences together in an invented space to re-envision the city, its icons and natural resources, and its gang members, who could seek redemption as protagonists in their own stories. I would argue that these dramatic enactments strengthened the local culture in a city where people had long demonstrated the capacity to overcome adversity and learn from the past in order to craft the future, a capacity that psychologists characterize as resiliency.[65] Storyhouse nurtured the confidence to employ "strong, accessible language and engage in useful and reasonable thinking, theorizing, and storytelling. With flexibility, with open minds. With optimism." It produced roadrunners who got flattened and popped right back up. Though Storyhouse engaged in all three dimensions of place-based activism, it excelled in this attitudinal dimension, igniting passions and engaging company members and audiences in "social dreaming" and imagining a preferred future.[66]

## Critical Placemaking: Sparking a Change of Hearts and Minds

In general, placemaking is the intentional manipulation of public space, no matter the size, from a street corner to a city or a nation state.[67] It requires the place agency "to be in, act on, or exert control over a desired part of the built and natural environment."[68] Further, whoever has agency determines the beneficiaries of the placemaking process—for example, whether it benefits neoliberal market forces or grassroots ones. Though youth, especially youth of color, typically lack placemaking authority at even the smallest scale, sometimes they illicitly seize it through vandalism, graffiti, or protests.[69] But evidence abounds that they lack authority even to occupy public space and can wind up in the criminal justice system or the morgue for merely being there. In downtown areas where placemaking is about branding a city to attract investment, low-income adults also typically lack placemaking authority except in the form of protest, which is often about resisting marginalization in their own neighborhoods.

In short, Storyhouse's constituency lacked placemaking authority, yet its organic gardening project legitimized the physical presence of mostly African American and Latino/a workers, giving them permission to act upon and control public space. In contrast to the highly publicized social practices of the youth who had contributed to stereotypes of Detroit as a gang-infested war zone, this project granted them the right to dance and have fun, but it also tasked them with the responsibility to clean up trash-filled vacant lots, including picking up their own refuse and moving around heavy boulders. Their presence offered a resolution to the conflict between longtime residents, who justified their placemaking authority on the basis of having sustained their neighborhoods through devastating disinvestment, and downtown elites, who justified theirs "on the basis of dollar returns and enhanced city image."[70]

Into this tug of war paraded the Storyhouse work crew with parents in tow, no doubt sweating and covered in soil, carrying tools and turning the physicality of labor into a ritualistic drama. What an incredible counternarrative to the dominant ones that either commodified or demonized African American culture in order to draw whites and money back to the city. In their place were workers who had earned the right to Detroit's waterfront by cleaning up lots that were "owned yet untended by the city and real-estate speculators."[71] I would argue that the place-based dramas portrayed in Storyhouse's waterfront performances offered a powerful tactic for changing hearts and minds about who should have the right "to use, shape, and regulate downtown spaces."[72] Storyhouse brought an enjoyable event to Detroit's tourist-oriented waterfront that featured personal and collective responsibility, not profits, as the stars of a commons where resources sustain not just the elite, but the entire community.

## Conclusions: A Troubled but Promising Exemplar

To bring Part I of the book full circle, I conclude this section with observations of the shortcomings that limited Storyhouse's transformational aspirations—namely, centering the norms of white supremacy, having a constrained artistic vision, and most problematically emulating corporate America's social stratification. Then I attribute these shortcomings to the omnipresence of neoliberal capitalism and offer a means for Storyhouse to overcome them.

### Centering the Norms of White Supremacy

Lillian and Lamar Montgomery, two mid-career Caucasian artists, arrived in Detroit via Utah after spending their formative years in Wyoming. During the 1990s when they were establishing Storyhouse, the population of Wyoming was 94 percent white, with persons of Hispanic origins representing less than 6 percent of the population and African Americans representing less than 1 percent.[73] Despite the Montgomerys' avowed commitment to social justice, they surrounded themselves with the kind of people who were most familiar to them—other Caucasians—instead of looking to Detroit's majority population of African Americans or the Mexican Americans who filled the surrounding neighborhood. In addition to Lillian, who had assumed singular leadership by the time of the 2004–2005 study, an influential board member (and likely other board members), the only full-time staff member, and the puppet director were all Caucasian.

Today, the executive director is Caucasian, and a nine-member board is led by two Caucasians who are part of powerful, majority-white organizations, as is one of the two African American board members. In addition, Storyhouse's partners, past and present, have consisted of mainstream institutions (public schools and government and social service agencies) that have notoriously failed Detroit's majority African American population. Yet more progressive organizations, such as the Boggs Center, were not among its partners. Co-founded by a Chinese American and African American couple, the center has a significant track record running a nationally recognized summer youth program and was strong enough to survive its cofounders' deaths, yet Lillian seems not to have tapped its expertise. Thus, Storyhouse's performances created future visions of the commons, but its administrative structure assigned Caucasians the leading roles in that future. Because Lillian was invested in maintaining her invisible privileges at the top of the social order, she failed to bring into leadership positions the persons of color who would have been necessary to decenter white supremacy.

## Having a Constrained Artistic Vision

A review of Storyhouse's portfolio reveals that its distinguishing artistic practices—the original plays, celebrations, performances, and activities aforementioned—took shape early on. As the company expanded in size and range, those practices remained unchanged until Lillian's departure in 2016, staying within the traditional boundaries of community-based theatre except for a transitory involvement with gardening on vacant lots. Yet, this latter work presented a compelling arena of expansion because it aligned with Detroit's leadership role in a growing urban agriculture movement. Gardening had become an extensive bottom-up "industry" in Detroit as a result of the immense amount of vacant land that covered one-third of the city and represented 150,000 vacant lots. In 2013, the city even adopted legislation legalizing between 350 and 1,600 gardens, ranging in size from backyard plots to small farms that together were yielding 165 tons of produce per year "for sale through a dozen farmers' markets, direct sales to restaurants, Community Supported Agriculture (CSA) networks, and soup kitchens."[74]

This explosion of urban agriculture posed an extraordinary opportunity for Storyhouse to expand its influence by partnering with some of the many farmers and volunteers who were making the city a more beautiful, healthier place, replacing the wage labor that had proven so fickle for poor Detroiters with meaningful productivity. I can imagine Storyhouse animating a sense of possibility in a commons that the farmers and volunteers had invented out of despair, performing rituals about the cycle of life and celebrating the laborious tasks of restoring place. Such rituals would not only have heightened the cultural meaning of the city's new urban agricultural commons, but it would also have opened a more robust funding stream for Storyhouse. For example, in 2019, the National Endowment for the Arts' budget was $162M, but that year the U.S. Department of Agriculture's budget was almost 900 times that, at $140B. Extending the organization's portfolio beyond the boundaries of the arts to infuse Detroit's grassroots community revitalization practices with new heart-centric ways of working would have expanded its funding stream, allow-ing it to acquire the scale and complexity to propel systems change.[75]

## Emulating Corporate America's Social Stratification

Initially, Storyhouse envisioned bringing together "a bunch of people" of all ages to have fun and work toward "a common goal," but this commitment to intergenerational programming dissipated, likely in response to age-specific funding requirements. The first dissipation occurred in 2010 when Storyhouse separated its school, professional theatre, and puppetry program into distinct operations, with the school having intergenerational classes but a separate teen company. By 2020–2021, a much-simplified agenda mir-rored the age-segregation of the education system and consisted of offerings for children, ages eight to fourteen, and for teens, ages fifteen to eighteen who aged out of the company after high school. Nor did Storyhouse keep its most promising alumni on as staff, as occurred in the other exemplars in this book.

Having youth who did not ascend into staff positions and staff who did not ascend into senior positions because they left to get better-paying jobs com-bined with a failure to involve the youth, parents, and community members in decision making. The outcome was a governance structure that lacked the inclusiveness that is often a hallmark of community-based organizations. Nor was the board engaged enough to meet its responsibility to grow second-generation leadership and ensure succession planning,[76] leaving Lillian at the top of a stratified social hierarchy, exercising sole control over Storyhouse's ar-tistic vision and management.

At the bottom was the largest group, children taking classes off-site at ele-mentary and middle schools. Next came a smaller group of teens writing and rehearsing plays onsite for performances that occurred around the city. An oc-casional group of parent and other volunteers was somewhere in this lower strata, chauffeuring, attending performances, and so forth but with no decision-making authority. Higher up was a group of paid and volunteer staff who worked in the building and at schools and other sites, its status diminished by short tenures and lack of a home base. Much higher up came Lillian with the title of founding director, a Ph.D. who sometimes underwrote projects and had control over budgeting and personnel and likely had the only office in the tiny building. At the very top was the board of directors, disconnected enough to have been blindsided by Lillian's sudden departure. Thus, Storyhouse evolved from an organization where "the intergenerational thing" was key to helping the youth learn to interface with all different ages to one that was more akin to corporate America, where the CEO is deemed 320 times more valuable than the typical worker. Such organizational flaws prevented Storyhouse from itself being the commons that it hoped to create.

## Realizing the Emotional Realm of Place-Based Activism

The foregoing shortcomings in Storyhouse's justice-oriented aspirations mirror those of many activist youth organizations and the foundations that support them. They are typically not-for-profit, but they operate within a neoliberal framework, amplifying its relentless calls for young people to exercise responsibility and self-reliance. Neoliberalism does not necessarily guarantee equal rights to low-income youth but rather offers them an opportunity to self-improve by acquiring the skills to succeed in the marketplace. Making low-income youth responsible for their own economic and social well-being neutralizes the activism of justice-oriented organizations like Storyhouse, forcing them to compete for grants while demanding measurable improvements in a population that needs services (like free food) and that capitalism has deemed to be "at risk" for economic failure. Storyhouse "pushes against this individualizing focus,"[77] but it could go even further by forthrightly confronting the all-encompassing encroachment of neoliberal capitalism into the nonprofit sector. To realize the full potential of its activist agenda, the company must make "unlikely alliances" outside of the arts,[78] especially with organizations that are expert in circular economic strategies. Such alliances would help Storyhouse free itself from the clutches of funders by multiplying the small grants it receives as sustainable sources of income that also benefit the larger community. They would not change but rather deepen Storyhouse's artistic practices and surely result in a more democratic commons than the one that exists in Detroit today—one that takes shape "between the real and the fictional—between the actual world and the dramatic one" where transformation can happen.[79]

## Notes

1. Using a pseudonym is required by the participating institutional review boards that established the terms of conducting the research.

2. Reynolds Farley, Mick Couper, and Maria Krysan, "Race and Revitalization in the Rust Belt: A Motor City Story," *Michigan Sociological Review* 20 (Fall 2006): 8, https://www.jstor.org/stable/40969161.

3. After one of Storyhouse's cofounders completed a structured telephone survey, which led to its selection as a case study, three University of Michigan GRAs administered nine additional open-ended interviews with constituents. The transcript

that I constructed from their much longer verbatim documentation of both these protocols contains only the responses that inform my theoretical framework. The GRAs were supervised by Professor Lorraine Guitiérrez.

4. Among the sixty constituents the director identified as possible interviewees, just nine were able to complete interviews with the GRAs, the lowest response rate of the six case studies in the Ford Foundation research. The GRAs attributed the low response to scheduling snafus, all likely as a result of Detroit's state of decline. Per contracts with the Human Subjects Review Boards of the various participating academic institutions, the names that appear in the narratives are pseudonyms.

Staff study participants included: Lillian, forty-nine, Caucasian, and founding executive director (completed the initial survey); Lamar, fifty, Caucasian, founding youth director, high school teacher and parttime staff, and Lillian's husband; Josephine, fifty, Caucasian, and puppetry director; Angie, under thirty-five, Caucasian, and full-time staff; and Francesca, fifty, Latina, and artist-in-residence.

Youth study participants included: Rufus, sixteen, African American-Native American-Eastern European, and eleventh grader; and Jena, twenty, Caucasian, college freshman, and Josephine's daughter.

Parent study participants included: Gloria, over fifty-five, African American, and mother of Bridget (a tenth grader); and Hazel, forty, African American, and mother of Dayton (a fifth grader). The board member was Kordell, under thirty-five, and Caucasian.

5. Drawing from the literature, I define "critical awareness" as young people sharing their personal experiences with peers in order to understand the societal systems that perpetuate the injustices in their lives; "collective agency" as young people perceiving a common purpose and becoming confident that they can work together to change their circumstances; and "collective action" as young people working together to change unjust conditions. See the section on critical pedagogy in the Introduction for more information on how I have used this educational philosophy in framing the book.

6. My GRA administered a single interview via Zoom and transcribed it using Temi. The interview was with Hattie Ahearn, over fifty-five, Caucasian, and executive director.

Unlike the other programs in this book, Storyhouse had changed leadership three times, so Hattie was unable to identify possible interviewees who would have been around in 2004–2005. In addition, Lillian and Lamar were experiencing health crises, eliminating their participation.

7. The refocused dimensions of critical pedagogy are: "place awareness" (or helping youth understand the systemic causes of injustices in their neighborhoods); "place agency" (or equipping them with the capacity to transform these injustices); and "critical placemaking" (or engaging them in a participatory process of transforming their neighborhoods).

8. Bill McGraw, "Life in the Ruins of Detroit," *History Workshop Journal*, no. 63 (Spring 2007), https://www.jstor.org/stable/25472916.

9. Maria Elena Rodriguez, *Images of America: Detroit's Mexicantown* (Charleston, S.C.: Arcadia Publishing, 2011).

10. McGraw, "Life in the Ruins of Detroit."

11. Farley, Couper, and Krysan, "Race and Revitalization in the Rust Belt," 1–67.

12. Rodriguez, *Images of America.*

13. June Manning Thomas, "Neighborhood Response to Redevelopment in Detroit," *Community Development Journal* 20, no. 2 (April 1985): 89–98, https://www.jstor.org/stable/44256327/.

14. Thomas, "Neighborhood Response to Redevelopment in Detroit."

15. Thomas, "Neighborhood Response to Redevelopment in Detroit."

16. Rodriguez, *Images of America.*

17. McGraw, "Life in the Ruins of Detroit," 297.

18. Tara Clark, "Detroit's Empowerment Zone: Evaluation of Success," *Virginia Policy Review* (Fall/Winter 2013): 44–60, https://pages.shanti.virginia.edu/VPR_Journal_Team/files/2013/02/Lynch.Benjamin_VPRFallWinter.ClarkResearchFINALCDC.44-60.pdf.

19. Rodriguez, *Images of America.*

20. Rodriguez, *Images of America.*

21. Rodriguez, *Images of America.*

22. Lizabeth Jenkins-Dale, "Soo Theatre Project Announces Ken Miller as Executive Director," *Sault News* Online (March 26, 2016): B2.

23. Department of Justice, *Crime in the United States: Uniform Crime Report* (Washington, D.C.: Federal Bureau of Investigation, 2004), https://www2.fbi.gov/ucr/cius_04/summary/index.html.

24. "Quick Facts: Detroit City, Michigan; Michigan," 1–3, Washington, D.C.: United States Census Bureau, https://www.census.gov/quickfacts/fact/table/detroitcitymichigan,MI/PST045219.

25. Isaac Ginsberg Miller, "Place-Branding Detroit: Beloved Community or Big Society?" *Berkeley Journal of Sociology* 60 (2016): 6–17, http://www.jstor.com/stable/44713555, quoting Malik Yakini, lifelong Detroiter and co-founder of the Detroit Black Community Food Security Network, no source provided.

26. Alesia Montgomery, "Reappearance of the Public: Placemaking, Minoritization and Resistance in Detroit," *International Journal of Urban and Regional Research* (2016): 776–99.

27. Ariel Guevara, "Mirror News: A Solution for Southwest Detroit," *ULOOP Inc.* (February 1, 2016).

28. Annalise Frank, "Mexicantown Avenue to be Remade as Shared Street," *Crain's Detroit Business* 34, no. 21 (May 28, 2018).

29. Montgomery, "Reappearance of the Public."

30. Merrit Kennedy, "Controversial Emergency Manager of Detroit's Public Schools Resigns," *The Two Way*, February 2, 2016, https://www.npr.org/sections/thetwo-way/2016/02/02/465279038/controversial-emergency-manager-of-detroits-public-schools-resigns.

31. Stephani Etheridge Woodson, "Performing Youth: Youth Agency and the Production of Knowledge in Community-Based Theater," in *Representing Youth: Methodological Issues in Critical Youth Studies*, ed. Amy L. Best (New York and London: New York University Press, 2007), 284–303, http://www.jstor.com/stable/j .ctt9qg0pf.16.

32. Tim Prentki and Sheila Preston, "Introduction," in *The Applied Theatre Reader*, ed. Tim Prentki and Sheila Preston (New York and London: Routledge, 2009), 9–15.

33. Jan Cohen-Cruz, "A Hyphenated Field: Community-Based Theatre in the USA," *New Theatre Quarterly* 15, no. 4 (November 2000): 364–78.

34. Jan Cohen-Cruz, "Early Antecedents," in *Local Acts: Community-Based Performance in the United States* (New Brunswick, N.J.: Rutgers University Press, 2003), 17–34, http://www.jstor.com/stable/j.ctt1b4cwtm.6 JSTOR.

35. Sharon Verner Chappell and Melisa Cahnmann-Taylor, "No Child Left with Crayons: The Imperative of Arts-Based Education and Research with Language 'Minority' and Other Minoritized Communities," *Review of Research in Education* 37 (2013): 243–68, https://www.jstor.org/stable/24641963.

36. Geraldine Pratt and Caleb Johnston, "Turning Theatre into Law, and Other Spaces of Politics," *Cultural Geographies* 14, no. 1 (January 2007): 92–113, https:// www.jstor.org/stable/44243683.

37. Prentki and Preston, "Introduction."

38. Julie Dunn and Madonna Stinson, "Learning through Emotion: Moving the Affective in from the Margins," *Springer* (June 29, 2012): 205.

39. Alexis Jemal, "Critical Consciousness: A Critique and Critical Analysis of the Literature," *Urban Review* 49 (2017): 602–26.

40. Shawn A. Ginwright, "Peace Out to Revolution! Activism among African American Youth: An Argument for Radical Healing," *Young* 18, no. 1 (2010): 93.

41. Melvin Delgado, *Music, Song, Dance, and Theatre: Broadway Meets Social Justice Youth Community Practice* (New York: Oxford University Press, 2018).

42. Doreen Mattingly, "Place, Teenagers, and Representations: Lessons from a Community Theatre project," *Social & Cultural Geography* 2, no. 4 (2001): 445–59, https://doi.org/10.1080/14649360120092634, referring to R. Elizabeth Thomas and Julian Rappaport, "Art as Community Narrative: A Resource for Social Change," in *Myths about the Powerless: Contesting Social Inequality*, ed. M. Lykes Brinton et al., 317–36. Philadelphia: Temple University Press, 1996.

43. Jemal, "Critical Consciousness."

44. Delgado, *Music, Song, Dance, and Theatre*, 6, 3.

45. For example, see Linda Charmaraman, "Congregating to Create for Social Change: Urban Youth Media Production and the Sense of Community," *Learning, Media, and Technology* 38, no. 1 (2013): 102–15, and Rebecca A. London et al., "The Role of Community Technology Centers in Promoting Youth Development," *Youth & Society* 42, no. 2 (2010):199–228.

46. Marion Coddou, "An Institutional Approach to Collective Action: Evidence from Faith-Based Latino Mobilization in the 2006 Immigrant Rights Protests,"

*Social Problems* 63, no. 1 (February 2016): 127–50, https://www.jstor.org/stable /44014898.

47. Delgado, Music, *Song, Dance, and Theatre*, 157, referring to Teresa A. Fisher, "If Obesity Is So Bad, Why Are So Many People Fat? Interrogating, Exploring, and Understanding Obesity through Theatre," unpublished dissertation topic proposal (New York: NYU Steinhardt School of Culture, Education, and Human Development, 2009).

48. Mindi Rhoades, "LGBTQ Youth + Video Artivism: Arts-Based Critical Civic Praxis," *Studies in Art Education* 53, no. 4 (Summer 2012): 317, https://www.jstor.org /stable/24467920.

49. Tim Prentki, "Citizen Artists and Human Becomings," *Journal of Aesthetic Education* 50, no. 2 (Summer 2016): 77, 80, https://www.jstor.org/stable/10.5406 /jaesteduc.50.2.0072.

50. Dorothy Heathcote, "Drama as a Process for Change," in Prentki and Preston, *Applied Theatre Reader*, 201.

51. Alina Campana, "Agents of Possibility: Examining the Intersections of Art/ Education, and Activism in Communities," *Studies in Art Education* 52, no. 4 (Summer 2011): 278, https://www.jstor.org/stable/41407910.

52. Campana, "Agents of Possibility."

53. Campana, "Agents of Possibility," 281.

54. Robin D. G. Kelley and Jeffrey J. Williams, "History and Hope: An Interview with Robin D. G. Kelley," *Minnesota Review*, nos. 58–60 (Spring/Fall 2002–Spring 2003): 93–109.

55. Delgado, *Music, Song, Dance, and Theatre*.

56. Miller, "Place-Branding Detroit, 6–17, quoting Malik Yakini.

57. Ginwright, "Peace Out to Revolution!"

58. Ginwright, "Peace Out to Revolution!," 85.

59. Ginwright, "Peace Out to Revolution!," 85.

60. Rhoades, "LGBTQ Youth + Video Artivism."

61. Fran H. Norris, "Behavioral Science Perspectives on Resilience," unpublished Report Prepared for the Community and Regional Resilience Institute (CARRI) (Washington, D.C.: Meridian Institute, June 2010).

62. Thomas F. Gieryn, "A Space for Place in Sociology," *Annual Review of Sociology* 26 (2000): 463–96, http://links.jstor.org/sici?sici=0360-0572%282000%2926 %3C463%3AASFPIS%3E2.0.CO%3B2-S.

63. Lee Cuba and David M. Hummon, "A Place to Call Home: Identification with Dwelling, Community, and Region," *Sociological Quarterly* 34, no. 1 (Spring 1993): 113, https://www.jstor.org/stable/4121561, referring to Fritz Steele, *The Sense of Place* (Boston: CBI, 1981).

64. See, for example, Kevin M. Kruse and Julian E. Zelizer, *Fault Lines: A History of the United States Since 1974* (New York: W. W. Norton), 2019.

65. Markus Keck and Patrick Sakdapolrak, "What Is Social Resilience: Lessons Learned and Ways Forward," *Erdkunde* 67, no. 1 (January–March 2013): 5–19, http://www.jstor.org/stable/23595352.

66. Kris D. Gutiérrez et al., "Youth as Historical Actors in the Production of Possible Futures," *Mind, Culture, and Activity* 26, no. 4 (2019): 291–308, https://doi.org/10.1080/10749039.2019.1652327.

67. Siobhan McEvoy-Levy, "Youth Spaces in Haunted Places: Placemaking for Peacebuilding in Theory and Practice," *International Journal of Peace Studies* 17, no. 2 (Winter 2012): 1–32, http://www.jstor.com/stable/41853033.

68. Alesia Montgomery, "Reappearance of the Public: Placemaking, Minoritization, and Resistance in Detroit," *International Journal of Urban and Regional Research* (2016): 19.

69. McEvoy-Levy, "Youth Spaces in Haunted Places."

70. Montgomery, "Reappearance of the Public," 787.

71. Montgomery, "Reappearance of the Public," 785.

72. Montgomery, "Reappearance of the Public," 796.

73. United States Census Bureau, "1990 Census of Population: Social and Economic Characteristics—Wyoming," U.S. Department of Commerce: Economics and Statistics Administration, https://www2.census.gov/library/publications/decennial/1990/cp-2/cp-2-52.pdf.

74. Flaminia Paddeu, "Legalizing Urban Agriculture in Detroit: A Contested Way of Planning for Decline," *Town Planning Review* 88, no. 1 (January–February 2017): 114.

75. Alexis Stephens, "Lessons on Collaborative Practice between Artists and Community Developers," *Community Development Innovation Review* (November 13, 2019), https://www.frbsf.org/community-development/publications/community-development-investment-review/2019/november/lessons-on-collaborative-practice-between-artists-and-community-developers/.

76. Prabhir Correa, "Surviving a Leadership Transition, *Times of India*, Business (December 8, 2020), https://timesofindia.indiatimes.com/blogs/developing-contemporary-india/surviving-a-leadership-transition/.

77. Soo Ah Kwon, "Introduction," in *Uncivil Youth: Race, Activism, and Affirmative Governmentality* (Durham. N.C.: Duke University Press, 2013), 17.

78. Kwon, "Conclusions," in *Uncivil Youth*, 121–30.

79. Dunn and Stinson, "Learning through Emotion," 205.

# PART II

## Wai'anae, Hawai'i: Activism through Organic Farming

In this part of the book, I present an exemplar of how community-based organizations can cultivate citizens who contribute to the physical realm of the commons, defined as the public space of democracy where they join with others in a participatory process of making tangible improvements in the sociospatial fabric of their neighborhoods. For this exemplar, I take you to Ho'oulu 'Ōpio Farms, my pseudonym for a social enterprise located along a highway that hugs the west coast of O'ahu, Hawai'i's third-largest and most culturally diverse island.[1] To be exact, the farm, established by a group of community members in 2000, was located in Wai'anae, a quasi-rural, quasi suburban town that hosted Hawai'i's largest homeless encampment. My research team studied Ho'oulu 'Ōpio in 2004–2005, four years into its tenure, and then I revisited it at the height of the Covid-19 pandemic in 2020–2021. The farm was dedicated to reclaiming the ancestral agricultural know-how that colonialism disrupted, leaving in its wake a native population mired in intergenerational poverty and diet-related disease; its mission was to grow organic produce for an impoverished, predominantly Native Hawaiian community, while also "growing" young people and helping them rise above their colonial stereotype of being "lazy, undisciplined, and hypersexual."[2] As you will see, both crusades were literally grounded in *aloha 'āina* (love of the land).

You will read a narrative from the 2004–2005 study with excerpts from a seventy-two-page, 34,000-word transcript of a survey and seventeen interviews that graduate research assistants from the University of Washington School of Social Work and College of Education administered.[3] Study participants, consisting of one of the cofounders, staff, mentors and interns, parents, and board members, responded to questions about the organization, its setting, and its activities.[4] I have organized the narrative according to the dimensions of critical pedagogy (critical awareness, collective agency, and collective action), though the protocols did not ask about this educational philosophy.[5] Except for one person, study participants lived near Ho'oulu 'Ōpio, most had spent their lives there, and several were blood relations. You will also read a narrative from the 2020–2021 study with excerpts from a sixty-four-page, 30,500-word transcript of four interviews that my research assistant at The New School conducted.[6] Study participants, consisting of the other cofounder, the development director, and two staff who had been interns around the time of the initial study, responded to questions intended to weigh my framing of the organization's 2004–2005 curriculum as critical pedagogy. Their interviews confirmed the validity of my framing and revealed a deepening and expansion of Ho'oulu 'Ōpio's initial mission.

This four-section part of the book presents Ho'oulu 'Ōpio as an exemplar of what I theorize as body-centric critical pedagogy within the physical realm of place-based activism based upon its engagement of youth in the labor-intensive work of growing crops to improve health within the surrounding community. In the first section, you learn about Wai'anae's ecology and culture and have a brief introduction to Hawai'i's sovereignty movement, which blossomed around the time of Ho'oulu 'Ōpio's founding. You also learn about the farm, its surroundings, educational mission, and the dedication of staff to realizing it. In the second section, you hear from the 2004–2005 study participants about their experiences in a recently established organization, presented within a critical pedagogy framework and in the third, you hear from the 2020–2021 study participants about its evolution, outcomes related to the dimensions of critical pedagogy, and future trajectory. I begin the fourth section by assessing both narratives to conceptualize the organization as exemplary of body-centric critical pedagogy. I then ground this pedagogy in the commons as the physical realm of place-based activism, refocusing its dimensions as place awareness, place agency, and critical placemaking.[7] I conclude with observations of Ho'oulu 'Ōpio's use of physical labor to advance a democratic commons with access to land, water, healthy food, and political agency.

Though you will eventually encounter all the study participants, here I introduce the organization's leaders to establish not only their familial bonds but also their community connectedness. Ezra, a New Zealand business consultant, and his Native Hawaiian wife, Aulani, cofounded Ho'oulu 'Ōpio. Aulani explained that, when they met, the farm was a seed of an idea "from both our parents and our grandparents who were farmers . . . [and] that seed was planted in us" to grow food and ourselves. Her sister, Alani, a former store manager, ran the farm's café. Bruce, an elder, community activist, and retired teacher, mentored Ezra and Aulani in creating the organization; he served on the board, as did his business owner son, Bruce Jr., and daughter-in-law, Lynette, and, though retired, he also worked as its first employee for almost a decade. Another elder, Luana, whose son was an intern in the inaugural class, had recently joined the board as vice president, replacing Jenny, a founding board member. Of this group, only Aulani participated in the 2020–2021 study, though she did not participate in the earlier one.

# Historical Context

In order to appreciate Hoʻoulu ʻŌpio's deep commitment to the land, you need to understand the ethos of its very unique context, so I begin this section by characterizing Waiʻanae's ecology and way of life and the impoverishment that occurred there in the wake of postwar colonization. Then I portray Native Hawaiians' resistance to their degradation, which climaxed a few years before the organization came into being and helped shape its mission. I end by describing Waiʻanae as a cultural context, as well as Hoʻoulu ʻŌpio's community-embeddedness, dedicated staff, and entrepreneurial prowess.

## Wai'anae, Hawai'i

Looking through the eyes of Waiʻanae's *Kanaka Maoli* (first people), you can sense the sacredness of its landscape. Named for its *wai* (fresh water streams) and the plentiful *ʻanae* (full-size mullet) that inhabited them, they perceived its landmasses as the bodies of mythical creatures, its caves as the dwelling places of gods.[8] Hoʻoulu ʻŌpio elder Bruce said that knowing native folklore helped the youth understand their spiritual connection to this landscape.

> When they're grounded, they hear about the places around them and how and why they are important, . . . the stories of that mountain, the stories about that beach, the name "Waiʻanae" [large mullet], the indication of what climatic conditions were at the time when the first people arrived. . . . It gives them some connection to the past. And in some cases, because we don't have large mullets anymore, our sense of future, too (Bruce).

In the 1950s, Waiʻanae was still a place of magical beauty, communicating sacredness to its native inhabitants and nourishing their bodies, as another Hoʻoulu ʻŌpio elder, Luana, experienced in her childhood.

> We were raised on the land. We grew everything that we ate. And my tutu had *loʻi* [irrigated terraces]. . . . When it would rain really heavy, the mountain would get so saturated, the water would just come down, you know. It would feed into the *loʻi*, then we will have all this *opai* [shrimp]. . . . Way back then, when the water was clean, we used to eat snails. . . . Itʼs all the ecosystem (Luana).

Unbridled construction of military bases and tourist facilities spoiled Waiʻanaeʼs sacredness, eroding soil and polluting runoff. Its namesake, the large mullet, became extinct in altered coastal and estuarine habitats; its residents became low-wage laborers in a capitalist economy, its fresh water pilfered by plantation and golf course owners. By 2004, when the initial study began, Waiʻanae had become one of Hawaiʻiʼs most economically devastated regions.[9] Home to the stateʼs largest native population, almost one-quarter of the residents lived below the poverty line—more than double that of Oʻahu—almost half qualified for food stamps, and many were homeless.[10] As café manager Alani elaborated:

> The largest part of our community here is on welfare, food stamps. Most who have jobs are having to commute every day into Honolulu. . . . We have a lot of homeless people—5,000 on our side of the island who used to live on the beaches. They had to leave the beaches, so they are going inland or to other parts of the island, or they have a place where people put their cars and tents, waiting for one development to build homes for homeless people (Alani).

Intern Keola spoke of generations of homeless families, disturbed that there were "a lot of kids who live on the beach with their parents or were born on the beach. Itʼs a third-generation family. . . . We could use some of those taxpaying funds to help out our communities—to get some shelters for the moms out here who live on the beach and in the tents." Poverty restricted access to a nutritious diet for about one-third of Waiʻanaeʼs households, making it the stateʼs most food-insecure locale and contributing to its high rates of obesity, diabetes, and poor health.[11] Luana said that diabetes is "really high on this side of the island. We have high blood pressure, you know. Way back in the 1800s, our *kupunas* (elders) hardly got these diseases, but because of the Western diet, we all get all kinds of diseases." To the problems of homelessness and poor health, Bruce added environmental racism.

We are shouldering the burden . . . of the economic success for
everybody on that side of the mountain range. We have the power
plants. We have the industrial plants. We have municipal solid waste
disposals. We have the construction dumps. We have the dumping
from DFS. We have the largest military. . . . We have a four-lane
highway that blocks people from going to the beach. . . . As a result,
we have higher rates of fatality than any other place on O'ahu (Bruce).

Given Wai'anae's impoverished conditions, many outsiders assumed that
its residents were dropouts and substance abusers, and many youth had internalized these stereotypes. Alani explained that "the youth haven't been given
the chance or haven't taken the initiative to go beyond their community to
college or a job because they label themselves because they have been so
labeled—mainly the young men."

Another intern, Patrick, elaborated, saying that "everybody thinks that
Wai'anae youth are a bunch of hard asses—you know, dumb kids who don't
do right. And that we're ignorant. But what I mean is that a lot of the kids in
Wai'anae, you know, are really smart. They just don't know it, or they don't
put their talent to full use." Some young people, seeing few educational opportunities, headed into the military or, as Luana's son, Makalo, said: "A lot of
kids here drop out of school and do nothing," yet he insisted that "it's not as
bad as people think. People think of Wai'anae as a ghetto area, but it's not really
like that."

For residents, community pride, activism, and doggedness defined
Wai'anae's identity, rather than its marginality.[12] As former board member
Jenny noted:

It's very community-oriented, definitely. I mean people in the
Wai'anae Coast don't let anything goes on without their input, you
know. They're very vocal people. . . . I don't know why people say,
"don't come to Wai'anae." You know, Wai'anae people are really
friendly, and I think they get the raw end of the stick. . . . I have to
think it's the best place to be homeless (laughs). If you're going to be
homeless, be homeless in Wai'anae (Jenny).

Sometimes outsiders characterized the area as being "local," implying that
residents were backward, but residents described themselves as having a strong
sense of pride and capacity for bucking outside development, using the term
to indicate the sense of belonging, fortitude, and self-sufficiency that united
the community.[13] According to mentor Aleki: "From one coast to the other is
a big neighborhood. Everybody knows each other. It's a beautiful place, with

ocean and mountains, . . . [and] what we have is what we get for ourselves." Bruce added: "That's why all the homeless people move here, because people out here is a-caring." Nor was food insecurity a barrier to hospitality. According to Keola: "The positive part of this area is that we have a lot of *aloha* out here. . . . We're like family, like 'come, come eat.'" Mark, an intern who dropped out of Hoʻoulu ʻŌpio because he needed a higher paying job to deal with a "financial problem" at home, also affirmed residents' generosity, saying that "if you need help, you can pretty much ask anybody on the street."

## Hoʻoulu ʻŌpio Farms

A resistance movement launched in 1893, immediately after U.S.-backed insurgents overthrew the Hawaiian monarchy, but it exploded on the one-hundredth anniversary of that takeover. In marking this cataclysmic event, activists took stock of native people's suffering—their "declining health and increasing incarceration, landlessness, homelessness, child morbidity, child and spouse abuse, drug dependency, and despair." Believing that these pathologies originated in the theft of their land, language, culture, and identity, activists organized marches, rallies, and legal actions to reclaim the "Hawaiian-ness that had been discouraged, removed, minimized, and lost through time."[14]

As Luana explained: "When I was a youth . . . we were taught not to speak Hawaiian. We had to learn English you know. Hawaiian was not considered a second language. . . . It was like taboo." Having begun to reclaim their language in the mid-1980s, the resistance movement spurred Hawaiians to use education as a window into their Hawaiian-ness and capacity to seek *pono* (correct or proper) relationships between people, the heavens, and the earth. Hoʻoulu ʻŌpio took shape within this heightened cultural renaissance and reflected its commitment to adopt Hawaiian ancestral concepts of *aloha ʻāina* (love of the land), *ohana* (devotion to family and community), and *kuleana* (responsibility) as guides for behavior. Initially formed as a community development corporation (CDC), the farm began operations in 2001 on a five-acre leased site. The third cohort was underway at the time of the initial study.

### Being Embedded within the Local Community

In 2004–2005, Hoʻoulu ʻŌpio was located on a church campsite along a four-lane highway that featured seventeen fast food restaurants within as many miles. Nearby were mostly vacant housing projects, a gambling den and meth house, abandoned chicken farms, farms that raised fighting chickens, and a stream that had been dry for fifty years. Alani's café and other convenience stores were also nearby. Within this run-down landscape, Hoʻoulu ʻŌpio's improvements stood out, as Jenny boasted. "They built all these stuffs. . . . They put in all that (pointing to the sink, workspace, and plants). This wasn't here. They put in all this gravel, you know. They've made this place."

Hoʻoulu ʻŌpio offered a ten-month internship in agriculture for twelve high school graduates, occurring August to May, that combined hands-on farm work with classroom learning. Most interns (75 percent) were Hawaiian, with the remainder being Japanese, Korean, Filipino/a, and other nationalities; they were seventeen to twenty-five years old, with females making up 60 percent of cohorts because high rates of illiteracy, alcoholism, and incarceration limited male participation. Interns were paid to work eighteen hours per week and were obliged to volunteer an additional two hours, though some contributed much more. As Mark explained: "Usually we would work on Mondays, Wednesdays, and Fridays but on occasion, I would go on a Tuesday or when we had [the farmers' market] on Saturday morning. . . . I went there a lot just to help. I wasn't getting paid for it, but I went there just to hang out." The interns learned the farming cycle by working alongside mentors (who had been interns) to prepare soil, plant, weed, thin, nurture to maturity, harvest, and begin the cycle over again. According to Bruce, they also engaged with Alani and others at the farmers' market, in the public schools, at community events, and even within their families, trying "to make things better."

As a foundation for their hands-on work, the interns attended classes led by Ezra and Aulani on topics ranging from colonialism to conflict resolution. Aleki described the internship as "an alternative for college or the Army, where you get leadership training," while Krushi emphasized its holistic approach, noting that "we teach them organic farming and other personal skills and opening up with people. We teach customer service as well—how to laugh with people, how to . . . talk in big groups." The interns honed their communication skills with seventh graders, helping them create gardens in their schoolyard, taking them on trips to the farm, and, according to Amura, mother of eighth-grader Cairo, to the Makaha Valley "to check the stream out." They also worked with high school students, but Mark said that he preferred "going to the intermediate school and helping the younger kids. It's easier than going to the high school. . . . I just graduated from high school, and I know most of the kids there. It's harder to get through to them, because they are at a certain age where they do whatever."

According to Ezra, Hoʻoulu ʻŌpio emphasized family and community involvement, explaining that, "as part of training, [the interns] have to bring brothers and sisters, and family members to the farm, have to eat food, do evaluation based with family members." On monthly "give days," as few as four and as many as sixty youth and adults lent a hand with seasonal tasks. In addition, community members purchased fresh-cooked meals at the café and fresh produce at the weekly farmers' markets and at the island's health food stores. Hoʻoulu ʻŌpio strengthened its connections to family and community through a five-member board of directors consisting of relatives of the inaugural class of interns and one of the interns and a fifteen-member advisory board consisting of parents and community members. The group, which encompassed business, education, and agricultural expertise, was further enriched by partnerships with the public schools, a community college, a research university, a private school for children of Hawaiian descent, two health clinics, and local businesses. Hoʻoulu ʻŌpio was truly a community-embedded organization.

## Having Staff Who Gave 1,000 Percent

Study participants consistently characterized Hoʻoulu ʻŌpio as a commitment, not a job, declaring that the organization was about helping, giving, caring—behaviors that the leaders modeled and everyone else emulated. Alani explained:

> So much of it is giving of yourself. It is volunteer time—giving back. We have Uncle Bruce, who could just be Santa Claus in disguise. He could be retired; he has eleven children and grandchildren. He is in Vegas right now with his family, and he gets a call on his cell from somebody at the farm, and his response is: "What do you need baby? Uncle can help you." And he's on vacation. His son is Uncle Bruce, Jr. . . . He has a yard that I think the Jolly Green Giant would love to live there. It's always huge and they bring bags to donate to the café—fresh fruit for our smoothies, avocados, bananas, and some of the stuff they only grow on the cooler side of the island. All organically grown. And his wife is on the board, and she's a teacher, and they give of their time as well as to the farm and the youth. We need to hand out flyers, and they're there.
>
> My sister, who I love and will always be proud of, gives 94 percent plus—1,000 percent of her time with her children and her new grandchild who is here with me cooking, who is there every minute of the day for the students. She teaches a class in Hawaiian language. And Ezra her husband, head of the farm who is there teaching, and you know one of his majors was business—one of the top loan officers—who gave up to run the farm. He wanted to be full-time committed to the farm, and he is up there teaching the kids about organics and lives and breathes the youth and the farm and being

youthful in what they do and respectful in what they do. That is every board member and every staff. "Tired? Grouchy? I don't want to get up. Too many mosquito bites, but let's go again." That's farming. Things have to be taken care of, and people help each other (Alani).

## Securing Government Funding for a Movement

Ho'oulu 'Ōpio's budget during its first year was $275K, but it immediately ballooned to $475K, all coming from federal, state, and local governments, an anomaly among the Ford study organizations, as governments were significantly more conservative in their approach to youth than foundations. Ho'oulu 'Ōpio was able to meet government requirements for educating an impoverished, low-achieving population while also subverting the Western education that had contributed to its marginalization.[15] In addition, the organization had achieved a remarkable degree of self-sufficiency by its third year, when one-third of the budget came from agricultural products and the café, contributing almost $160K toward supporting thirty-five staff, including the twelve interns. Explaining the rapid expansion, Luana boasted that the organization had "a terrific grant writer. And that is . . . Ezra. He's very well educated. He knows how to write grants, you know." I would add that Ezra knew how to run a business and that the youth had his back in demonstrating the organization's worthiness. According to Mark:

> Ezra works hard to get grants and get money to pay us and pay the bills. That's why we work hard up there. We don't put up any bad images while we're wearing Ho'oulu 'Ōpio shirts. If we do that, it might screw up grants for us, and we really don't want that to happen (Mark).

Luana explained that government grants had funded the interns' international travel to participate in indigenous farming conferences. "They already have gone to New Zealand. It's a cultural exchange, you know. They teach their culture. They also teach the way they grow their food organically. I guess it's sharing their love for the land." Within the global sovereignty movement, Ho'oulu 'Ōpio was amplifying indigenous approaches to reclaiming colonized land, and it was getting the U.S. government to fund its efforts.

Now that you understand the context and shape of the organization, I explore how Ho'oulu 'Ōpio helped the interns use their hands to grow food and themselves.

# 2004–2005 Narrative

In this three-part narrative, you hear from the 2004–2005 study participants about Hoʻoulu ʻŌpio's curriculum. Though the protocols did not ask about critical pedagogy, I have conceptualized the narrative to illustrate its three dimensions, showing how the curriculum helped the interns discover their ancestral agricultural heritage (critical awareness), learn organic farming from near-peer mentors (collective agency), and become advocates for healthier eating habits (collective action).

## Encouraging Critical Awareness

### Countering a Consumerist Mindset

Hoʻoulu ʻŌpio honed a pedagogy that sought to reverse the consumerist mindset of the interns. As Krushi explained: "We work with youth from seventeen to twenty-five who have just graduated from high school. All they want to do is make money; they don't want to think about land, community, health. 'How can I get a nice car? How can I raise the kids that I already have? . . . How do I make money to go to a club?'" Bruce attributed the interns' mindset to a society that not only emphasized "the individual and not . . . the community," but that also emphasized "the individual's consumption . . . because it helps in the marketplace." He also blamed their disconnection from the land, explaining that "often times, youth don't have a sense of where they come from. . . . There is no value in the land that they walk on. There is no value in the spiritual places that surround them." Bruce said that Hoʻoulu ʻŌpio's mission was to help the interns become grounded in place—for example, by understanding the connection between Maui, the Hawaiian mythological god, and Wai'anae, "where Maui grew up." He believed that knowing their history would contribute to the interns' self-esteem, provide them with a foundation for further learning, and, according to Ezra, disrupt the myth that:

> Captain Cook discovered Hawai'i, but he didn't discover Hawai'i. He stumbled across it after many Pacific Islanders had lived here for a long, long time. That in itself is a way people perceive the start of society here—through a white, Caucasian lens. So, we encourage kids to look at culture and the history of this place through both a Western and Hawaiian sense of the truth (Ezra).

To lay this foundation, Ho'oulu 'Ōpio's pedagogy included interviewing local elders to learn about Wai'anae's agricultural legacy. For example, Joshua said that he talked "to older people who knew the community back in the old days and how that place was and how it changed a lot. Like I get opinions on how older people acted with younger people and what they thought about." Ezra believed that this exploration of the past gave the interns a perspective on their current situation.

> For example, 90 percent of our fresh vegetables and other things are being imported now. We emphasize that this was not always the case. Ships were coming here before the Western contact, but some people lived pretty self-sufficiently. . . . It's important for youth to understand that their ancestors had it going on. Their ancestors might have had it tough, but they were industrious and smart and able to take care of their community (Ezra).

In addition to oral history, Ho'oulu 'Ōpio's pedagogy drew upon music to help the interns understand that, as Takashi put it, "what has happened in the past has created the present for us." For example, Ezra described how the interns "deconstruct a song that we give them and after that they look at a song that they like. We use a Somali song that talks about the oppression of African people and the movement of African people around the world. . . . We really try to get them to look at the complexity of the issue." Elaborating on the multiple media that Ho'oulu 'Ōpio used to raise the interns' awareness of their cultural context, he said:

> We try to teach them through videos and stories of what has happened around the world so they can understand the global context of what their situation is. We also try to look at their history and culture as an asset for them—somewhat of a road map for them. We try to look at

their own lives and the lives of their community—that we do have values, and we do have road maps to get to a better place for our community (Ezra).

## Nurturing a Love of Farming

To reach its goal of providing the community with fresh produce, Hoʻoulu ʻŌpio had to convince at least some of the interns to choose farming as a career—a hard sell, according to Takashi, because many youth bought into the stigma attached to farm labor. The mentors played a vital role in leading the interns toward a love of farming, serving as near peers who could expand their views of farming as a cultural practice. For example, Makalo said that he wanted to help the "youth see a bigger picture, not see this just as a normal job. It's not all about making money, but about helping the community, providing the community with food security, helping the community become self-sufficient and healthy. What we want youth to see is about that bigger picture and not about making money." For Darde, mentoring was about providing an alternative to the commercialization of food.

> The media doesn't put value on food and the sacredness of food in the way we promote it. I think it's difficult for the students to really understand that because there's so much influence by television. But after working with a lot of students, they become much more aware. Because of our discussions that we have—political or philosophical—a lot of students become enlightened. . . . Mainstream media's ongoing narrative is pretty self-centered, and that doesn't really work on the farm. It's the diversity and shared effort that is the value we promote (Darde).

He hoped to reveal alternative career pathways to the interns by using farming as "a template for creating employment that is not only financial security but also dignity. It's also pride and ownership, and there's also a sacredness connected to it." Aleki, instead, emphasized helping the interns explore their agricultural legacy, explaining that "being in the internship I think affects a lot on understanding where they're coming from. We address the past, the history of farming, everything that we were good at" before losing the land. To expand the interns' perspective, Ezra provided classroom instruction, including, according to Mark, in current events, "like stuff that has been happening lately—stuff to make us open our eyes. The internship makes you see more." Instruction also took the form of informal discussions in the field. As Krushi explained: "When we're in the field, there's always conversation going on, always talking, nobody is quiet. . . . We talk about the presidential debate, food issues, the war, animal issues that not a lot of teenagers in the community get to talk about." Conveying the effect of these experiences, Patrick said:

> Hoʻoulu ʻŌpio Farm has given me a different outlook on things—on subjects. We always have heated discussions on the politics of Hoʻoulu ʻŌpio Farm. So, I think it has given me a different outlook on life, and taught me a few lessons along the way, kind of like not to be afraid of work. Everybody's like: "Oh, it's hard work. Oh, you shouldn't do it." But in reality, it's not so terrible (Patrick).

Alani praised the interns' openness to farming, saying that "these youth are so interested to do this. They're willing to be out there and do the hard work in the dirt and pulling weeds. We had girls with Hawaiian gold bracelets and their nails just done, and they can give that up, . . . giving up their free time to be at a job that's not air-conditioned. It's not comfortable; it's farming." Takashi confirmed the internship's success, saying that "in the last two years, we had eighteen youth go through the internship, we've had four stay on as farmers. That's over 20 percent. That's like back-breaking dirty work. Well, four of eighteen want to farm and they're not making much money. But they are passionate."

## Activating Collective Agency

### Instilling a Work Ethic

Many of the interns had witnessed child abuse, drug addiction, and incarceration in their families, and some had personally engaged in criminal activities. For example, Keola said: "I wasn't doing too good in my life. Over here where we live, the community is kind of corrupted and all with high crime and stuff. I was trying to get away from my old friends and start all over and stuff." Ignoring their history, Bruce and Ezra told prospective hires that the position required only "love, respect, and the willingness to work," but Bruce said that incoming interns were "the floaters, they jelly fishes that come here. And after this, they learn how to persevere." And the first step toward learning to persevere was learning to work together as a team—and to work hard. Explaining how the interns discovered the value of teamwork, Takashi said that sometimes fifteen youth and adults would "get down and weed for thirty minutes, and you turn around and go wow! We call that *laulima* [many hands working together]. You can really jam on a work and get it done." According to Bruce, such experiences kindled a work ethic and contributed to a sense of *ohana* (family), compassion, and *kuleana* (responsibility).

To help the interns carry out their *kuleana*, Hoʻoulu ʻŌpio established a clear organizational structure with Ezra overseeing the farm, Alani overseeing the café, Aulani overseeing education, and, according to Makalo, the mentors being in "like a supervisor position." Explaining the farm's "chain of command," Keola said:

> The interns who worked on the farm before are hired in some kind of position, and so it goes on down the road. I have my boss and his wife, and there's other people under him. And then there's the manager. He tells us what to do, and we do it. . . . We are only interns. We don't have a say, you know, but we can speak our minds and say how we feel about things (Keola).

The interns accepted their subordinate role with varying degrees of buy-in. Keola, who was the most senior, saw possibilities for negotiation, saying that "our boss always lets us have input. Sometimes the plan is not good, and he won't do it. And if it's not good, he'll let us change it." But the more junior Joshua expressed frustration.

> Our boss says that we got to do this, this, and this. In order to do that, we need to do something else first, and we are all riding on him. . . . Sometimes he overrides us. Sometimes we just get mad and we keep talking. And yeah, I wish we did have that authority to tell him that we got to do this first in order to get those other steps done (Joshua).

Ezra elaborated on Hoʻoulu ʻŌpio's youth development approach, explaining that "the kids have a say in what goes on. We make sure that when they have a say, they have to back it up with action as well. The old saying is, 'if you going to talk the talk, you got to walk the walk.'" Expressing the more traditional view of an elder, Bruce said that the interns "should have—be queried or questioned on what they think. They have to earn the right [to take part in decisions]. . . . They have to demonstrate their sense of responsibility and understanding of what is asked of them." Ezra emphasized the importance of setting high expectations for the interns' performance, faulting Western neoliberal education for helping "nurture a culture and environment that doesn't seek out excellence—that doesn't evaluate the curriculum to improve upon it." He complained that out-of-school youth programs mirrored the school system in "babysitting kids" and that "what they really do is sports, and the programs don't necessarily evaluate the kids' response to teamwork, to instruction, to self-improvement. They are basically programs that fill kids with soda and basketball courts after school instead of excellence."

Ezra explained that Hoʻoulu ʻŌpio countered the incoming interns' exposure to neoliberal mediocrity by pushing them "to want to learn, to want to go to college, to run a business," adding that he hoped to empower the interns by holding them to high expectations and giving them an increasing voice in running the farm as they advanced.

## Developing Technical Expertise

Growing crops without using pesticides or fertilizers is labor-intensive and includes controlling weeds and pests, applying compost, rotating crops, and many other soil-management techniques. Somehow a business major who had worked as a loan officer had obtained the agricultural expertise not only to run an organic farm, but to run it as an educational enterprise. Ezra hired Darde—a former intern who had "done some informal training, growing up with gardening" but had no management experience—as farm manager. Together, these two novices figured out how to farm sustainably while also motivating "jelly fish" interns to become team leaders. Darde and Jenny both discussed how Hoʻoulu ʻŌpio developed expertise among team members.

> I would sit with the director and manager weekly and plan what we'll do. And then also we had monthly meetings to bring everything together and then work with the students to implement the programs, depending on whether we needed to harvest or weed or do some nursery work. I would work one-on-one with the students. The students, in return, would work with other students as teachers as well. We try to train group leaders (three to four people), and it's based upon their interest and what they want to learn about, . . . agriculture or nursery work (Darde).

> The youth, they have their duties whatever they are in charge of. A lot of times, Ezra gives the youth one vegetable or whatever that they are the expert on, and they really become the expert on it. Because initially, you know, they come here, and they don't know anything. But they get to know so much about farming, what bugs are out there and what works with getting rid of the bugs. They become experts themselves, I think. They know more than me (Jenny).

As you might imagine, some interns were less invested than others or were freeloaders, so Darde provided instruction in collaboration.

> We . . . teach them that they have different ways and styles of working and, as long as the task gets completed, they should respect each other.

For example, if we work with a student who is unhappy because another student doesn't work that much, we have to talk to that person and say: "You should just do your work and the others will catch up." . . . We encourage students to help each other and inspire each other (Darde).

## Providing Near-Peer Mentors

Through direct and indirect mentoring, Hoʻoulu ʻŌpio's pedagogy conveyed ancestral and political values while helping the youth acquire both technical and social skills. As roles and relationships shifted, a novice in one situation became an expert in another. For example, Aleki appreciated the behavior that Ezra modeled, saying that "Uncle Ezra [is] very willing to listen to us. It's a blessing to find somebody with so much experience who can help you, but also become your friend and mentor, and not just boss you around." At the same time, Aleki, who was a same-age role model for the interns, explained that:

A lot of the guys look up to me. They like the way I talk, and they think I should run for the president sometime. I look at things from the grown-up point of view but also from the youth point of view. I don't take sides. I'm an adult, but I just became an adult (Aleki).

Krushi elaborated, saying that "when youth have problems, they'd rather come to us than come to Ezra. But sometimes you also need an authority figure, because they need somebody older to tell them what you can do and what you can't do." Moving "down the road," Keola served as a role model for the high school students.

A lot of the kids now . . . don't know how to speak properly to people. So, when they come out to Hoʻoulu ʻŌpio, they see other kids a little bit older and working for this internship, and they like it. It gives them influence. I talk up to the high school students, talk straight up to them, and they like that. They see all the improvements in us (Keola).

## Providing Leadership Opportunities

Luana summed up how Hoʻoulu ʻŌpio helped the interns move into leadership roles, explaining that "the experienced ones, the ones who have been there for a couple of years, they become counselors or leaders or teachers, yeah. So, Makalo has excelled to that level." Bruce explained that the interns advanced by being assigned responsibilities and then receiving direct feedback about their performance.

> They charge the youth with making sure that the proper amount of vegetables are harvested for whatever mode of sales is taking place, whether it is at the local farmers' market, at the [clinic], or the larger [hospital]. "You know what the orders are, you know what the orders should be, you guys go do it." They get feedback. If there's too much vegetables in the cooler at the end of the day, they overestimated. If there's not enough, they underestimated (Bruce).

Patrick noted that the farmers' market helped the interns "try out our customer service skills, interact with people." Krushi said that they also had an opportunity to advocate good eating habits because "all the people who come to the farmers' market . . . listen to the youth who farm the land, harvest all the veggies, and tell them to eat those veggies because they're very healthy for you." Neil said that:

> For every farmers' market, the staff would push [the interns] to get up and help the customers, talk to them, ask them questions. Just bring up anything so that we can get feedback. Every farmers' market we go to, we get good feedback. Like people tell us about the good vegetables that they got from the previous markets (Neil).

Although the interns may not have had a say as laborers on the farm, they were pushed to move out of their comfort zones as leaders within the community, which Krushi believed community members valued. She said that parents and other adults "want to see the youth really take charge . . . —want to see them organizing things, putting stuff together, really going at it." Takashi went further in positioning the interns as leaders, saying that ultimately there will be "a few youth who will come back and run this show in their own fashion over time."

## Creating a Space for Collective Action

### Creating Advocates for Self-Sufficiency

Mark pinpointed the driving force behind Hoʻoulu ʻŌpio's mission to increase the supply of locally grown food, saying that "it's a one-way-in and one-way-out situation in Waiʻanae. There's no way around, no way out." Luana, who had experienced more bad times than good, recognized that Hoʻoulu ʻŌpio was preparing the interns for possible disruption of the food supply.

The internship is like teaching our youth how to survive—how to help them with their budgets, you know, grow their own foods. Yeah, they have them thinking that what happens if the economy drops? What happens if the Matson ships no longer can come for whatever reasons? How are people going to survive? We are so conditioned to go to the store and buy packaged food, you know (Luana).

Turning the problem of limited geographic access into an opportunity, Neil said that the farm was promoting "food security so the community can be food-sufficient or have local access to organic food," and Mark acknowledged the intern's responsibility to move the agenda forward.

If we like want anything to change, we got to do it ourselves. We cannot really be sitting around expecting the people in office to change everything with the snap of a finger because they have not been able change stuff for how many years already? . . . If you want something to change, you got to do it yourself (Mark).

## Creating Advocates for Healthy Living

In addition to teaching the interns how to grow organic produce, Ho'oulu 'Ōpio prepared them to market it to a clientele that, as Takashi noted, had unhealthy eating habits.

Hawai'i is still the fat capital of the world. Our population of nearly 50,000 people . . . consume[s] more beer per capita than any other part of the Hawaiian island. We've got so many 7-Elevens and fast-food stores, local drive-ins that serve tasty local foods, but very greasy and fattening. Hawaiian population is one of the sickest populations in the U.S.; the diet is a huge reason (Takashi).

Takashi added that the interns "had the exposure and enjoyment of growing food that's really good for everybody and being able to bring it home and share it," which Ho'oulu 'Ōpio saw as a way to change the eating habits of family members, as occurred with Luana.

The first week my son was at Ho'oulu 'Ōpio, when he first joined right after high school . . . he came home and went to clean up my whole refrigerator. Oh, he threw everything away. He threw all my food away, okay? . . . He told me: "Mommy, I'm tired of seeing you suffer already with this disease." Yeah, he taught me how to take better care of myself, you know (Luana).

After family members, the interns turned to the eating habits of community members. As Aleki explained: "Our goal is to have a community where the children are fit; they grow up fit, everybody is able to work hard, and the obesity rate drops. That's one of our dreams. We want our community to eat well." To achieve this dream, he said that "we try to improve their eating habits. . . . We try to get the communities to have a different outlook, a different perspective on food. We have a café, so they have an alternative—a healthy one." Though most interns arrived at Hoʻoulu ʻŌpio expecting a job, Makalo explained that, "after a while, they realize that it's not all about [a job]. It's also about the community and helping the community to be healthier." Jenny said that the interns tackled the community's poor eating habits by "taking the product out, you know. Talking to people and stuff," and Keola elaborated:

> We go up to the high school to talk to the kids. We also bring a lot of high school kids up here to work with us. We go out to the community colleges, and we go to places where some of the people don't think that organic vegetables are healthy. We try to educate them to eat healthy, because we have a lot of obesity out here.

Keola expressed pride in the quality of Hoʻoulu ʻŌpio's produce, noting that "when we go to the comprehensive center—it's like a low-income hospital where we serve the people—there's a lot of elderly people who are sick and all, and they just love our vegetables. Because that stuff is better than the regular food. . . . We put in the best—real vitamins and all that." Alani said that "the community has noticed their kids' changes in eating habits, for example I can't remember the last time I brought dressing for salad because the salad is so good on its own. The community has commented about how they are feeling better and eating better, looking forward." Ezra added that sometimes the interns' campaign for healthy eating habits went further during concerts and other activities when they encouraged people not to consume alcohol or informed them about environmental racism and social inequities.

## Building a Cohort of Shared Values

Many study participants believed that the experience at Hoʻoulu ʻŌpio cultivated enduring relationships among the interns. For example, Bruce said that farming exposed them to "a tradition to get the job done, to get the crops out regardless of what the climatic challenges are," explaining that as they worked together to overcome the challenges of farming, "there is definitely a sense of *ohana*, of compassion, a sense of teamwork" and tolerance. Takashi agreed, noting that "there's a lot of really good friendships. Some of them came into the internship friends, some of them made friends through the activities. They confide in each other, look after each other." Ezra offered that the interns "have a great sense of humor, a good sense of camaraderie, and a commitment to each other. I think once they know each other, . . . they will stand by those other people or kids through thick and thin." With his typical panache, Keola boasted that "we are tight, and we cruise together all the time. I guess the youth in the internship are my new crew now. . . . Last night, we got to make *laulau*, and I was with the people in the internship—even my boss. We get along best when we are at our boss' house. That's the best time; everybody just clicks." Being more analytical, Patrick said:

> We've pretty much become brothers and sisters. We're involved in each other's lives. . . . It's a close-knit group. It's like living with brothers and sisters. Everybody has their day when they don't feel right, . . . but you know, for the most part, everybody's cool with each other. We all talk, and now we all get along very well (Patrick).

Though the parents, staff, and youth all praised the sense of *ohana* at the farm, it was Joshua who said that "Ho'oulu 'Ōpio pretty much changed" his life, explaining that he went from being a "troubled kid" to someone that his parents and even his neighbors could love. Throughout his interview, Joshua revisited what the farm meant to him, saying that it provided him with a lot of friends, including Ezra, to hang out with and discuss life. He valued that the youth treated one another like family, that they were always there for conversation no matter the problem, and that they would always be there. In speculating about his future, Joshua ended the interview by saying:

> My dreams are to become a successful welder, to have my own house, and to be able to give back to the Ho'oulu 'Ōpio internship. It doesn't matter if I give back through work, or money, or more land. Like if I had land and like I didn't need the land, I would give it straight to Ho'oulu 'Ōpio and thank them for all the stuff they gave me (Joshua).

Takashi believed that what bound the interns together was their shared experience of caring for the land and wanting to give "their children experiences they have experienced—the healthy *'āina*, the earth," noting that:

> Two years ago, I sat down with youth and said: "If we gave you a full scholarship to go to college if you'd come back and be a taro farmer afterward, would you do it?" Barely any raised their hands. But then I said: "If we restore a stream and make taro patches there where you could come back and bring your friends and family," nearly all the

hands went up. We're realizing that although there are a few who will become organic farmers, many will participate in a community endeavor that's like what they have experienced in the farm (Takashi).

## Building a Community of Support

After declaring that "the general community is really important" at Hoʻoulu ʻŌpio, study participants provided examples of how the organization engaged various constituencies. For example, Ezra described the monthly workdays when volunteers do chores on the farm, saying that the event "attracts all kinds of people. Lots of people outside our community come, some from corporations, and the funders that have donated money to us. They bring their staff and make sort of like a staff-building day." He said that the interns "are put in the position of leadership and given a group of people to work with," which encourages the volunteers to recruit other youth who would not normally "be attuned to giving back." Ezra also described fundraisers that bring community members to the farm.

> One of the things we do there is prepare a meal and have the kids write to people who might be interested. We cook; some of the stuff is cooked at our café and a lot of stuff comes from their garden at the school or the farm. It's really just a way to have a celebration for kids where they can show off their work to their parents. It's also a way for the food to be shown and how they are growing it (Ezra).

Alani described a space in the parking lot of the café where the interns set up the farmers' market. She said that customers can gather on a patio deck in the shade of banana trees, noting that:

> The community has benefited by having a place where they can come and meet and have a cup of coffee and everybody says it's kind of like old Hawaiʻi, in the porch kind of setting, not fast food and so commercialized. They can come and sit and talk all day if they like. They exchange stories about what's going on in the community (Alani).

Finally, Bruce described the community that Hoʻoulu ʻŌpio was building among farmers, explaining that the farm "is basically there to create like an extension agency for creating organic farming, and to get the knowledge out to the farmers in the area. Not only changing the behavior, but impacting the environment, having more nitrogen places in the ground. Not nearly as much pesticides."

# 2020–2021 Narrative

This section brings you forward fifteen years to hear from a cofounder and three current staff at Hoʻoulu ʻŌpio who were there around the time of the 2004–2005 study. They offer a deeply informed appraisal of how the organization matured, given its early beginnings. Unlike the protocol for the initial study, this one asked study participants to share their recollections and current view of Hoʻoulu ʻŌpio's strengths and shortcomings, its outcomes related to the dimensions of critical pedagogy, and its future trajectory and that of the youth it serves. As you read this narrative, keep in mind that, whereas the 2004–2005 study participants were diverse constituents responding to general questions, the ones in 2020–2021 were long-time insiders responding to specific questions related to critical pedagogy. Another difference is that advances in technology allowed for a more accurate transcription of the interviews than was possible earlier. That said, let me introduce the 2020–2021 study participants.

Kai and Mekeke both encountered Hoʻoulu ʻŌpio in high school. Kai became an intern in 2008 right after graduation, and Mekeke followed him the next year. Having climbed the managerial ladder, Kai had recently become the "middleman between our co-producers" (the customers, interns, and apprentices). Mekeke interned until about 2010, then advanced to apprentice and a Bachelor of Arts degree in Hawaiian Studies at the University of Mānoa before becoming general farm manager. Linda encountered Hoʻoulu ʻŌpio in the youth food justice movement while she was working for a real estate company. Inspired by the movement, she left real estate in 2008 and became a buyer for Hoʻoulu ʻŌpio's produce at Whole Foods Market, and then in 2018 became its director of development. And you already know the cofounder, Aulani. To give you a feel for Hoʻoulu ʻŌpio's workspace, I will share that Mekeke referred to Auntie Aulani and Uncle Ezra as "a bunch of radicals" who have become "a little bit more poised"; Kai described her teaching the interns the hula "for four weeks at a time on every single Wednesday"; and in response to the protocol question about her race, Aulani replied: "So I'm *Kanaka*, meaning human, human being."

## Strengths and Shortcomings

Aulani unequivocally identified Hoʻoulu ʻŌpio's early potency as: recognizing the land as teacher, family, and self-sufficiency; valuing people, particularly young people; and understanding Waiʻanae's need to reclaim its land and reverse its health and education deficits. She explained that, to improve the community's access to food, employment, and education, Hoʻoulu ʻŌpio married land, people, and growing food—that growing food became the enterprise, and the social mission of the enterprise became the empowerment of youth through meaningful work. Aulani additionally called out Hoʻoulu ʻŌpio's early community organizing savvy, stating that "we were really good at, you know, bringing together and just leaning into this work with others in a way that we could resource all of the different program needs and operation needs." Linda agreed, noting that the organization's clarity of purpose revealed a complex understanding of, and approach to, food sovereignty, food self-sufficiency, and community-based economic development. She said that "as a partner but not a staff member, I had such a strong sense of why Hoʻoulu ʻŌpio existed, what it was trying to do, and how that related both to the community within Waiʻanae and the broader community in Hawaiʻi, and, of course, beyond."

As young interns, Kai and Mekeke both treasured their deep relationships with mentors, which they attributed to Hoʻoulu ʻŌpio's small size early on. Mekeke said that the farm "felt more like *ohana* kind of, or like family," and Kai appreciated that he did different jobs every day, saying that "we were kind of doing something different every single day because we had a smaller, tight-knit group." Kai acknowledged the benefit of spending more time in a single job but said that Hoʻoulu ʻŌpio's current size meant that mentor/intern interactions and repetitions "are slightly stretched out more." On the other hand, Linda said that, though Hoʻoulu ʻŌpio offered the promise of doing things differently, it initially lacked the scale to propel systems change. And Kai and Mekeke felt that it lacked the community relationships and reputation to support needy interns. Mekeke remembered that when she "first started on the farm, it was just like 'head down ass up,' you know, like work the land. You know, you do good in school and, you know, you'll get to that next place. But . . . there's some people who can't excel as quick, you know, and need a little bit of help and support." She added that "we always had to . . . fight for our own reputation and to build that positive outcome that we wanted the farm to be."

Yet, Mekeke also said that she was intrigued by the prospect of helping formulate a trajectory beyond hoping that young people would stick out farming and go to college. "It was like I could help build that kind of platform for me and my community." And Kai marveled that Hoʻoulu ʻŌpio had evolved from having just one track to having multiple tracks that allowed the interns to begin after high school and then "step up in leadership" from being a group leader to developing a specialization as they transitioned from community college into apprenticeship and a baccalaureate degree. Furthermore, he said that Hoʻoulu ʻŌpio had shifted the community's perception of youth as lazy, *kolohe* (destructive) troublemakers to recognizing that they are Waiʻanae's largest demographic and "the biggest asset we have." Thus, while study participants somewhat regretted the loss of intimacy that came with growth, they were unequivocal in praising the organization's trajectory. Asked about Hoʻoulu ʻŌpio's shortcomings, Aulani began by lamenting the dearth of innovative, solutions-oriented thinking in government, the private sector, and even the nonprofit sector. Then she concluded: "Our only shortcoming is that because we were a young organization, we didn't really see how important this movement was going to be to our community. So maybe we could have stretched ourselves to do more."

## Developing Critical Awareness

### Understanding How the Land Feeds

Thinking back to her early experiences at Hoʻoulu ʻŌpio, Mekeke recalled that Uncle Ezra, Auntie Aulani, and staff reminded the interns daily that food justice, social justice, and emotional and health justice are all connected. She said that those conversations engaged her "really quickly because I just wanted to learn more about food and land." She recalled stories about how Native Hawaiians were not only taken away from their land but also from their style of food production as large industrial ag brought in sugar cane, pineapple, GMO seed, and hemp—one-crop production with "tons of pesticides or herbicides and all, no *aloha ʻāina*, you know, no reciprocity to the land, no relationship with the food." Recalling his early experiences, Kai said that "it was kind of cool to like understand that, you know, we have this land that could feed our community." His awareness of how the land feeds increased when he explored food insecurity at a youth-led conference in California during his first year on the farm. Linda, who also attended, remembered hearing about the problems that indigenous people had inherited and "really radical community-based visions" for overcoming them.

Despite his exposure to food justice, Kai said that he continued the poor diet he had grown up eating until he was diagnosed at age twenty-four as prediabetic, a disease that his mother and older brother already had. Only then did what he had learned about multi-billion-dollar fast-food corporations and how they "make all their money off of poor communities" sink in. Kai remembered going to "the farmer's market and seeing how people loved this healthy food. And it's like, understanding culturally, why do I not love this healthy food? Why didn't my community members grow up loving this healthy food?" Mekeke added that, as interns, they began to see the injustice of growing up eating fast food without access to land and water to grow their own food.

Aulani said that Hoʻoulu ʻŌpio started to make a difference after the staff understood how the emotional burden of food and education injustice was affecting families generationally "in a real visceral way." To promote healthy eating habits, she said that Hoʻoulu ʻŌpio began embracing a more holistic "wrap-around" approach, exploiting peer mentoring and role modeling to engage youth and their families in activities that promote "not just their physical well-being but also their mental, spiritual, cultural, and emotional well-being." Kai added that Hoʻoulu ʻŌpio had created more diverse learning spaces, and Mekeke described a summer intensive that prepares recent high school graduates for the challenges they will face in college by adding tutorials in emotional intelligence and holistic health to their farm work and college courses. At the closing session, when the youth testify about what they have learned, Mekeke said that she never leaves "without crying because you just see a transformation. . . . Even if it's only ten weeks, it lights up a space in them of like hope and drive and, you know, motivation for them wanting to be better."

## Holding Space to Gather for the Mission

When asked to cite an activity at Hoʻoulu ʻŌpio that helped the interns understand injustice, Aulani responded that "we have time to be present and to bring presence of issues into our circles" at the beginning and end of every day. Portraying the circles as "holding space to gather for this mission," she explained that Hoʻoulu ʻŌpio's work was about acknowledging and healing society's dissymmetry and dissonance, saying that the circles offered a sacred space to "ensure that everybody is on the same page, you know. So many things that we stop for and we make room for—to acknowledge and to affirm that this is still the work that we do for our community and that, you know, our work reverberates further than we know." Describing the circles as a space of engagement where the interns learn that their voice matters, Kai said that, pre-Covid, everyone would hold hands and chant *E Hō Mai* (Grant Us) to start the day and that afterward "different interns would be sharing what they're going to do for the day, you know, or different managers, apprentices would be sharing into the circle." To end the day, he said that the interns were responsible to consider their progress "so each person had an opportunity to just give reflections every single work-day." Kai believed that the circles showed the interns the importance of finding their voice, explaining that, in the Hawaiian language:

> There's this term called *'ewalu mau maka* [eight different ways of looking], which stands for eight eyes, right. And it's just this looking at a problem or looking at anything from eight different ways. And I think its understanding that each person's individual voice contributes to those eight different perspectives and understanding the power in that (Kai).

For Aulani, holding space helped everyone, the young people and the staff, transform "the kinds of deep racial divides, deep social equity issues that we're challenged with as a society today"—it helps them "be present with the *kaumaha* [grief] because that is the only way that it will change." She said that sharing the burden "welcomes a whole bunch of resources, not financial or even influence or political power. It's like it invites *aloha* into what would be a very detrimental situation. It invites love, it invites, you know, compassion, invites kindness."

## Inspiring Collective Agency

### Revealing Opportunities for Agency

Kai recalled his early awakening to Wai'anae's historical abundance, explaining that he had learned how, before his ancestors lost their land, they had diverted water to feed kalo patches and that people thrived. Now, he said:

> Wai'anae has the largest concentration of Native Hawaiians, while we are also having some of the lowest test scores, you know, the lowest access to food, highest health-related disease, diet-related disease, deaths, you know what I mean? And understanding that all those plays a part in sort of this systemic racism that kind of occurred years ago, you know, but we're still feeling these ramifications of it now (Kai).

Mekeke said that one of racism's legacies was the stereotyping of youth within the community and even their families—a "kind of generational trauma" that "started when we were displaced from our land, when we were, you know, taken away from our traditional foods and our ways of practice and thinking of like what is healing, and, you know, what is medicine." Linda recalled that during one of her early visits to the farm, she had observed the youth grappling with how they were perceived and not "just passively accepting what that view might be, but they were trying to grapple with it, to understand it, and to change it." Kai said that, in recent years, Hoʻoulu ʻŌpio had become more assertive in helping the youth see their agency.

> We are a community that is so used to coming from a place of lack, right? And sometimes our approach to things is as if we're coming from a place of lack and not a place of abundance, you know, not necessarily in capital, but abundance in the capacity to produce change. And now we approach these things, and we're teaching the interns to approach things, in a way of you're coming from a place of abundance in terms of your capacity to change something (Kai).

Linda pointed to Hoʻoulu ʻŌpio's environmental justice tours for new interns and staff that start with the community's historical abundance and progress to its current degradation as the repository of the island's waste, explaining that the tours framed social justice as something that takes place over time and in place; they situated "Wai'anae, not only as a space of victimhood, but as a place of abundance and agency, depending on the choices that we make as a broader community."

## Inculcating a Sense of *Kuleana*

According to Aulani, Hoʻoulu ʻŌpio teaches young people love, respect, and the willingness to work, "like turn your hands down and feed yourself" so that they have the agency to choose what they ingest and learn. She said that by showing up for their *kuleana* every day—washing cilantro, weeding a kale bed, solving an irrigation issue—the interns saw firsthand that if they do not know how to do a job, the trucks will not deliver the food, people are not going to eat, Hoʻoulu ʻŌpio is not going to get paid, and they will not receive their stipends or tuition. She said that "it's this interdependence that I think is taught through nurturing and nourishing this relationship with land and the production of food for a community. That's our theory of change; it's very simple." Aulani believed that, apart from the farmers' market, working the land provided Hoʻoulu ʻŌpio's most powerful experience.

> When they actually hear testimony from people who are, you know, depending on this food and for all kinds of reasons—for health reasons,

for economic reasons, for access reasons, for cultural reasons, right—they kind of understand how important this work is. But the greatest change comes from the interactions that happen between our peoples and the land, and that's unquantifiable and unqualifiable because that is theirs to experience (Aulani).

Mekeke offered Hoʻoulu ʻŌpio's compensation policy as another example of encouraging responsibility, explaining that the interns receive a full tuition waiver and fixed monthly stipend for the first semester, but then their stipend becomes an aggregate of grade point average and farm performance, a policy that resulted in differing pay scales. She said that some interns were in the top or middle tier while others were struggling, but the mentors show them "what they have to do to improve, which might be 'just come to the farm five minutes earlier to show that you're prepared.'"

### Gaining Confidence in the Mission

When asked to recount an activity that helped the interns become confident in their ability to make a difference, Mekeke described an experience that she had when Michelle Obama visited the farm. She explained that the First Lady came in early November, which "was a massive deal, like newspapers everywhere, the news everywhere," and then she returned for an unpublicized visit.

> So she came back a second time a month later because she wanted to show her two daughters the farm. And then they came, and they planted a couple trees in our garden, and you know, and we got to eat lunch with them and just like talk stories with them. And I think having those two experiences, like one was like really heightened with secret service everywhere on the mountains . . . and the second one, it was just like, wow, she just wants to be here. So I think for me and for a whole bunch of our interns and our staff, you know, that second time I think it made me a little confident in like what we do, it really did. And it made me love what I do more cause to see the impact that it would have on the First Lady. And it wasn't just her; like she wanted her daughters to come here and experience what she felt that first visit, you know, and that *ohana* feeling, that family feeling (Mekeke).

Reflecting upon that experience, Mekeke added that "right now the biggest challenge in this pandemic is how we bring people to the farm to feel what the farm is about, you know, and not only to like physically see the interns, but to feel in-the-moment of like what *aloha* is."

## Growing a Community for Making Change

Aulani lamented that, while none of her peers shared her space of food justice, educational justice, social justice, and environmental justice, Hoʻoulu ʻŌpio had "grown" 300-plus young people who shared this space. Linda noted that near-peer mentors were immensely powerful in the space because they enabled the interns' access to education, knowledge, and know-how and provided examples of the possible. For Aulani, the mentors showed how, even in struggle, you can hold onto your identity, heritage, and the places you love. She expressed joy that Hoʻoulu ʻŌpio had connected the interns to "their counterparts in other parts of the community—food, education—and like that's a cohort and that's a community that like, you know, when we planted Hoʻoulu ʻŌpio, we were planting seeds. Now the tree, the *kumu*, the tree is creating even more fruit and more trees."

Aulani added that she and Ezra were the elders and have *kaikaina* (siblings) who "are mentoring their younger siblings. And so, yeah, it feels really quite incredible that [Kai and Mekeke] would have that experience along with us in developing Hoʻoulu ʻŌpio to where we are today and that they have tangible, hands-on work that they did." She also acknowledged Hoʻoulu ʻŌpio's early collaborators, who not only committed to the organization's vision but also stepped out of their comfort zone to support it. She provided as examples Uncle Bruce ("he had a lot of know-how, he knew how to do things, he knew people who knew how to do things, and he was such an amazing resource for us"), the chair of a local community foundation who brought in social justice philanthropists, and a banker who helped detail a ten-year financial model that not only positioned Hoʻoulu ʻŌpio to invite conventional investment but that "really created an exciting dialogue about how we can create new tools for organizations like ours with a really strong social mission."

Linda included in Hoʻoulu ʻŌpio's space "all of the community members who have lifted up the organization over the years and helped bring it to fruition": the grocery stores and restaurants, farmers' market, CSA members, residents in other communities who purchase its products at Whole Foods, and the education institutions that were "helping brown people get college degrees." She said that Hoʻoulu ʻŌpio's success lay in seeing the complexity of the community and in weaving the social relationships that, over time, helped the organization engage in change making. Explaining how Hoʻoulu ʻŌpio grew the interns to engage in this community with the same *kuleana* that she has, Aulani said:

> What we're teaching today is: you honor, you love, you respect those relationships you make with, you know, *ʻāina* because *ʻāina* will teach

you how to interact with people, no matter who that person is. They can be the head of a foundation, they can be an internationally known financial person, right. They can be the uncle down the street, but if you have that there (patting her heart), you know, it's really something special (Aulani).

## Creating a Space of Collective Action

### Offering Support to Beat the Odds

Mekeke recalled that, during her second year on the farm, when she was about twenty years old, the interns tried to purchase eleven acres of land next to their rental property and "not under like Uncle Ezra and Aulani, but under the non-profit," which she identified as a land trust. She recalled thinking: "We ain't got money. Like this is $1.1M. Like how do we get this? And we did presentations of like what we did on the farm and like what we wanted to do and grow food and show like the impact of how being on the land helps young people like me go to college and feed ourselves." Mekeke remembered hearing derogatory comments at the community meetings—"Oh, what's a bunch of eighteen- to twenty-five-year-olds going to do on that land? They're just going to steal whatever gets there, you know, or are not take care." She said that purchasing the property "just made me realize like, man, there's so much people trying to not have us do this, you know"—that people in their own community did not think they deserved the land or would take care of it.

Then Mekeke recounted that the following year in 2011, Ho'oulu 'Ōpio learned of a plan to rezone a large piece of agricultural land for industrial use. Linda explained that the property had been farmed until the 1980s when Japanese investors purchased it to develop a golf course and then sold it to other investors to develop an industrial park. To help the interns fight the rezone, Mekeke said that Ho'oulu 'Ōpio was "super supportive" in getting the resources and information they needed "and even sometimes helped us go to city hall to do our testimonies." She remembered that, once again, the interns encountered "a lot of fellow community members that didn't really give a rat's butt about us, you know, and our hope to like continue to grow food. . . . And some of these people were teachers in our local high schools and they were like, shoot, brushing us off, like 'I teach at these schools, these kids are bad.'" She said that she felt emboldened by learning how to reason and not just protest, explaining that the mentors "taught us how to be on the same level as a politician and speak our mind but be very clear and emotional and loving in what we want and what our needs are for our community."

Linda said that, because of the intensity of the proposed land use, Hoʻoulu ʻŌpio collaborated with two other organizations, recalling how the interns testified "that this wasn't the only option, that there were young people in the community who were ready, willing, and able and wanted to take empty ag land, fallow ag land and make it productive." Mekeke remembered that the interns stayed involved for six to eight months, finishing their farm assignments early so that they could meet with lawyers and the elders and attend community meetings. She recalled that eventually the city approved the rezone, though with a really close vote, but then, after the economy tanked, the funding vanished, and the land sat fallow for another six years. Linda reported that, despite this setback, Hoʻoulu ʻŌpio was able to purchase a smaller twenty-one-acre parcel in 2016 that had been fallow for almost forty years, recalling the joy that the interns experienced in bringing "useless, dry, dusty, empty land . . . into a relationship with themselves" as they cleared it, built irrigation, planted perimeter trees, and harvested the first crops.

## Being Patient in Beating the Odds

According to Mekeke: "Being patient ended up being our justice cause . . . we weren't ready in 2011 and 2012 to put that land up in production, but now we are, you know. So last year we just closed the funding for the 256 acres of land, and now we're growing on it." Kai said that Hoʻoulu ʻŌpio needed twelve months to raise $3M to purchase the land, but because the banks would not allow that length of time, Kamehameha Schools—in a first—guaranteed the loan. Mekeke marveled that she had "been on the farm to see all that happened, right. Like to challenge the people back then about land use, and then here we are now, like having the land under the nonprofit and using it as a catalyst for young people and organic food." She said that Hoʻoulu ʻŌpio would help replenish the watershed of the ancient *ahupuaʻa* (narrow wedges of land) that flowed from mountain to sea, rebuild the forestry system, and bring a diversity of food to Wai'anae.

However, to restore Wai'anae's ecology, Hoʻoulu ʻŌpio must also fight the blatant environmental racism that Bruce talked about in 2004–2005, including a plan proposed by the construction landfill company for Oahu to double its disposal site in Wai'anae. According to Linda, the plan "was effectively paused because of community pushback" against hosting the large diesel trucks that transport waste. She said that the interns and apprentices had discussed whether Hoʻoulu ʻŌpio should try to buy the land that was targeted for expansion, noting that they coordinated with the elders in order "to be in action with fellow community members." Revealing the effectiveness of that strategy, Aulani reported that an elder had arrived unexpectedly one morning to advise her against communicating with the landfill company because "they're very kind of like off kilter" after seeing the community's united opposition to its application.

## Bringing Joy to a Pandemic

All the study participants spoke with pride about Ho'oulu 'Ōpio's contribution to feeding the community during the pandemic. Mekeke explained that its expanded acreage offered enough space for socially distancing about one hundred workers "where we can be together as an essential business, providing food for our families and mentor young people and feed our community." Kai figured that, with businesses closed and people unemployed, the demand for the interns to distribute boxes of produce directly to families and through the local hospital had increased four- or five-fold. He calculated that the interns were providing 800 pounds of food weekly within and beyond Wai'anae, figuring out packaging, delivery schedules, and storage space while planting more fields (making the time that study participants took for this project quite remarkable).

Kai was amazed that, "you know, it was just free food going into our community weekly. It was just insane. And some of these families were even families of our interns, right. Where their parents have lost their jobs, you know, during this pandemic or haven't got their unemployment checks coming in." He added that the pandemic had shown how fragile Hawai'i's food system is and had elevated the importance of local agriculture, giving Ho'oulu 'Ōpio more leverage in achieving its vision. According to Aulani:

> The pandemic has just given us such clarity about how important we
> are to this work. Our work is important to these challenges and not
> only that, but like there's such a willingness to share our joy, you know,
> this is a joyful work. . . . We've sort of exposed all of the things and like
> now we can really look at it and go: "Oh man, we gotta really work
> hard to make sure we end up in a good place and that we honor
> everyone that makes up this place." So that is both a joy, but also a
> *kāhea* [call] to action (Aulani).

## Future Visions

### Becoming Better Human Beings

Considering Ho'oulu 'Ōpio's evolution, Mekeke concluded that, though the organization had extended its influence, the constant had been taking care of the land and growing good food and good people. "The growing of people is

not just providing them jobs but really working alongside them, being mentored by them, challenging them, you know, to their belief systems and their
upbringings and challenging them physically on the farm, you know, mentally
in school." She also identified as a constant having a space where everyone
can push each other to do better. As Ezra had in 2004–2005, both Mekeke
and Kai described Hoʻoulu ʻŌpio's high expectations for the interns. Kai said
that the farm provided "a space where like you're not expected to change who
you are to be better, right. But you're expected to elevate who you are to be
better." Mekeke explained that another constant had been providing a space
that helped the interns go to school, get an education, take home organic
veggies, and thrive with the land because:

> You know, we don't farm the land; I think the land farms us, you
> know, and it cultivates us into better human beings. We just have to be
> open to that. So that's that safe space. I think that is what gives us a
> chance to listen and to focus and be intentional and to slow down, you
> know, on the dailiness here on the farm. . . . And to do it along peers
> and along mentors, I think is what makes us better, you know. We're
> hoping that it makes them better to do good in school and hopefully it
> transfers to their family. And then our students can have these oppor-
> tunities to start healing from within (Mekeke).

Having a physically safe space where she could be challenged while challenging others was among the top three gifts that Hoʻoulu ʻŌpio had given
Mekeke over the years. "I think your truest and honest actions come when
you feel safe, you know, when you feel trust, when you feel love." She noted
that Hoʻoulu ʻŌpio had made its space feel safer by bringing in specialists
who could help the young people deal with the traumas they experience in
their families. Mekeke believed that this deepened involvement had made
the farm a lot more loving and paid dividends both in terms of the interns'
accomplishments and farm sales. She said that Hoʻoulu ʻŌpio had definitely
evolved in "going down in here in your heart and to your gut all the way to,
you know, how do you get young people to get good grades in school? You
know, how do you get them to interact with their families in a loving way
and a respectful way?"

## Becoming Experts in *Aloha ʻĀina*

When asked to envision the interns' future contributions, Mekeke declared that
their leadership would be from the physical ground up, working the land as "a
*kākou* (inclusive) thing" that encompasses everybody, even ancestors. She said

that Ho'oulu 'Ōpio's leadership team would consist of "young people who are in year one all the way to, you know, apprentices who are in year five to the mentors who've been here since the beginning twenty years, all the way to, you know, our mama *ʻāina*, you know, to our land on mother earth, who's been here for millions of years." Aulani said that Ho'oulu 'Ōpio's greatest gift to itself was having created multi-generational leaders who will "take their place in our communities, whether they're teachers or educators or social workers, or mechanics, or some other calling." She characterized the interns as:

> The subject matter experts in *aloha ʻāina* [love of the land] where basically no matter what professional pathway or profession that they choose, that they are all capable of teaching, you know, the people around them—their partners, their friends, their families, their children, their children's children—to have a deep and abiding love for the land (Aulani).

When asked to envision the organization's future contributions, Linda said that Ho'oulu 'Ōpio would continue to exemplify the creativity that can be unleashed by marrying social purpose with enterprise, by investing in young people, and by empowering them to be agents of change for themselves and their families. Kai and Mekeke envisioned other localities repurposing Ho'oulu 'Ōpio's template to establish community-driven businesses and even education programs or services that generate revenue and reinvest it to uplift youth and their families. Kai also envisioned Ho'oulu 'Ōpio training young people to work their own or other farms. Aulani noted that Ho'oulu 'Ōpio's community counterparts were doing great work warding off a cascade of negative forces, "continuing to educate people, continuing to feed families, continuing to create bountiful, prosperous places." However, to sustain their efforts, she said: "We're going to really need to buckle down and . . . really like deepen our practice in order to . . . bring as much investment and resources to these incredible latent community organizations." Then, Aulani added:

> The organization itself is an endowment and a legacy to our community and our future children. Along with that, our hope is to create not just the farms that produce food, but the homes that produce housing, that we, you know, provide an endowment that provides educational scholarships, that we also think about creating other vehicles like a land trust or a community development financial institution . . . to be able to share resources, to share expertise—to share. My grandmother said basically if you share, you're gonna be okay, because somebody

else will share with you, you know. So I think this is like kind of our way to create a caring and sharing economy (Aulani).

Study participants perceived several roadblocks to advancing Hoʻoulu ʻŌpio's mission. Kai listed "acquiring land and land that has access to water" and getting people to make the cultural shift to view food and education differently. Linda listed finding "the creative and intelligent and expansive-thinking individuals to join the team" and overcoming the increasing challenges that young people face in pursuing a college education. Both Linda and Mekeke listed growing the organization so that it "retains all of its culture and the depth of experience that youth have been able to have at a smaller scale," but Aulani maintained that no roadblocks existed that could not be overcome through "love, respect, and willingness to work." Alternatively, when asked what resources Hoʻoulu ʻŌpio would need to advance its mission, Kai and Linda mentioned financial capital, but all the study participants emphasized social capital, and Mekeke was the most eloquent.

I think to me, the biggest resource that we need to engage in is our community. . . . We hope to do some big things in ten years, and we'll need a lot of help, you know. We'll need a lot of people sharing our stories, you know, and our mission and our movement. And we need other people to have their own kind of social justice program, whether it's growing a farm or creating their own type of other business. We need more people. We need more indigenous people. We need more brown people doing that 'cause we're the ones that already have all the answers 'cause our ancestors and our people have been living this earth for years, you know. And not only living but had systems and understanding the knowns and unknowns that we're facing today. So it's like, how do you build up, how do you make re-known our indigenous practices. Because our ancestors could feed themselves for years and years and years. . . . And so it's like, how do we as a collective recapture those types of knowledges and practices (Mekeke).

# Theorizing the Narratives

In this last section of Part II, I first theorize Hoʻoulu ʻŌpio's curriculum as body-centric critical pedagogy, and then I ground it as the physical realm of place-based activism occurring within Waiʻanae and beyond. To do that, I integrate Western concepts of hands-on learning with indigenous views of body-centric knowledge as a means of responding to Grace Lee Boggs's call for a new kind of activist citizen. Figure 5 offers a visualization of the relationship between body-centric critical pedagogy and the physical realm of place-based activism.

## Organic Farming as Body-Centric Critical Pedagogy

According to Paulo Freire, all human beings, no matter their level of literacy, are capable of joining with others to look critically at their world, thereby developing a new self-awareness, dignity, and sense of hope. Freirean pedagogy engages young people in self-reflection and dialogue that examine contradictions in their lived experiences. It gives them the mindset to join forces and transform oppressive social structures[16] and recognizes that learning occurs within a geographic locale and cultural context. In indigenous cultures, Freirean pedagogy engages young people in diagnosing the wounds that colonialism inflicted. Deconstructing those wounds, or decolonization, involves them in confronting the dominant systems of thought that perpetuate injustice and in acquiring the insight that can lead to their intellectual and cultural liberation.[17]

Hoʻoulu ʻŌpio needed to adapt these principles of decolonization to Waiʻanae, where the youth were not only unaware of the historical trauma that Native

Wai'anae, Hawai'i
Physical Realm of Place-Based Activism

| Place Awareness Cognitive | Place Agency Attitudinal | Critical Placemaking Behavioral |
|---|---|---|
| | | |
| | | Improving the Commons Hands-on |

Hoʻoulu ʻŌpio Organic Farm
Body-Centric Critical Pedagogy

Collective Action
Behavioral

Critical Awareness
Cognitive

Collective Agency
Attitudinal

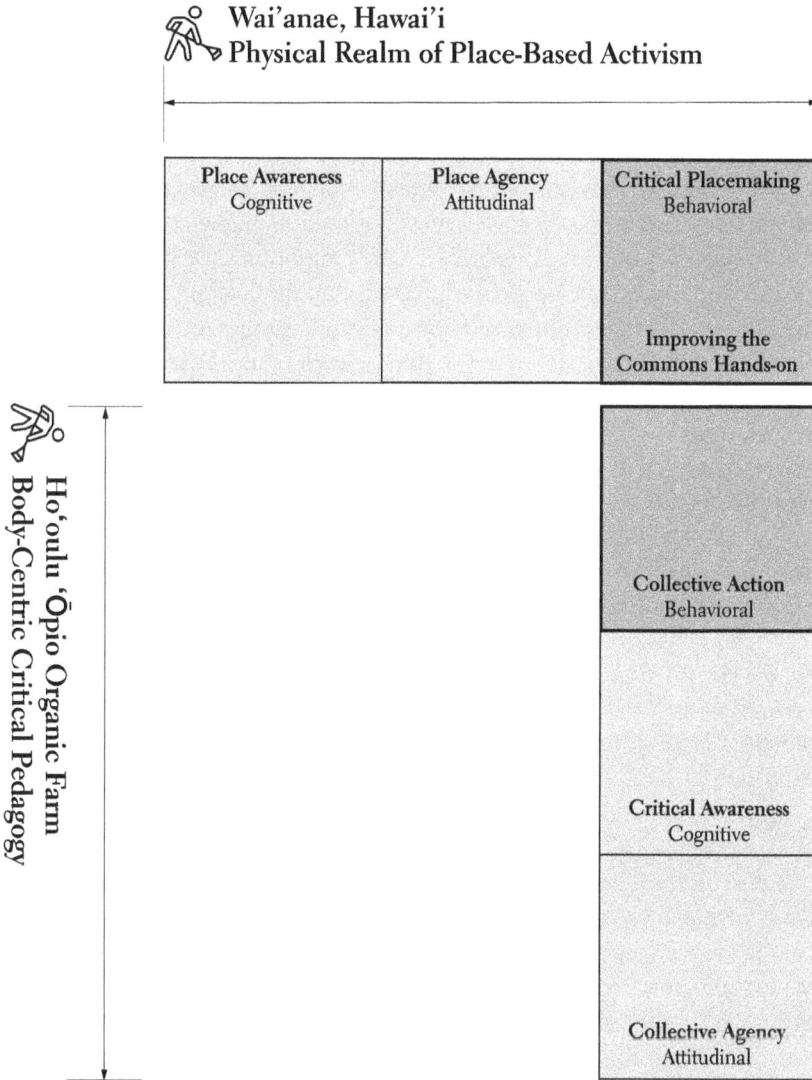

Figure 5. Body-Centric Critical Pedagogy and the Physical Realm of Place-Based Activism
Image credit: Sharon Egretta Sutton, 2023

Hawaiians had experienced but also had internalized a consumer culture that stereotyped them as lazy and stupid. The staff needed to help them shift from wanting to make money to buy stuff to wanting to improve the community. Guided by the wisdom of Wai'anae elders, they adopted an educational approach that centers concrete experience and is known as "experiential education."

From a Western perspective—and one that John Dewey advocated—this approach involves real-life learning, active learning, learning by doing, learning through projects, and learning by solving problems.[18] Having proven especially effective with older students, experiential education promotes learning through hands-on experimentation and reflective observation.[19]

Dewey argued that experiential education benefits society because it helps students become active, engaged citizens,[20] and its many advocates believe that it prepares them for the job market by promoting such competencies as critical thinking, decision making, effective communication, sense of responsibility, and ability to collaborate.[21] Several studies suggest that learning outdoors enhances these outcomes,[22] making experiential education an effective overlay for enacting critical pedagogy on an organic farm. However, from a Hawaiian perspective, an experiential education overlay offers even more profound insights that go to the heart of indigenous thought systems. Drawing from an interview with Hawaiian historian Rubellite Kawena Johnson, activist scholar Manulani Aluli Meyer posited knowledge as both spiritual and body-centric, conditioned by Hawaiians' relationship with nature, family members (including ancestors), God, and mythological deities. Meyer identified the five physical senses of sight, taste, smell, hearing, and touch as the basis for how Hawaiians actively learn about and experience their world, citing Johnson to explain that the process "is not something passive. We are active in our understanding. We are engaged in it. Knowing something becomes something *we create*."[23]

Meyer drew parallels between similar Hawaiian words to define an indigenous way of "learning through the senses," proposing that to see is to know, to taste is to try to learn, to listen is to invoke a spirit or deity, to touch is to "grasp" through the hands or the mind so that one's body becomes an instrument of knowing and cultural expression. She concluded that, for Hawaiians, knowledge is something they *cause*, and awareness is an accumulation of what they learn through their bodies: "It is deeply embedded in other, in elder, in spirit."[24] To help the interns, who had been programmed for failure, acquire such knowledge and distinguish the wounds of colonialism, Ho'oulu 'Ōpio's pedagogy needed to connect their bodies with the dignity of growing food for the community. To accomplish this connection in the early days, Ezra, Aulani, and the mentors engaged the interns in hands-on experiences of oral history, music, chanting, and hula during the workday and in making laulau after hours.

As Ho'oulu 'Ōpio expanded, the young peoples' academic work moved off the farm to the community college and university, requiring a transition to these more traditional learning spaces. However, what continued to ground them was the body-centric learning that occurred in the farm's muddy fields, where they used their hands to clear underbrush, dig up rocks, pull weeds, build irrigation, grow crops, and plant trees—a distinguishing feature of Hoʻoulu ʻŌpio's pedagogy that I will return to later on. To impart a love of farming, Ezra employed peer mentors, or "social interlocutors," to help the neophyte interns reach beyond societal stereotypes and seek out excellence.[25] This scaffolding of expertise reflected the Hawaiian belief that knowledge is not singular but rather is deeply embedded in other people who form continuous links in a chain of cultural practices.[26]

Hoʻoulu ʻŌpio's pedagogy equipped the interns with the farming know-how that generations had lost after colonizers stole their land and way of life, and it set high expectations for them to "be better" human beings by reclaiming their own history and culture. To overcome the generational trauma that they had experienced, it utilized peer mentors who had themselves benefitted from knowing that "their ancestors had it going on." The mentors, apprentices, and interns began their day by literally holding the space of a circle and ended it by sharing into that circle. The staff, who primarily lived in the community and worked in partnership with local organizations, developed a whole-person approach that positioned the young people to confront oppression, engaging them in marketing their crops, sharing their expertise with schoolchildren, convincing adults to eat healthier, testifying at community meetings, and growing and distributing tons of organic food. Hoʻoulu ʻŌpio's body-centric take on critical pedagogy helped the young people "see themselves, not as victims, but as masters of their own fate."[27] Through concrete experiences, their bodies became instruments that know in their hearts down to their gut. By learning to love the land, they were able to listen to spirits and grasp decolonization through hands turned down to the soil. Some will become farmers, but no matter their professional pathway, they will be able to teach others to experience a deep and abiding love for the land.

## Illustrating Place-Based Activism's Physical Realm

I hooked the previous section around Western and indigenous concepts of hands-on, body-centric experiences to demonstrate how Hoʻoulu ʻŌpio reinterpreted critical pedagogy. Here, I ground that pedagogy in Boggs's concept of "community activism" or "community-building activism" to validate my claim that farming can help young people develop the place awareness and place agency to engage in critical placemaking in their communities. Boggs argued that place—locality—offers an ideal focus for activism because people experience multiple issues in and through it. She believed that, unlike struggles around race, gender, or other identities that "tend to isolate rather than to unite different constituencies," struggles around place bring people together.[28] An analysis of Ho'oulu 'Ōpio's pedagogy helps me elaborate Boggs's argument to show how caring for place—or *malama 'āina*—can help young people achieve their right to self-determine life-sustaining resources in the commons. I follow the Freirean praxis of awareness, agency, and action to show that, by using their hands to cultivate ever-expanding, community-owned farmland, the interns and apprentices learned to love the land (*aloha 'āina*) and to feed themselves, their families, and their communities.

### Place Awareness: Inspiring a Love the Land

In a move that turned out to be devasting to the first people, Hawai'i's native leaders agreed to replace its indigenous system of shared control and use of the land with the Western system of private property ownership and commercialization, simultaneously enabling colonization of the people and their land.[29] In the Western worldview, land is "property to be bought and sold as real estate"; in the Hawaiian one, it is *'āina*, which translates to land but literally means "that which feeds" and includes the mountains, streams, winds, animals, and trees that are living manifestations of deities and ancestral gods.[30] *'Āina* shaped the first peoples' understanding of their "spiritual relationship to all elements and resources that sustained life, inclusive of land, sky, and sea." Ho'oulu 'Ōpio set out to nurture the young peoples' awareness of the ancestral meaning of *'āina*. Helping them learn to value the land's practical purpose was straightforward; it enabled the growing of healthy food, provided nourishment for the interns' and apprentices' families and neighbors, and created a revenue stream that contributed to their stipends and tuition. To cultivate this perspective on the land, the leaders and staff emphasized working hard—physically on the farm and mentally in school—and being responsible in growing and marketing food. They encouraged the young people to take pride in their work and see that excelling at their duties could change stereotypes of themselves as destructive troublemakers.

Mentors worked alongside the youth, pushing them to be their truest selves. But Ho'oulu 'Ōpio wanted to go beyond this practical perspective and inculcate a deeper understanding of the land as a guide for their relationships with other people and nature. To awaken this deeper understanding, the leaders and staff helped the young people learn to love the land and their connection to it, to respect indigenous farming techniques, to value the spirituality embedded within places, and to understand how the cycles of nature governed their daily lives. They envisioned growing an increasing number of young people who would share their knowledge with friends, partners, children, and children's children. In short, Hoʻoulu ʻŌpio began an iterative process of place-based activism by awakening within the youth an ancestral understanding of the land as "that which feeds," envisioning that their numbers would multiply and help refuel more just and sustainable relationships among people and with nature.

## Place Agency: Modeling Lost Indigenous Practices

In 1921, after the number of persons with Hawaiian blood in the colonized Territory of Hawaiʻi "had declined to 23,000 from nearly 500,000 a century earlier," the U.S. Congress adopted legislation that gave the survivors rocky ten-acre agricultural plots that lacked access to water, while protecting the thousands of cultivated acres owned by sugar and pineapple barons.[31] To restrict the number of persons who qualified for this "gift," given that most territory residents had some Hawaiian blood, the legislation restricted the homestead plots to persons who could prove they had 50 percent or more Hawaiian blood instead of accepting the traditional indigenous view that practicing *aloha* and *malama ʻāina* indicated Hawaiian identity. A later amendment reduced the original allotment of 203,000 acres by carving out public land (mainly for military bases and a few parks) and residential areas to accommodate wage laborers. However, during the Depression, *malama ʻāina* prevailed as wage laborers nationwide sank into poverty. The homesteaders "drew on the *malama ʻāina* that had sustained their people through scarcity and suppression for a century," reviving exchange-based subsistence by catching fish and trading them for crops grown further inland. Their 1930s response to economic crisis continued and seeded the postwar "cultural renaissance and bids for sovereignty."[32]

Hoʻoulu ʻŌpio adopted an ethos of *malama ʻāina* to guide the youth and their families in practicing, experiencing, and living their cultural identity.[33] With heads down, asses up, and hands turned toward the soil, the leaders and staff set about helping them restore, reestablish, and reaffirm "the relationships between people and places through actions based on *aloha ʻāina*."[34] Believing that decolonization required only the willingness to work, along with love, honor, and respect, Hoʻoulu ʻŌpio reclaimed the lost indigenous knowledge needed to prepare the young people as engaged citizens who could assume responsibility for making change. The work ethic it inculcated resulted in academic success, helping the interns and apprentices learn to get the job done no matter what, their self-esteem, pride, and confidence increasing as they built lasting connections to the farm and to one another. This iterative process of being taught practices for reinhabiting stolen land and then teaching them to others heightened their sense of place, as Uncle Bruce said it would. Thus, Hoʻoulu

'Ōpio advanced place-based activism by modeling a counternarrative of *malama 'āina* and self-sufficiency.

## Critical Placemaking: Seeking *Proper* People/Place Relationships

Scholars and practitioners characterize critical placemaking as the processes through which disparate voices come together to reclaim privatized public space. In the Hawaiian context, it involved reclaiming the land and resources that colonizers stole,[35] including the foreign traders who brought diseases to Hawai'i that killed thousands of indigenous farmers, resulting in the abandonment of irrigation systems and cultivated gardens;[36] the foreign investors who purchased land after supplanting Hawai'i's traditional land tenure system with a Western concept of fee-simple ownership;[37] the powerbrokers who overthrew the Hawaiian monarchy and converted its *ahupua'a* (ecological systems) into plantations;[38] and the U.S. military that partitioned 600,000 acres of land in O'ahu and built accommodations for 50,000 troops, which tourism obscured by portraying the area as a tropical paradise.[39] All these abuses altered Wai'anae's geography, one compounding the other to make healthful living ever more elusive for its native population.

To help the young people reinhabit this place in a nonexploitative manner, Ho'oulu 'Ōpio's organizers needed to reeducate them to experience "intimate, organic, and mutually nurturing relationships" with their surroundings.[40] That is, reeducate them to cultivate Wai'anae's fallow pastures, strengthen its social fabric, improve the health of its population, and advocate for protecting its resources. The youth physically engaged the regenerative process, first cultivating five acres of land and then developing the political savvy to convince community leaders that they could cultivate twenty-six and then 281 acres. They began clearing the land, restoring its natural systems, planting it with a variety of organic crops including traditional produce, and learning to cook traditional dishes that they prepared with hand-made implements. They encouraged younger youth to follow in their footsteps, helping them make gardens in their schoolyards and teaching them how to garden at home.

Initially, the interns provided food for a café where people ate well and lingered to talk stories. On monthly workdays, they engaged their families and neighbors in seasonal tasks, recreating a farming culture that agribusiness had devalued as backward. Sometimes they put on concerts that raised money, entertained, and showed off their organizational skills. As catalysts for getting overweight adults to adopt healthier eating habits,[41] they took on the fast-food industry's shameless exploitation of their community, selling organic produce at a farmers' market, taking veggies home and giving them away, and, at every opportunity, instructing their families and customers in good eating habits. Joining with the elders, they advocated for reclaiming Wai'anae's stolen ecological resources, not only testifying at meetings against contamination from the U.S. military occupation, a proposed expansion of an industrial waste site, and the tourist industry's piping of fresh water from their community, but also taking high school students with them to amplify their voices. And recently, they ramped up production in order to supply tons of free food to families hit by the pandemic.

Ho'oulu 'Ōpio created a context for the young people to engage in decolonizing Wai'anae's commons, their willingness to work making it the area's third-largest private landowner. The older youth engaged the younger ones in the process, sharing knowledge and becoming continuous links in a chain of cultural practices while working collaboratively to advance self-sufficiency and demand control over the spoils of the commons. By listening to spirits and grasping decolonization through their hands and minds, they developed a first-hand understanding of their culture, their hard work generating strong familial bonds and a deep connection to the farm. Ho'oulu 'Ōpio grounded its praxis in a Hawaiian sense of the truth and instilled the capacity to seek proper relationships between people, the heavens, and the earth. It helped an expanding cohort of young people become caring activists who worked hands-on to improve the health of the land and the people, its pedagogy empowering them and their families with the agricultural and entrepreneurial expertise to reinhabit the land that colonizers exploited. By centering learning in culture, spirituality, and nature, Ho'oulu 'Ōpio's pedagogy created a counternarrative to education's increasingly market-driven purpose.

According to the 1960s progressives, education's purpose was to improve social mobility for marginalized populations, and so they proposed reforms to equalize outcomes.[42] Then the structuralists posited its purpose as legitimating inequality by intentionally preparing poor students for low-level employment that kept them at the bottom of society.[43] The culturalists agreed but assigned agency to the poor, positing that they adopted rebellious behavior to disqualify themselves for the meaningless jobs that were their destiny. They also accepted that mental work merited higher rewards than manual work, thus affirming class and gender divides.[44] Now the neoliberalists posit that education's purpose is to assure American competitiveness and, like the progressives, have proposed reforms but ones that reflect the corporatization of American society. None of these narratives have resulted in educational equity.[45]

Ho'oulu 'Ōpio disrupted these narratives and freed the young people from either reproducing or resisting the forces of neoliberal capitalism. Instead of seeing manual labor as meaningless, they embraced it as a sacred pathway to finding their place within the community. Instead of rebelling against the norms that enable mainstream success, the youth have become a counterculture of farmers who have acquired the skills to move up a ladder of self-sufficiency. Instead of distinguishing manual and mental labor, males and females alike seamlessly shift from being farmers who work in the mud to being entrepreneurs who oversee sales to being co-producers in the marketplace or graduate students in the university, demonstrating that "the work of decolonizing . . . requires labor of the mind, the heart, and the hands."[46] Ho'oulu 'Ōpio realized place-based activism by engaging growing numbers of young people in critical placemaking on ever-increasing acres of land where they practice *aloha* and *malama 'āina* to reclaim their ancestral identity. Though Ho'oulu 'Ōpio engaged in all three dimensions of place-based activism, it excelled in the behavioral dimension, involving the interns and apprentices in working hands-on in the mud to grow food, eat well, and reinhabit the land.

## Conclusions: Exemplifying the Physical Realm of Place-Based Activism

To bring Part II of the book full circle, I conclude this section with a synthesis of Ho'oulu 'Ōpio's achievements as an exemplar of the physical realm of place-based activism. Within a context of increasing economic and educational inequality and magnifying threats from climate change on an island that is dependent upon imported food, this organization is an undisputed leader in sustainable Native Hawaiian agricultural and educational practices. Twenty-two years old at the time of this writing, Ho'oulu 'Ōpio has expanded its peer mentoring concept to begin in K-12 and continue through graduate studies and advanced career opportunities. It has produced tons of locally grown organic crops, supported hundreds of youth in pursuing college careers, cultivated hardworking community leaders, improved individual and community health, created hundreds of jobs, and stimulated economic development. Ho'oulu 'Ōpio has deepened its partnerships, extending its reach locally, nationally, and internationally, and it has returned 281 acres of stolen land to community members. In the next ten years, it plans to increase agricultural production ten times and youth education four times and to build affordable housing.

I attribute these achievements to a pedagogy that physically grounds young people in caring for the *'āina*, helps them adopt the inclusive Native Hawaiian concept of *kākou*, and engages them in "really leaning in" to improve the commons with their whole selves, emotionally, socially, spiritually, and physically.

Through this pedagogy, Hoʻoulu ʻŌpio supports young people in reinhabiting the commons of Waiʻanae in a nonexploitative, loving manner while placing ownership of that commons in the hands of the community, which assures that everyone will have access in perpetuity to food, education, meaningful work, and shelter. And—importantly—it assures that everyone can participate in dispensing its wealth.

## Notes

1. Using a pseudonym is required by the participating institutional review boards that established the terms of conducting the research.

2. Wende Elizabeth Marshall, *Potent Mana: Lessons in Power and Healing* (Albany: State University of New York Press, 2011), 2:49, muse.jhu.edu/book/1889.

3. Three University of Washington GRAs were supervised by me and Susan P. Kemp. After one of Hoʻoulu ʻŌpio's cofounders completed a structured telephone survey, which led to its selection as a case study, the GRAs administered thirteen open-ended interviews via telephone, and then one Native Hawaiian GRA, Alma Trinidad, administered four face-to-face and later used the data in her doctoral dissertation. The transcript that I constructed from their much longer verbatim documentation of both these protocols contains only the responses that inform my theoretical framework. Per contracts with the Human Subjects Review Boards of each of the participating academic institutions, the names that appear in the narratives are pseudonyms.

4. Staff study participants included: Ezra, forty, Caucasian, cofounding administrative coordinator and former business development consultant, and Aulani's husband (completed the initial survey and an interview); Alani, forty-nine, Hawaiian-Caucasian, café manager, and Ezra's sister-in-law; Takashi, forty-eight, Japanese-Hungarian-Jewish, coordinator of the intermediate school program, and founding board member; and Darde, twenty-eight, Portuguese-Chinese-Japanese-Hawaiian-German-Russian-Polish, and founding farm manager (on break to pursue art activities).

Mentee study participants had all been interns. They included: Krushi, twenty, Hawaiian, had worked for a little over a year; Aleki, twenty-one, Samoan, inactive in the Army Reserve, had worked for a little over a year; Neil, nineteen, Hawaiian-Portuguese, learned gardening at home, had worked for four months; and Makalo, twenty, Hawaiian-Guatemalan-Japanese, intern in inaugural class, had worked for two years.

Intern study participants included: Keola, twenty, Portuguese-Hawaiian-Chinese, and in this tenth month; Joshua, twenty, Hawaiian-Samoan, and in his eighth month; Mark, eighteen, Hawaiian-Caucasian, and in his seventh month before being forced to get a higher-paying full-time job; and Patrick, twenty, Hawaiian-Caucasian, and in his seventh month. The internship lasted ten months.

Parent study participants included: Maleah, forty, part-Hawaiian, and mother of an eleventh-grade daughter, Natalia; and Amura, thirty-eight, Hawaiian-Caucasian, and mother of an eighth-grade son, Cairo, who began the program in elementary school. Board member study participants included: Bruce, fifty-five, part-Hawaiian, elder founding member, and father of Bruce Jr., who was the current board president; Luana, fifty, Caucasian-Okinawan-Portuguese-Spanish-Hawaiian, newly appointed vice president, and mother of Makalo; and Jenny, forty-one, Hawaiian-Japanese-Portuguese-Chamorro, and former member who had recently completed her term.

5. Drawing from the literature, I define "critical awareness" as young people sharing their personal experiences with peers in order to understand the societal systems that perpetuate the injustices in their lives; "collective agency" as young people perceiving a common purpose and becoming confident that they can work together to change their circumstances; and "collective action" as young people working together to change unjust conditions. See the section on critical pedagogy in the Introduction for more information on how I have used this educational philosophy in framing the book.

6. My RA administered these interviews via Zoom and transcribed them using Temi. Study participants included: Aulani, fifty-five, *Kanaka* (human being), cofounding program and organizational coordinator; Kai, thirty, African American-Filipino, food processing and quality control manager, formerly an intern; Mekeke, thirty-one, Filipina–Hawaiian–Puerto Rican, general farm manager, formerly an intern; and Linda, thirty-nine, Caucasian, food processing and quality control manager, and formerly in real estate and a buyer for Whole Foods.

7. The refocused dimensions of critical pedagogy are: "place awareness" (or helping youth understand the systemic causes of injustices in their neighborhoods); "place agency" (or equipping them with the capacity to transform these injustices); and "critical placemaking" (or engaging them in a participatory process of transforming their neighborhoods).

8. Trisha Kehaulani Watson, *Ho'i Hou iā Papahānaumoku: A History of Eco-Colonization in the Pu'uhonua of Wai'anae* (Ann Arbor, Mich.: ProQuest Dissertations and Theses, 2008).

9. Watson, *Ho'i Hou iā Papahānaumoku*, referring to Unites States Department of Commerce, "Wai'anae ç" Community Report, DZM Hawai'i and National Oceanic and Atmospheric Administration.

10. Watson, *Ho'i Hou iā Papahānaumoku*.

11. Christy Inda et al., "Home Grown: The Trials and Triumphs of Starting up a Farmers' Market in Wai'anae, Hawai'i," *Community Development* 42, no. 2 (April 1, 2011): 181–92, referring to Office of Planning, State of Hawai'i Food Security Task Force (January 2003).

12. Watson, *Ho'i Hou iā Papahānaumoku*.

13. Marshall, *Potent Mana*.

14. Lynette Hi'ilam Cruz, *From Resistance to Affirmation, We Are Who We Were: Reclaiming National Identity in the Hawaiian Sovereignty Movement, 1990–2003* (Ann Arbor, Mich.: ProQuest Dissertations Publishing, 2003), 3, http://search .proquest.com/docview/305327402/.

15. As reported in the Ford Foundation study that underpins this book's investigation, government grants provided the primary funding for just 30 percent of the Ford study organizations. Those organizations were significantly less likely to embody a transformative philosophy, defined as having a commitment to both youth and community change. Hoʻoulu ʻŌpio contradicted this finding. Scoring 4.25 out of 5.0, its transformative philosophy was above the mean of 4.08, and yet its only grants were from the government. For more information about the Ford Foundation study, see Sharon E. Sutton et al., *Urban Youth Programs in America: A Study of Youth, Community, and Social Justice Conducted for the Ford Foundation* (Seattle: Center for Environment Education and Design Studies, College of Architecture and Urban Planning, University of Washington, 2006).

16. Paolo Freire, *Pedagogy of the Oppressed*, trans. Myra Bergman Ramos (New York: Seabury Press, 1970).

17. Alma M. O. Trinidad, "Sociopolitical Development through Critical Indigenous Pedagogy of Place: Preparing Native Hawaiian Young Adults to Become Change Agents," *Hūlili: Multidisciplinary Research on Hawaiian Well-Being* 7 (2011): 189, referring to bell hooks, *Black Looks: Race and Representation* (Boston: South End Press, 1990).

18. Anna Leis et al., "Student Farms at United States Colleges and Universities: Insights Gained from a Survey of the Farm Managers," *NACTA Journal* 55, no. 1 (March 2011): 9–15, https://www.jstor.org/stable/10.2307/nactajournal.55.1.9, referring to John Dewey, *Experience as Education* (New York: Collier Books, 1938).

19. Gail Hansen, "When Students Design Learning Landscapes: Designing for Experiential Learning through Experiential Learning," *NACTA Journal* 56, no. 4 (December 2012): 30–35, https://www.jstor.org/stable/10.2307/nactajournal.56.4.30, referring to David A. Kolb, *Experiential Learning: Experience as the Source of Learning and Development* (Upper Saddle River, N.J.: Prentice Hall, 1984).

20. William F. Heinrich et al., "Critical Thinking Assess across Four Sustainability-Related Experiential Learning Settings," *Journal of Experiential Education* 38, no. 4 (2015): 373–93.

21. Leis et al., "Student Farms at United States Colleges and Universities."

22. Hansen, "When Students Design Learning Landscapes."

23. Manulani Aluli Meyer, "Our Own Liberation: Reflections on Hawaiian Epistemology," *Contemporary Pacific* (Spring 2001): 132, citing from an interview with Rubellite Kawena Johnson on April 11, 1997.

24. Meyer, "Our Own Liberation," 132.

25. In his zone of proximal development theory, Soviet psychologist Lev S. Vygotsky proposed that social interlocutors guide neophytes in achieving culturally appropriate development beyond what they can achieve on their own, a theory that John Dewey among others criticized as propagandist. I use the terms because Hoʻoulu ʻŌpio specifically drew upon elders and near peers to advance interns' knowledge of Hawaiian values and practices. For more information, see Michael Glassman, "Dewey and Vygotsky: Society, Experience, and Inquiry in Educational

Practice," *Educational Researcher* 30, no. 4 (May 2001): 3–14, http://www.jstor.com/stable/3594354.

26. Meyer, "Our Own Liberation."

27. Lynette Hi'ilam Cruz, *From Resistance to Affirmation*.

28. Grace Lee Boggs, "A Question of Place," *Monthly Review* 52, no. 2 (June 2000): np, https://monthlyreview.org/2000/06/01/a-question-of-place/.

29. Watson, *Ho'i Hou iā Papahānaumoku*.

30. J. Kēhaulani Kauanui, "Properties of Land: That Which Feeds," in *Paradoxes of Hawaiian Sovereignty: Land, Sex, and the Colonial Politics of State Nationalism* (Durham, N.C.: Duke University Press, 2018), 77.

31. Judith Schachter, "Living on the Land: Mālama 'Āina from Past to Present," in *The Legacies of a Hawaiian Generation* (New York and Oxford: Berghahn Books, 2013), 20.

32. Schachter, "Living on the Land," 31.

33. Trinidad, "Critical Indigenous Pedagogy of Place."

34. Ke Kilohana, "Hana Lima: Decolonial Projects and Representations," in *Detours: A Decolonial Guide to Hawai'i*, ed. Hokulani K. Aikau and Vernadette Vicuna Gonzalez (Durham, N.C.: Duke University Press, 2019), 120.

35. Trinidad, "Critical Indigenous Pedagogy of Place."

36. Stuart Banner, "Preparing to Be Colonized: Land Tenure and Legal Strategy in Nineteenth-Century Hawai'i," *Law and Society Review* 39, no. 2 (June 2005): 273–314, https://www.jstor.org/stable/3557617.

37. Banner, "Preparing to Be Colonized."

38. Laurel Mei-Singh and Vernadette Vicuña Gonzalez, "DeTours: Mapping Decolonial Genealogies in Hawai'i," *Critical Ethnic Studies* 3, no. 2 (Fall 2017): 173–92, https://www.jstor.org/stable/10.5749/jcritethnstud.3.2.0173.

39. Mei-Singh and Gonzalez, "DeTours."

40. Trinidad, "Critical Indigenous Pedagogy of Place," 192, referring to David Orr, *Ecological Literacy* (Albany: State University of New York Press, 1992).

41. Kenneth R. Jones, "Influences of Youth Leadership within a Community-Based Context," *Journal of Leadership Education* 7, no. 3 (Winter 2009): 246–64.

42. Stanley Aronowitz, "Preface to the Morningside Edition," in *Learning to Labor: How Working-Class Kids Get Working-Class Jobs*, by Paul Willis (New York: Columbia University Press, 1977), ix–xiii.

43. Samuel Bowles and Herbert Gintis, *Schooling in Capitalist America: Educational Reform and the Contradictions of Economic Life* (New York: Basic Books, 1977).

44. Paul Willis, *Learning to Labor*.

45. Richard Neumann, "American Democracy at Risk," *Phi Delta Kappan* 89, no. 5 (January 2008): 328–39, https://www.jstor.org/stable/20442493.

46. Kilohana, "Hana Lima," 120.

# PART III

## Harlem, New York: Activism through Critical Inquiry

In this part of the book, I present an exemplar of how community-based organizations can cultivate citizens who contribute to the intellectual realm of the commons, defined as the public space of democracy where they simultaneously build the habits of mind to decide how they want to live and then work together as critical thinkers to achieve that ideal. For this exemplar, I take you to Academe, my pseudonym for a nationally recognized youth organization in Harlem,[1] once the nation's largest African American ghetto and the undisputed spiritual homeplace for this population.[2] You learn about a program that was initially conceived as a community service project by two Harlem-born undergraduate students. After offering activities in area high schools, the pair established the organization in 1994 when they were twenty-one years old. Academe, which my research team studied in 2004–2005 and I revisited at the height of the Covid-19 pandemic in 2020–2021, targeted African American and Latino/a youth, helping them develop the capacity to self-determine their future through socially critical study of their history and culture and by supporting them as scholars and change agents in the surrounding neighborhood.

I have created a narrative from the 2004–2005 study using excerpts from a fifty-three-page, 25,000-word transcript of a survey and fourteen interviews that graduate research assistants from the City University of New York Environmental Psychology Program administered.[3] Study participants, consisting of both cofounders, staff, youth, parents, and a volunteer, responded to questions about the organization, its setting, and its activities.[4] Some lived in the neighborhood and others came from around the city, but they were all persons of color. I have organized the narrative according to the dimensions of critical pedagogy (critical awareness, collective agency, and collective action), though the protocols did not ask about this educational philosophy.[5] I have also created a narrative from the 2020–2021 study with excerpts from a sixty-one-page, 29,000-word transcript of four interviews that my research assistant at The New School administered.[6] Study participants, consisting of one of the cofounders and three staff who had attended Academe as youth, responded to questions intended to weigh my framing of the organization's 2004–2005 curriculum as critical pedagogy. Their interviews confirmed the validity of my framing and revealed a deepening and expansion of Academe's initial mission.

This four-section part of the book presents Academe as an exemplar of what I theorize as mind-centric critical pedagogy within the intellectual realm of place-based activism based upon its development of young people as leaders who use their minds to build community. In the first section, you learn about Harlem, an African American neighborhood that transitioned from cultural mecca to slum during the 1960s and 1970s but was just beginning to redevelop as Academe opened its doors. You learn about the organization, its dedicated staff, and the rooming house it upgraded as its home. In the second section, you hear from the 2004–2005 study participants about their experiences in an organization that was beginning to have roots, presented within a critical pedagogy framework, and in the third section, you hear from the 2020–2021 study participants about Academe's evolution, outcomes related to the dimensions of critical pedagogy, and future trajectory. I begin the fourth section by assessing both narratives to conceptualize the organization as exemplary of mind-centric critical pedagogy. I then ground this pedagogy in the commons as the intellectual realm of place-based activism, refocusing its dimensions as place awareness, place agency, and critical placemaking.[7] I conclude with observations of Academe's use of critical inquiry to create a loving, intergenerational commons.

# Historical Context

In order to help you understand the place that animated Academe's mission, I provide a snippet of Harlem's remarkable naissance and decline, which was followed by creeping gentrification during the time that the organization came into being. I provide the 2004–2005 study participants' view of the neighborhood, along with their insights into the organization, its staffing, programmatic approach, and homelike setting.

## Harlem, New York

Harlem, the nation's most iconic African American neighborhood, took shape in farmland north of New York City in the late 1800s and early 1900s. Its speculative tenements, apartment buildings, and brownstones, intended for a white middle class that never appeared, offered African Americans a "promised land" within an otherwise inhospitable city.[8] Racist social codes helped Harlem materialize as a segregated "city within a city" with its own churches, cafes, clubs, theaters, political organizations, and newspapers.[9] The area soon became a preferred destination for African American artists and intellectuals seeking a spiritual homeplace, migrants escaping the Jim Crow South, and veterans returning from World War I, determined to win equal treatment at home.[10] The political activism and cultural expressiveness of this group, which produced the 1920s Harlem Renaissance, along with the area's many places of worship and unique architectural characteristics, distinguished Harlem, making it a powerful symbol of "race progress."[11] Yet even in its heyday, Harlem was indisputably a ghetto.

Aware that African Americans were barred from white neighborhoods, landlords levied exorbitant rents for subdivided spaces. To pay their bills, tenants, even in the nicer buildings, took in roomers, making some blocks among the city's most densely populated, with the most disease and mortality.[12] Harlem's impoverishment became all too apparent during the Great Depression, when its Jazz Age illusion of the good life vanished. Then, just as Harlem's population peaked in 1950 as a result of migration from the South, deindustrialization and suburbanization dealt a fatal blow, enabling the exodus of low-skill jobs. In the wake of Harlem's 1964 race rebellion, many white Americans realized that a demographic transformation had befallen the neighborhood,[13] and the 1968 Fair Housing Act pushed it even further, enabling the exodus of small businesses and well-to-do African Americans. Harlem's remaining residents, mired in poverty, were powerless to save the neighborhood's once-stately architecture from decay.[14] By 1970, America's cultural mecca was unequivocally a slum, plagued by declining "opportunities for mobility, increasing poverty, overcrowded schools, onerous tax burdens, disinvestment, and police brutality."[15]

During the 1970s, Harlem lost housing stock to demolition, arson, and abandonment as landlords walked away, leaving taxes unpaid. Many residents also walked away, driven out by the pathologies of poverty,[16] but, as Academe's cofounder Sean explained, though "there's a lot of what you experience in a ghetto community, at the same time, it does give a lot of love." In that spirit, longtime residents, many of them women, organized and advocated for urban homesteading, affordable housing, accessible healthcare, decent schools, and functioning infrastructure. To take care of the neighborhood and its derelict real estate, they formed community design centers, community associations, and community development corporations. Their activism, reflecting Harlem's legacy as a segregated city-within-a-city, eventually influenced its redevelopment.[17]

Initially, activists rejected top-down redevelopment, demanding total community control despite the diminishing population and housing stock. However, after Mayor Ed Koch showered global corporations with subsidies and offered regulatory flexibility to developers in the 1980s, their demands for community control morphed into an acceptance of outsiders as partners. To stay in the housing game, eventually activists embraced public-private partnerships with powerful nonprofit intermediaries. Neoliberal privatization and commodification worked. After years of decline, Harlem became a sought-after destination for a mostly African American middle class, though not in sizable numbers.[18] In the mid-1980s, as the crack epidemic worsened, Harlem was still in decline. Then a turn-around occurred when the Harlem-based borough president, David N. Dinkins, pressured Koch into adopting a ten-year plan to create new and renovated housing.[19]

As mayor, Dinkins and then Rudy Giuliani kept building housing, and, though this construction did not make up for earlier losses, by the 1990s, the area was finally on the mend.[20] Yet at the time of the first study, Academe's other cofounder, Lucas, described Harlem as:

> Inundated with drugs, lacking in schools, with an infrastructure that supports the drug trade (diamond and gold shops, high-end clothing stores that only take cash), barber shops, and low-end food stores. . . . There's no restaurant that a postal worker or teacher would grab a meal at. There is one cleaners, no good produce—nothing that a community needs (Lucas).

Still, the population and housing stock increased for the first time in the postwar era. A shopping mall, Starbucks, and Pathmark supermarket opened, crime plummeted, rents skyrocketed, and upscale (mostly African American) families began restoring brownstones. Sean said that, in the last five years, the neighborhood had "become increasingly gentrified—an increasing number of wealthy folks, an increasing number of white folks, which has brought the pros and cons of gentrification." Around the time of the 2004–2005 study, gentrification took off after Harlem's main commercial spine, 125th Street, was up-zoned to accommodate office towers, hotels, and high-end condominiums, escalating rents and pricing out many lower-middle-income residents. As the number of affluent whites increased and new businesses displaced old mom-and-pop shops, the neighborhood's character began to change.[21] According to codirector Gretchen, demographic shifts produced tension between African Americans and the increasing Dominican and Latino/a population and between long-term residents and newcomers, many of whom had little affinity with the community's culture. Some called the police to intervene in the street life that had been a defining feature of Harlem for decades[22] and that Gretchen characterized as "a lot of people living their lives outside."

However, Academe's After-School Program director and Harlem resident, Camila, acknowledged that there was "a lot of drug dealing on each block, a lot of hanging out, drinking." And staff member Darden said that "all kinds of things can be going on," adding that neighborhood mores were informally monitored by "a group of elders who sit out and keep eyes out." Still, Camila affirmed Harlem's cultural cache, saying that "it's a caring community. It's pretty safe. All the young people know all the elders . . . [who] grew up in this community themselves." And Sean, who had been priced out by gentrification, described it as "a very strong and supportive community" with "a lot of older folks playing cards, watching the children; a lot of family connections." He also took pride in its beautiful architecture, especially Sugar Hill, the center of the Harlem Renaissance. However, the sixteen-year-old Vanessa, who lived about eight blocks away from Academe, was the most appreciative of this loving ghetto.

> Around here, there's always people on the streets and there's always music. Everyone knows everyone. The majority of the people are African American and Latino. It's a busy neighborhood. There's a lot of little stores, like grocery stores and sneaker stores. And buses are always passing; you never have to wait long. There's one elementary school that everyone who lives around here has gone to, like my mother and aunt and me. . . . My whole family lives in a five-block radius, so I grew up here. Sometimes I hear stories about robbery or rape, but mostly because it's busy, it's never deserted. You always see someone you know (Vanessa).

## Academe

Sean and Lucas established Academe within the gentrifying slum where they had grown up, intending to support the adolescent African American and Latino males who were being sucked into the school-to-prison pipeline. After formalizing the organization in 1995 and with Gretchen's guidance, they expanded the program to include adolescent girls in 1998. In its tenth year at the time of the first study, the organization had grown to support over 130 African American, Caribbean, Latino/a, and South East Asian youth, ages seven to twenty-one. Its annual budget of about $750K came primarily from foundations, but individual donors, including parents and even youth, were also supporting Academe's evolving comprehensive approach. As Sean explained:

> When we first started, all we had were the [single-gender] chapters. In the beginning of creating these chapters, we realized they needed more than that. They needed an after-school program. We also recognized the need for them to have summer-month activities, because it's a long time to not be in an organized program. We knew they needed job opportunity, and they needed money. A lot of kids didn't have opportunity to experience college life. The opportunity to experience a campus would be life-changing (Sean).

The Pathways Program began first and consisted of school-based, single-gender chapters with up to eighteen members who, over a period of years, attended weekly adult-led study sessions covering history, literature, and revolutionary movements. Session coleaders were available 24/7, and, as Sean pointed out, they also took the youth on "retreats for three days in the wilderness—being able to give them an opportunity to get away from the stresses in their lives—being able to be amongst your peers and experience the wilderness." The mixed-gender Freedom Program came next and provided a platform for the members to undertake campaigns and community service projects. Lucas said that "activism is what the whole platform of the Freedom Program is about: providing opportunity and space for youth to develop long-lasting social change for their community." Though the youth study participants had spent multiple years in the Pathway Program, they primarily talked about the youth-led Freedom Program, as you will see later.

In addition, the After-School Program offered academic tutoring, acting, poetry, sports, and drumming and, according to Lucas, encouraged the youth "to use their talents—drawing, painting, graphic arts, fashion design." He pointed with special pride to the Resistance Ring, "a group of ten fifteen- to twenty-one-year-olds who use spoken word to address social justice issues." These programs were enriched by a summer International Studies Program, jobs, day camps, wilderness retreats, and college tours along with prison visits, rallies, and a newsletter. Explaining Academe's breadth of activities, Sean said that "we try to incorporate a holistic model that engages every aspect of their development. In the instances where we can't provide for them, we try to find that support in the community. Our responsibility is to provide them with whatever they need." Deepa, whose three children attended Academe, vouched for this claim, disclosing that it even provided financial help "with notebooks, pencils, and pens. . . . Some kids even get served lunch over there."

## Having a Cohesive and Caring Staff

For the cofounders, working with youth was a calling, as Sean recollected.

> I was passionate about working with youth. I felt connected to them. I felt the need to provide support and guidance similar to what I had received as a young person. [In college], I felt like I was getting this elite education with other privileged people, and I felt a little out of place. I wasn't really serving my community by being on campus. So, I decided to reach out to the local community. This really interested me and was aligned with my passion. I did it out of passion to give back and for the enjoyment of working with youth. It was also out of the recognition of the need to. I stayed because once you start an organization, it's like a child—and it's taken a long time to get to a point of sustainability. I've stayed also because I've enjoyed it; it has allowed me

to survive and sustain myself. I also feel like I am doing work that benefits my community and is in line with my soul (Sean).

The cofounders' passion spilled onto the staff, who according to another parent, Kendra, "genuinely care about the youth. They have an interest in what all the youth are doing and where they're going and where they'd like to see them going." Sean was unwavering in claiming that Academe had "the best staff on the face of the planet," and Camila explained why, saying that:

> We're a small staff, so it's critical that our minds and goals are similar. What's important is that we see the big picture for young people down the road, and that we enjoy working with youth. We're not necessarily all youth educators, but we all still like and respect youth. We see the long-term goals for youth as graduating from wherever they might be at in school, having passion for community, becoming critical thinkers, having an interest in learning about culture and history (Camila).

Darnell reiterated this commitment, saying that working with youth "will give you a mirror into yourself through them, because we are in the business of caring for each together." Sean credited the selective hiring of "a staff community that is an extended family . . .—folks who are dedicated and really care about kids." He said that Academe tells prospective staff that "they have to be on 24–7 duty. You are working your forty hours plus; you have to carry a cell phone and be willing to respond to their needs whenever they call on you." Lucas said that his weekly time commitment was at least fifty hours and could easily expand to seventy hours or longer if they took the youth on a retreat. "We are always on call. We are always able to be reached." To illustrate the staff's dedication, Sean mentioned twice that, for three months during the previous year, "we had them all volunteering because we couldn't pay them." Camila felt that not being paid "forced members and staff to work closely together and it showed members that we are here—that we'll work with or without the money. And that was important for them to see." Clarence, the volunteer, summed up by saying that the staff "can't always speak to the numerous needs of the youth—for example, homework, law, college applications, single-parent issues, safety, any number of trying situations—but they try to. The biggest need is for caring, and Academe provides that."

## Creating a Collective Space of Empowerment

Lucas stated unequivocally that "we are zealots for our young people. I believe in their ability to make change, and I believe in youth empowerment." The youth study participants emphasized that while the Pathways Program helped them find their voice, feel a sense of accomplishment, develop their identity, and realize their strengths and weaknesses, the Freedom Program helped them use their voice to take action and achieve results. Academe's narrow three-story brownstone, built for residential use in the early 1900s, offered the youth a homelike space of empowerment. Its east side flanked vacant lots where the city had demolished three condemned buildings, and then its west side was exposed when another building was demolished to create a parking lot, giving Academe a singular prominence on the block, especially after residents turned the vacant lots into a community garden. As Gretchen explained: "We are a freestanding brownstone so you can't help but notice us." Academe adapted the structure for commercial use, situating youth spaces on the top floor including a lounge, library, computer room, TV room, and game room because, as Sean said, "it is important for them to have their own space."

Academe situated administrative and programmatic spaces—reception, conference rooms, offices, and kitchen—on the lower two floors, allocating space in the cellar for recreation and a darkroom. According to Sanjiv: "There is plenty of space; sometimes we need bigger space; sometimes we use a gym at a school. . . . We have pictures and paintings and photos of kids' work on all the walls here—and people are making more." Demetrius was even more enthusiastic about the facilities, noting that "the space is perfect. It gives you that home feeling. It's like a house, not a like a Boys and Girls Club center." Lucas explained that Academe's space "reflects positivity, knowledge. It's filled with light and natural wood—youth friendly, beautiful. We said, within our budget, 'this is what we can do, make it open, collective, and cohesive.'" With pride, he said: "We own the building. We consider it to be liberated land. We want to encourage the community to have a voice by helping them to organize to improve things for adults and youth. We have a desire for true community ownership."

Sean agreed that "the home we've created, the brownstone, is a community center. And we've tried to keep the home feel, while turning it into a community space." In Vanessa's opinion, Academe offered the youth "a place to get away to sometimes, where you don't have to worry about anything, and you're comfortable there." At the same time, this home-like space hosted numerous social events, connecting this select group to a larger community of youth and adults and enhancing its sense of collective empowerment.

Now that you understand the context and shape of the organization, I explore how Academe helped the youth become critical thinkers and actors within the commons of their community.

# 2004–2005 Narrative

In this three-part section, you hear from the 2004–2005 study participants about Academe's curriculum. Though the protocols did not ask about critical pedagogy, I have conceptualized the narrative to illustrate its three dimensions, showing how activities broadened the young peoples' worldview (critical awareness) and cultivated their confidence (collective agency), while offerSing opportunities for them to speak out and engage in community service (collective action).

## Encouraging Critical Awareness

### Instilling a Sense of Self-Worth

Gretchen explained that to develop self-worth, Academe's members had to rise above the "really horrific things" in their surroundings, saying that she was "always struck by what they have to deal with to get to the brownstone. These include gangs and their temptations, things that go on in their houses, seeing their parents in jail. They are exposed to a lot." Darnell said that their surroundings cast a shadow over the youth "so they don't feel good about themselves. It can happen in their family, the media, or on a subconscious level at times. Our guys know that when they are walking down the street, they are suspects immediately."

Academe staff helped the members understand that discrimination affected them both as individuals and as a community, pointing out the lack of greenery, overcrowded schools, garbage-filled streets, and deteriorated subway station to make the youth aware of systemic, racially based bias. Gretchen explained that the youth "talk about why things are the way they are. . . . One of the schools we work with is the first school to be built in this area over the last fifty years. The kids have an understanding of the lack of services." Growing up in Harlem—then the city's number-one entry point for cocaine—put a tag on the youth that took a herculean effort by Academe staff to eradicate. Darnel explained that they talked to the youth about "setting their own standards and not letting limitations be put on them, either by themselves or together. All of what we do is goal setting—what are you trying to do, as opposed to society's definition of who you are." In his view, the challenge for Academe's staff was to convince the youth that they could "accomplish the goals that they set their mind to regardless of society or environment."

Gretchen agreed, saying that "we work to help them to understand their world, for example, the reasons why there are drugs in their neighborhood and their schools are underfunded." Academe provided an ideal learning environment because it not only lacked the biases and negative associations of their regular schools, but it also had a secular spiritual quality. In meetings, the co-leaders asked the members to spell out their moral convictions for becoming their better selves, and according to Sean: "We hold them to that. That's the power of self—recognizing your own self-determination. Ultimately that's what you strive for. That's what we try to help them develop within themselves." Darnell said that Academe staff helped the youth develop the collective courage "to be the exception, not the rule," explaining that "if you are pleased with yourself, that transcends everything else. Academe brings them together in a group and lets them know that they are not alone in what they are going through." Vanessa offered an example of the collective courage she developed after her chapter's field trip to a rehabilitation center in Connecticut.

> We came back later to the brownstone for a sleepover. We had to write oaths to ourselves and there was a candle ceremony where we read them to the group. We all cried and stuff. That day was my favorite because at the end of it we learned so many things. . . . We learned about ourselves and got in touch with ourselves (Vanessa).

## Opening Up a Wider Worldview

Academe was about helping youth reposition themselves in a society that had consigned them to second-class citizenship. Clarence explained that:

> What's been a driving force is the potential for something better. Staff try to model critical thinking and [are] committed to family and community. Images of themselves from the popular media aren't necessarily

positive for the self, but by reading texts and through discussion, they develop a new lens to look at themselves and the community (Clarence).

Darnell said that staff drew upon Harlem's history to inspire the youth "to become more conscious of their community—to be exposed to something different. They don't have to go on with the norm." Kendra agreed that knowing history was important and reported that her daughter had talked about the neighborhood's past. "She told me, I believe, that Alexander Hamilton has a house in this area. I remember that they talked about that, and they had a project about slaves in the neighborhood." Lucas commented that the "kids are blown away when they find out celebrities lived here. Sugar Hill—we are three blocks from Convent Avenue. It's beautiful, but walk one block, it's night and day. To see that and know the legacy is essential." Vanessa was also blown away when she attended a workshop on hip hop in different countries and the guest speaker, a female disc jockey who had grown up one block from her house, described the old neighborhood. "I just wish I could have seen it!" she said.

Though steadfast in grounding the youth locally, Lucas also recognized that Academe could not "merely expose them to the six-block radius around the brownstone and expect them to change." According to Gretchen, the staff introduced the youth to a wider world:

> We try to expose them to all kinds of things, from going overseas, to eating dinner at an Indian restaurant. One of my strategies is that I might not tell them where we are going, but I know once they are there, they will appreciate it. I also remember taking them to a movie with subtitles, and they really enjoyed the movie. It was "Real Women Have Curves." I definitely see them growing in acceptance of things that are outside of their immediate world. The idea of them feeling comfortable in the world is important (Gretchen).

She believed that the International Program was the most life-changing of Academe's offerings because it expanded the young people's minds and "their understanding of the world, themselves, and their place in the world. This is the first time that some kids are away from parents and have the opportunity to be independent." Gretchen saw the program as "an opportunity for those who are involved in the single-gender groups to deal directly with the stuff that they talk about in the chapters and live together for a month." Clarence was especially intrigued with travel in Africa because it countered America's exaggerated individualism and provided an opportunity for young people to "see Africa where the society is a collective. And as the students write out what the community means to them, it helps those who are more entrenched in what they think they already know. They see community modeled." However, Lucas saw even more profound benefits.

> To take them in black and brown hands and return them to the African continent—to witness the 4,000 years of African history in Egypt, the slave forts of Ghana. To have these kinds of experiences— there is no way they can't come back and believe in something else. When they went to Soweto, the toughest cats living in the projects were weeping at the poverty. It blew them away. The trip is not all positive; it's not all glory, but it's about global awareness and enabling young people to dream in a different way (Lucas).

## Animating a Vision of Social Justice

In Academe's vision of a socially just world, young people would have the re- sources to determine their own and their community's future, they would gain the tolerance and understanding to coexist with others, and they would be able to participate in decisions that affect them. As Lucas put it: "Social justice means that there is an ability for young people to have a say . . . in their des- tiny—to bring about reform in schools, police brutality," and Academe made certain that they could participate effectively by equipping them with a global understanding of injustice. Lucas said that "it's not about freedom per se, but instead being aware that what's happening in Iraq is connected to here—the sweatshops they are participating in when they purchase goods, the sense of poverty, which is the most pervasive and hopeless."

The study participants revealed Academe's success in helping the youth un- pack injustice—for example, Morgan, who had attended the program every weekday for three years, described how she "used to have a blank outlook on certain things. It helps me see things in a different light. It helps me understand my community and what's happening in terms of gentrification It educates me every day." Demetrius conveyed his understanding of movement history, explaining that "social justice means all American social classes having an equal say. I've learned that this is something that we've been fighting for, for many years since the Civil Rights Movement. Eventually, one day, it will be won." Clarence explained that Academe encouraged the youth to go beyond understanding injustice to having a clear vision of a better world by asking them: "'What do you see now? What do you want to see in the future?' And thinking creatively about how to change the environment." For example, Jen- nifer said that in the 1960s and 1970s, "there was a lot of racism and now we can change this," a view that Vanessa elaborated.

We want for the people in this community to have equal rights as everywhere else, including our apartments and the gentrification. It's not fair that we have to pay expensive rents for such poor conditions. Our schools could be a lot better. In the program, we have a ten-point platform, and it has all that stuff about what we stand for—no more police brutality; for people to know their rights (Vanessa).

## Fostering Collective Agency

### Providing Support Across and Within Generations

Academe was started by two young men who had the same experiences as those they hoped to serve. Sean explained that:

> When we first started this, I was a junior in college. At that point, we were reaching out to high school students four years younger than us. It isn't a lot of time, but it's a great expanse when you think about the issues that they are facing at that age—that we were facing too. So thinking about dropping out of school, growing up in a violent environment, questioning your relationships with women or men, your role in society—it's a critical point in life. We really feel like kids now are having to face these issues that older generations didn't have to face, like HIV/AIDS wasn't around, and in terms of gun violence (Sean).

Academe's staff believed that young people needed to have adults other than their parents or teachers who could provide critical feedback and that older people also needed to have a sense of the younger generation's experiences. As Sean explained, the organization's commitment to intergenerational bridge-building "has kept me aware of the reality of what it means to be young." Lucas added that "we need intelligence from both youth and adult experiences. We try to celebrate elders here; we have a board that ranges from eighteen to sixty-five; our staff ranges from twenty-one to forty-two. That kind of diversity is very important to us." Clarence stated that:

> There are no age limits on great ideas. Society is not limited by a person's age or experience. Youth at Academe are not necessarily viewed as young people, but as people who have something to offer and . . . teach me. This really helps me that it's not an age, but an environment that crosses generations. We have retired educators, et cetera. Once I saw six generations engaged around one topic (Clarence).

At the same time, the staff believed that the youth needed a space of their own where they could, according to Gretchen, "assert positive peer pressure. What they do with each other is really powerful—probably more powerful than what we do with them." Darnel agreed, noting that positive peer pressure allowed the youth to "relate to each other better. They seem to understand it or get it quicker if it's a peer of theirs." Having their own space allowed for hanging out, having fun, and being part of a youth community where everybody was, according to Sanjiv, "friendly and interested in each other." For example, Sanjiv described what he gained as a mentor in the After-School Program, claiming that he got "new meaning coming back and helping out and giving advice about college." He also spoke to the benefits he accrued from same-age and younger peers.

> My peers were very vocal in their ideas and wanted to project their ideas. This rubbed off on me. This is one of the best things that has happened to me—learning to communicate better and be more vocal about my feelings. The younger ones now help me in the same way, learning how to share my ideas with them. Often adults don't see that kids can be mentors too, learning from younger people and helping them change (Sanjiv).

Deepa concurred. "People need each other at any age. If people are isolated, they won't learn from each other. At Academe, people are together. . . . They all learn from each other."

## Providing the Support and Love of Family

According to Sean, many of Academe's members viewed the organization as an extended family that helped them "find their true selves—what their gifts and dreams are." Darnel added that, for the youth who had relatives living on the block, the organization was truly part of their family. Sean believed that Academe's familial relationships helped the youth develop "their human capacity to care and support and love each other. They see something that is really genuine about caring and supporting each other and helping them to lead healthy lives." As Demetrius framed it: "I need the support from all the brothers and sisters. I've got a family, but it's different than what you get from your family." Deepa agreed, saying that "there is a lot of feeling between [the youth]. From each other, they learn love of human beings." At times, Sean explained that Academe served as an extended family for overburdened parents who needed childrearing help.

> Sometimes when I am talking to parents, they are needing to vent; they need a place to talk about those issues they are going through.

One of the roles I have to play is the role of mediator, and I am fairly comfortable with that. It's really helping the kids to understand their parents and their parents understand their kids' view. It's very hard to do that in the middle of a conflict, but if there is someone else there to help you take a step back, that helps a lot (Sean).

Darnel was more hard-nosed than Sean and thought that "ideally, an organization is a support, but not the parent. The problem is it becomes the parent. The young person gets used to it and the parent gets used to it. We're not here that many days compared to school, home." For him, parents needed to weigh their work obligations against those of raising their children.

## Inspiring Collectivity beyond Individual Goals

In addition to serving as an extended family, Academe endeavored to create a sense of community among the youth, which meant helping them learn to negotiate differences. As Jennifer put it: "Before I came to the program, I was loud and disrespectful. Now I take differences and try to understand them and not judge. I am more positive and open minded." Camila pointed out that young people have issues with one another and "don't always have the opportunity—the knack to let stuff go." Kendra said that Academe helped the youth learn "how to communicate and talk about their feelings" if something was bothering them, and Vanessa agreed. She said that she valued the disagreements that occur in meetings when there are different opinions. "We need a safe place to have different opinions, even if those discussions get heated."

Kendra believed that Academe also helped the youth be more accountable to one another, noting that it had prepared her daughter "for being responsible—not just carrying out orders but being able to function in a social setting." According to Clarence, the youth developed accountability primarily through community service where they became "responsible citizens, working to better self and the community." He believed that service inspired the youth to have a sense of us-ness beyond their individual goals. Gretchen added that they transported lessons from the community back into the organization as they interacted with one another, noting that "they also try to hold each other to certain standards even if their method is not always the most constructive way to give feedback! They all know they are going through a process that has them thinking about social justice" and recognize that they need to live its tenets.

## Cultivating Young People as Leaders

The cofounders embraced an eclectic approach to youth leadership. Lucas declared that "youth should have a voice in the things that affect their lives" and complained that "too often, if they're at the table, it's a surprise. The idea is that they are supposed to be there." To make sure that the members had a voice in Academe, the cofounders created a youth council, anticipating that it would eventually participate in board of director meetings and further specified that the Freedom Program would be youth-led. Morgan spoke with pride about this program, declaring that "it's actually run by teens," and Vanessa elaborated its use of near-peer mentors, explaining that, though Gretchen and Sean were present, the summer workshops were run by alumni "who were part of the previous Freedom Program" who helped "the youth make decisions for what's going to happen." As Sean put it, the staff "definitely have influence, but [the youth] have the vote and the decision-making power."

In contrast, Lucas said that the Pathway Program delivered a specific curriculum that emphasized the role young people thirty and under have played in social movements worldwide. He described the young men in one chapter who started learning this history when they were eleven years old and were now perceived as leaders in their high schools. He said that the Pathway Program members had become "the most popular men and women trying to live in more conscious ways—knowing that their history is cool, that being revolutionary is cool." Sean noted that Academe supported varied forms of leadership from being a revolutionary to being a positive influence within your family or by making positive decisions in your life. For example, Camila said that Academe teaches the youth to have a voice in their families and helped them learn to speak their minds at home in a productive manner.

Toward youth leadership's revolutionary end, Sean said that the youth "are developing their voice around issues of injustice and liberation, and they are also concretely working to improve their community by organizing and educating adults to fight back against gentrification. Toward its other prosocial end, Lucas predicted that they will "personally gain their dreams—through education, starting a business, becoming a star singer. Larger than that, they will feel empowered and teach others what they learned." According to Josephina: "The program has helped [the youth] believe that they have what it takes to create change. They all appreciate how we try to arm them to be in the world." To make sure that "their voices are heard so people can hear the profound things they say," Lucas explained that Academe published both the spoken word generated by the Resistance Ring and the mission statements and oaths adopted by the chapter members.

## Requiring Collective Action

### Engaging Young People in Community Service

Lucas revealed his knowledge of Freire's concept of praxis when he stated that Academe was designed to "help youth become change agents both through constant dialogue and with action—providing opportunities for youth to become direct agents of change for their community and for one another and participating in political rallies." While the Pathways Program engaged the youth in dialogue, the Freedom Program offered opportunities for action. In fact, participating in community service was a program requirement and ranged from campaigns to mapping, beautification, and education, with some activities lasting a few hours and others continuing over many years. Regardless of their duration, Sean and Darnel said that the youth began by identifying a problem that they wanted to address, analyzing it, and then organizing other youth and community allies. According to Darnel, the Freedom Program:

> Works directly with community activism—what issues do you want to address, the feeling of accomplishment, seeing the possibilities of something getting done. The first one we did, we had a street fair and a campaign—and we stopped drug activity for that day. It had been a year-long thing to get the street fair and health fair up and getting [residents] to participate. And the sense of accomplishment was huge. A young woman left and went out to start her own organization (Darnell).

Sanjiv said that the Freedom Program helped the youth "become activists and do things for the community, like the project in the park nearby and a few others. We help the community inside Academe first, and then Academe can help the community all around." Vanessa, who was clearly captivated by this program, said that the youth helped the community "because we live here and we are trying to help make it better, for example our project on trying to build a community center. We are trying to give the community productive things to do." Noting such projects as a community garden with a gazebo and storage shed and murals installed in Manhattan parks, Gretchen said that the program was "where adults, facilitators, and youth come together to improve the physical, political, social, cultural, and economic infrastructure of our neighborhood." Darnel's list of projects included "a property where people want to make a school or a community center—we are working to make sure it

doesn't fall in the wrong hands—helping at the block party, in the community garden, cleaning up and keeping the brownstone clean." Bragging that
people were "surprised and impressed at the work we do," Vanessa listed getting out the vote on election night, campaigning to turn an abandoned school
into a community museum, and interviewing elders to collect oral histories
for the museum. She said that her Freedom Program group:

> Is working on the community museum. We want to build an exhibit
> about the past and present of the abandoned school, Public School
> [Anonymous], and so we are interviewing people who went to the
> school in the past to learn more about them. It has been abandoned for
> like twenty years. My mother went to that school (Vanessa).

Jennifer said that the youth were "active trying to bring together residents
and build community centering in the abandoned building." Morgan clarified that it was "under the possession of the Boys and Girls Club. We want
it to be completed 85 percent for community space. . . . We are working in a
coalition of 10,000 in the community—people in the area and in organizations.
We're working to try to get the building restored into what it's supposed to be."
Kendra said that her daughter felt strongly about the project and had gotten
petitions signed to advocate for its funding. And Morgan explained that the
building had been "abandoned for many years. People have tried before we
have," saying that she used to give up, but the Freedom Program had taught
her to work past the frustration because "you can't change something with a
negative attitude."

Sanjiv provided unreserved applause for the benefits of community service,
saying that the youth were "changing the world as we speak. And as we change
ourselves and grow up, tomorrow we can make the world a better place."

## Engaging Young People as Community Leaders

Gretchen explained that sometimes she engaged the youth in conducting research and sharing their findings with residents. Touting their capacities as
community researchers, she described the youth as "naturally curious and critical thinkers" who were "really reflective," with "a lot of physical energy and
stamina." She said that they not only had boundless get-up-and-go for roaming the neighborhood to collect data, but they discussed their findings in a
fun, informative way because, as Morgan noted: "We have a group with a whole
bunch of intelligence." Gretchen described one study where "their job was
to go around and map the physical structures of the community, and in the
process, they did research on issues they were interested in. They later did

presentations in our community garden and invited the public." Another study related to rent stabilization and began when Vanessa wrote an essay about her family having to pay exorbitant rent for a small apartment, which led to "a committee that's writing a report about that and looking into the legal aspects." To make sure that the residents were knowledgeable about their rights and equipped to take effective action, the youth made presentations on such issues as rent stabilization and gentrification. As Clarence explained, Academe youth "have enlightened the surrounding community," while elevating their role as community builders.

## Being a Force against Racist Policing

Like most African American neighborhoods, Harlem suffered from abusive over-policing, and Academe's staff and youth were not exempt from racial profiling, despite the organization's positive presence on the block. While Gretchen acknowledged that "we've all had bad experiences with the cops," Lucas described "an incident where our codirector was arrested for loitering outside the building. He refused to move. There were twelve cops called. We fought it and the cop was disciplined. Another incident was when we took a group to a park, and there was a shootout." Gretchen added that "we've also had a lot of our kids get summons for not having ID or spending the weekend in Rikers for jumping the turnstile." Over time, Academe staff negotiated a rapport with the police, which resulted in its block being designated as a PAL Playstreet, a supervised recreation zone in the public right-of-way that the New York Police Department supports in high-crime, impoverished neighborhoods. As Jennifer explained: "In summer, there is the PAL that blocks off the street during the day where kids can play outside and not be exposed to negative influences." Yet, despite having this officially designated recreation space, the youth (especially the males) knew that, in Darnell's words, they were "immediate suspects" whenever they were in the public domain.

## Being a Source of Community Liberation

From personal experience, I know that the residents of New York's ghettos often populate abandoned buildings with the spirits of former occupants, and that was the case with the brownstone. When two college graduates showed up to take over a building that many imagined to be haunted, the neighbors were more than a little apprehensive. As Gretchen explained: "They all looked at us sideways; it was skepticism," but then Academe had met with community leaders, welcomed residents in, and contributed "to their events, like the annual block party. We had to work to help them understand that we are here for the long haul." Clarence noted that Academe had redeveloped an abandoned rooming house into a thriving youth organization and created a beautiful community garden, recalling that "one youth member saw the organization grow by watching the building change from a window ('What is it? What are you about?'), and this has become a person who's speaking to the board members and getting funding." Sean explained that Academe was not just about youth development, but it was also "about liberating the community, controlling the resources, giving more power to the people." Noting that drug dealers were not "all the devil's spawn," Lucas said that:

> We try to form collectives and reach out as much as possible—to prisons, group homes, et cetera. . . . We've become a beacon—a young woman who lives across the street, she often speaks to people and says that this place used to be abandoned, and if they were bad, their moms would punish them by making them stay on the stoop all day. And now we're here and she loves what's going on here. This is their space (Lucas).

Because the cofounders envisioned community members as collaborators, building relationships with them took priority. At the time of the 2004–2005 study, they had just hired a community outreach coordinator to keep residents informed of Academe's work and respond to their requests for programming. Sean said that they were also thinking about forming a block association to help the organization "delve deeper into our connection to the broader community and that is the ultimate thing we want to see. [The organization] won't die because people will be willing to fight for it."

# 2020–2021 Narrative

This section brings you forward fifteen years to hear from a cofounder and three current Academe staff who were associated with the organization around the time of the 2004–2005 study. They offer a deeply informed appraisal of how the organization you have just learned about matured as its roots deepened. Unlike the protocols for the initial study, this one asked the study participants to share their recollections and current view of Academe's strengths and shortcomings, its outcomes related to the goals of critical pedagogy, and its future trajectory and that of the youth it serves. As you read this narrative, keep in mind that, whereas the 2004–2005 study participants were diverse constituents responding to general questions, the ones in the 2020–2021 study were long-time insiders responding to specific questions related to critical pedagogy. Another difference is that advances in technology allowed for a more accurate transcription of the interviews than was possible earlier. That said, let me introduce the 2020–2021 study participants.

Diego had the longest relationship with Academe, having joined the Pathways Program during its very first year in 1994, before the organization formalized. He became a staff member in 2004, the same year that Jeremy entered the program. The next year, Academe became aware of the permaculture garden that Jeremy helped develop while attending high school on the Lower East Side and hired him to create a new Environmental Program. Qadira joined her sister in the Freedom Program in 2004 while attending a selective high school that she characterized as "great" but deficient in non-Western history. Qadira became a part-time staff member while she was in college and maintained the position in graduate school. Then, in 2016, while completing a doctoral degree in Africana Studies, she became the full-time coordinator of the program that she had joined as a teenager. Sean, the cofounder, you already know.

## Strengths and Shortcomings

Study participants had differing views of Academe's early strengths. For example, Diego emphasized its small size, which he felt offered "an authentic space—something that [the youth] could invest themselves in." For him, such authenticity was not only important internally, but it was also essential to building trust within a community that was worried about gentrification. He said that "the neighborhood wanted to know if you for real, if you mean what you're saying, and you say what you mean. We were very intentional around [the organization's] purpose, very intentional around its engagement and its messaging." Diego also valued that Academe "was very communal, you know, really grounded in community and family." Sean broadened this insight, saying that the organization provided "a living example of what community really looks like" and that when young people "experience what real love feels like, what real community feels like, what real support feels like, then, you know, it creates a seed in their mind that there is another way."

Sean added that Academe's early strength was having a clear mission and "an incredible team of staff who were 100 percent dedicated to the mission." He said that the organization had a "very clear vision in terms of the programming that we were running and the model that we were implementing." Amplifying Sean's perspective, Jeremy named each of Academe's programs and made note that its "International Studies Program was thriving. We were going to new countries. A lot of young people were, you know, applying to that program. And one of our classes, our writer's collective class, was having a very strong group of young people with poetry." These strengths notwithstanding, study participants also identified shortcomings in those early years, not surprisingly stressing the lack of funding as the organization's most serious limitation. Sean recalled that by 2004, Academe had achieved some level of financial sustainability, but the situation was still precarious because the organization was "operating out of a very small brownstone" and did not have enough space for all its programs or the budget "to build out that team—the development team." Jeremy recalled the difficulty of finding funders that aligned with Academe's mission, explaining that some grants "would demand a lot of data and that's not really what we're all about. It's the quality of work, not the quantity of work."

In considering the present, Qadira identified as a current strength Academe's approach to "social, emotional learning," which she said had become more refined because of its "connectivity to the sociopolitical world in New York City. . . . I think one of the things that we do well now is how broad our coalition work is," which Jeremy characterized as essential to community change. He said that parents, school staff, community members, district leaders, and the borough president "all have to be involved for something to work at a grand scale. We can do it in a smaller scale, but if you want it to really make effect in our community, in our boroughs, it has to be involved with many people." Qadira agreed, saying that one of Academe's current strength was its capacity to organize broad coalitions.

Study participants also pointed to its expanded catchment area as a current strength. Whereas Academe initially served students primarily from the Harlem area, Qadira remarked that it currently offered programming for all New York City public school students of color. Sean pointed to the Freedom Program's expansion to three levels of training, including a first summer in the Freedom School followed by a second summer of "intensive organizing training" and a third to transition from organizing to being a spokesperson "who can go out and kind of educate the broader community on the issues that we're addressing." Qadira added that the program runs four to six weeks with two workshops per eight-hour day and "takes a more profound dive into social justice education in a shorter amount of time so that folks can come into the school year ready to organize."

Jeremy underscored the higher enrollments in the Freedom Program (which had grown from about twenty youth in one chapter in 2004 to about forty-five in two chapters), and in the Pathways Program (which had grown from four chapters for each gender to six). Additionally, he observed that the Environmental Program began with seven youth working in summer and had grown to about fifty in three different chapters who work year-round to tend the garden and its greenhouse and aquaponic systems. Jeremy estimated that Academe's enrollment had more than tripled in the last fifteen years because, in addition to the foregoing expansions, it had added "after-school programming for teenagers and there's multiple classes like the dance class, like we still have the writers collective and now we have lit media and we have an art class as well." Most exciting for Jeremy was Academe's construction of a six-story building. He said that, after spending twenty years "in a brownstone that's like four stories high," the new structure was "gonna quadruple the amount of space that we have in the next year and the amount of young people that we're gonna serve. It's gonna be amazing." Jeremy boasted that Academe also had renovated 15,000 square feet of storefront space that it would likely keep for social enterprises. In addressing current shortcomings, Diego said that "there's really not many honestly," but acknowledged that the lack of delineation between employment and family made it hard to fire people when they were not "hold-ing up their end. And so that's a shortcoming." All the study participants agreed that the early funding constraints still existed, which Qadira attributed to the nature of being a nonprofit organization with spending constraints and staff who wear multiple hats so that "there is far too much on anybody's plate to actually do, you know, in-depth meaningful work. And it doesn't mean that we don't do in-depth and transformative and meaningful work, but like we ain't focused on all of it at the same time. And so sometimes things get dropped." Diego agreed, saying that he had "been fighting burnout for the past two, three years." Qadira noted that lack of funding was "its own kind of emotionally tax-ing reality" because "we know so profoundly what the issues are and where the holes are, and we are best equipped to plug them," but we lack the resources and capacity to address them. Despite funding constraints and the burnout that accompanied them, study participants agreed that Academe was on an unstoppable upward trajectory, which Diego insisted was a result of its authenticity.

> Being an employee for sixteen years and just being a part of the family for twenty-six years, you know, it's amazing to see where we've gone. We started out with one little office at Teachers College at Columbia, and now we're on the precipice of having a multi-million-dollar, environ-mentally friendly, state-of-the-art youth facility. . . . In terms of integ-rity, like to maintain your integrity for twenty-six years and for that not to be compromised by money. And again with growth comes a lot of growing pains. So I'm not saying that anything is perfect, but I'm talking about our core tenets have not been interfered with. And that level of sincerity and integrity is the reason why I'm still here. . . . The love is unconditional, my employment is not (Diego).

## Developing Critical Awareness

### Helping Lions Become Historians

In addressing Academe's approach to developing critical awareness, study participants thought back to their early experiences. For example, Qadira recited the African proverb—"when lions become their own historians, hunt-ers cease being heroes"—to pinpoint her political awakening during a his-tory workshop that Lucas offered in the Freedom Program. Recalling the unsettling nature of her awakening, she said that "history is written by the winners. And if you are getting a Eurocentric Western education, like all your knowledge base and your viewpoint is going to be Eurocentric and very

Western." Likewise, Diego recalled his awakening, miming his recollection of Lucas saying: "Like you're seeing the effects of something but let me just tell you the in-between step that allowed for this injustice to happen." He added that Lucas would tell him:

> I know that feeling that you get that this isn't right because it's not. But instead of just dwelling in the abstract, let me show you who James Baldwin is. Let me show you who W. E. B. DuBois is. Let me show you who Shirley Chisholm is, right? Let me bring you into all of these historic—Frederick Douglass—let me bring you into all of these historical figures who most accurately confirm that feeling that you have (Diego).

He recalled reading his first book, which was by Malcom X, explaining that Lucas had given him several of his books and audiotapes. Diego recalled going "to sleep, listening to Malcolm. And to this day, there's still like phrases that I use . . . paying it forward" to the young people. Of the present, he said that the Freedom Program offers workshops on movement activists like the Southern Negro Youth Congress, the Black Panthers, Angela Davis, Huey Newton, and Assata Shakur, "just making sure that the young men and women who come through the organization understand that the struggle that they've been told in school—you know, Martin Luther King is a great man, but Martin Luther King is not it."

## Simulating Real-Life Situations

Thinking about his early years at Academe, Diego recalled how expert Lucas and Sean were in teaching the youth a lesson by using real-life simulations to catch them off guard. For example, he recalled a retreat when "they let certain guys in to eat and had other guys wait. They gave certain guys privileges and didn't give privileges to other guys." Diego said that this simulation helped his cohort experience what millions of people across the globe experience daily when something happens but "nobody asked for it, nobody voted on it, nobody was told about it." Sean described another simulation, a game that involved splitting the youth into two teams and then doling out fake money as payment for one team to harm the other. He explained that, after several rounds of abuse, he and Lucas would throw fake money into the air, which the youth would fight over. Then, they would end the game by bringing out the prize, a pizza covered with roaches, and they would say:

> "Yeah, that's what you get, and the question is, what did you learn from this? What was happening here? What did you do?" And what

they begin to tear apart is that "man, you know, for money, we did everything, anything to harm our brother." And that's what happens in our society. That's what capitalism does to us. It puts us into these positions where we're willing to do anything, whether it's harming our own community, whether it's harming our environment, you know, whether it's even destroying our own families (Sean).

He provided a third example: camping trips when staff would "kidnap one of the kids in the middle of the night. And they'd be safe; they'd be with one of our staff in the woods somewhere. But all the other campers, you know, we would tell them, your brother has been kidnapped." Sean said that the simulation helped the youth understand "that when one of us is suffering and one of us is experiencing some kind of pain or need, that it is upon all of us to support that person." He felt it made them see the need for unity "without getting hurt but making them actually feel that reality."

## Providing the Language to Name Injustice

Sean explained that a core part of Academe's mission was helping young people:

Understand the circumstances that they're born into—the history behind the various social issues and injustices that they face. Within our Pathways Program, it's always been a part of our core curriculum and our focus to help youth understand the history of social injustice and to help them to begin to think about the obstacles in their lives, how do they overcome those obstacles, and then ultimately how do they fight for change so that those obstacles no longer exist (Sean).

Qadira recalled that "definitely the Freedom Program helped me understand the underlying causes of injustice. Like I can't even pretend that it didn't." She remembered that the program expanded her grasp of racial injustice and gave her "language to really understand what was happening and it gave me vocabulary." Referring to the workshops Lucas offered on "structural inequity and how it looks in New York City," Qadira said that she realized "that I wasn't crazy and that there were structures designed to keep me down." In Qadira's telling, she became "an African American Studies and sociology double major in college" and later changed to solely African American Studies as a result of her participation in the Freedom Program. Similarly, Diego said that, as a child, he "was always kind of inquisitive" and already felt that intrinsically "there's something wrong with the world."

I always had like this kind of perspective, but I never had like the outlet, the space to like unpack that. And Sean and Lucas they came in to kind of cultivate that space with the edge, you know, of guys. I'm like fifteen years old and they're like twenty-one. So they're not that old; they're old enough. They just, you know, from the outset, it was like social justice. Like that was something that they were very, very resolute and transparent about, which was like: "Yo! This country is founded on X, Y, and Z, but we're not into conspiracy theories; we're into intellectualism and fact. So we're going to ground you in a very particular way through literature that you may not be exposed to" (Diego).

In addressing the present, Qadira described Academe's current members' frame of mind as not unlike Diego's at fifteen, acknowledging that they "have a lot of experience or knowledge before they walk into our door, whether they are eight or sixteen." In Qadira's estimation, the youth came in knowing about injustice, but Academe provided "vocabulary for understanding the ways they already feel the world—the things that they already know." Jeremy added that Academe guided the youth in engaging "that fight, that struggle, that anger but learning how to use the right vocabulary . . . to express their feelings to a public or community."

## Encouraging Collective Agency

### Offering Guidance in Critical Thinking

Though Qadira said that she was "aware how awful the world was early on," at Academe she learned to move beyond anger and arguing with people to working on policy and strategy. Reflecting the 2004–2005 study participants' thoughts about intergenerational bridge-building, she said that, as a teenager, she valued encountering adults who were not her family or teachers who would discuss her ideas, make suggestions for alternative approaches, "and who were actually engaging with me about tactics or even just ideas and creating space for ideation. Like that was huge." Qadira said that she found it "amazing" to be forced to dig deeper into her ideas.

That helped me understand my place in the world and how to fix it, but also to like converse with adults and ideate with adults and learn about, you know, historical movements and historical efforts and feel like we were all on the same page. Like, even if like the idea was wild crazy like they would never have been like: "No Qadira that ain't it." They'd more like ask me questions, like: "So why do you think you should do that cause that doesn't really make sense to me, but I want you to walk me through it" (Qadira).

Noting that all the staff were persons of color, she said that conversations with them produced a "creative space" that helped build her confidence by showing her that "institutions are made by people; people are changeable, and everything is changeable," but you need to have the right strategy, path, and momentum. As Qadira put it: "There are all these other conditions for sure, but people make the shift and people are moveable." In middle school, she realized that "if I knew the terrain and I played the game well, I could get what I wanted, but I didn't think about it in a larger way until Academe." Then she had to write a paper about a book that she felt was racist and had "all these really offensive imagery around black people and specifically African people. And I'm like one black girl in my whole grade." After receiving a C– on her paper, she recalled going to Gretchen and asking her whether the grade was because of her criticism of the book or because it was not a good paper. Qadira said that Gretchen read the paper, told her she received a C– because it was not a good paper, and helped her revise it. Qadira remembered submitting the revised version and receiving "like an A– or B+. And so I learned, again, like there are rules. If you do this well, like there's space for you to do what you need to do for yourself."

## Creating Agency through Knowledge

Sean explained that Academe's current curriculum incorporated many different resources—books, audiotapes, films, theater, physical activity—"to engage young people in an exploration of injustice." Among the topics that Diego listed were African/Latino/a history, sexism and misogyny, sexual responsibility, racist bias and bias reduction, and environmental justice. He said that whatever the subject matter, staff hoped that the young people would come away with something substantive that they could use for an academic paper or other such purpose. Diego was confident that Academe's curriculum armed the youth "with knowledge and opportunities that will help them to be agents of change in their own right," adding that the staff wanted the young people to "take advantage as much as possible."

Both Diego and Qadira saw critical awareness and agency as inseparable. Qadira said that, initially, youth development was a biproduct of Academe's organizing agenda, not its central purpose, but that more recently, activities had explicitly paired knowledge and agency. Explaining how this worked programmatically, Jeremy said that the Freedom Program members investigated a particular issue and then all the youth got involved, "going to meetings, creating flyers, creating awareness. So one group is learning about it and deciding how they want to fight about it, but the whole organization gets to learn about it and gets to fight about it." Diego was passionate about this approach, saying that being informed was essential to agency and provided "a foundation to combat everything that inevitably will come their way."

### Providing Opportunities to Speak Out

As was true in 2004–2005, study participants reported that Academe valued helping the youth find their own voice. Diego insisted that Academe put the youth "out there in a safe, prepared way, but they are speaking on their own terms, and they are voicing their opinion in an articulated fashion." He pointed to opportunities for self-expression ranging from writing poetry to showing up in spaces where they were typically not present—for example, at school board or city council meetings. Sean added that Academe engaged the youth "in conversation that helps them to expand their thinking, to open their worldview—their perspective—and to help them formulate their own opinions about issues." Like Jeremy, Diego highlighted Academe's International Studies Program as "a tremendous step in leadership because it's not just going to sightsee, you know. We visit other NGOs, and the young people are in effect emissaries of Academe." He noted that, when they represent the organization on radio stations, at public gatherings, or while facilitating school and community workshops, they were refining their own interests.

> What Academe in effect does is provide a platform for them to explore things that they like, whether it's environmentalism, media literacy, poetry, music, youth activism, traveling, you know? I remember a couple of folks that traveled with me as young people. They decided to work in government and work abroad. And they credited that to being a month away in Ghana. So, it's a visceral experience; it's a hands-on experience that we really try to give folks so that it kind of activates . . . them to want to do a certain work (Diego).

## Sparking Collective Action

### Supporting a Long-term Campaign

Pushing for the redevelopment of a condemned school took center stage in Academe's community work for many years. Jeremy recalled how the Freedom Program members had organized to prevent a group of industrialists from converting the building into high-end apartments, which would have violated legislation requiring its redevelopment to be 85 percent for community use. He explained that, because the structure had been vacant for about thirty years, the industrialists were banking upon amnesia, but the youth, in collaboration with many individuals and organizations, uncovered the building's history, raised awareness of the legislation, and, as Vanessa explained in 2004–2005, created a traveling exhibition using interviews with the school's alumni.

Qadira remembered being asked to join the effort and thinking: "Like, well that's huge. Like, what are we going to do? Like, this has been in this place 200 years. Like, what can you possibly expect me to do? I don't even live here." She said that, after the youth created the exhibit, they started appearing on radio stations and at community meetings. Describing how people reacted to their presence, Qadira explained that "it wasn't like, 'oh my God, like these annoying kids.' It was like 'damn, they are not gonna stop. They're going to bring it up again. What are we doing about this? We don't know the answers. Now we gotta tell them there's no answer.'" She recalled that she was "'like cool, y'all are afraid of me.'" Sean remembered that the young people entered the building knowing that "this is illegal. We're not supposed to do it, but we're going to do it anyway because this is what's right. And this is what we feel we need to do in order to get the word out." He explained that:

> We didn't sleep in there, but we went inside. We made this huge banner three stories high and we put it out the windows of the building and tied it there. And so, what we were able to do was make basically a billboard on the side of the building that said, you know: "Demand a Community Center. Call Reverend [Anonymous]" and put his phone number there. So it was an opportunity to enter this space, utilize the space, and kind of put our message on the building (Sean).

Jeremy said that these small wins "taught a lot of our young people a lot about social justice," but Sean noted that the campaign was not successful for many years and "that's the way campaigns are. You know, they don't necessarily produce the results in a short period of time."

## Creating a Space for Community Change

In discussing Academe's early commitment to creating liberated space within the community, Diego recalled the annual block party that dated back to 2004. Acknowledging that it had been "a good way to ingratiate ourselves to the community," he recalled how the Freedom Program members invited residents into the brownstone to learn about their social justice campaigns. And Jeremy recalled how Lucas and Sean became stewards of the adjoining garden, which a group of residents had been using for barbecuing and getting high. He said that, after the pair bought the brownstone, they asked him to "come and help, you know, get this garden to the way you had the other garden,'" referring to his earlier project on the Lower East Side. Diego said that Jeremy helped the community view the garden as a space "where we could grow fruit, we could grow vegetables" and provide "employment for our sons, daughters, nieces, nephews." He said that the garden was an example of Academe being very strategic in a communal, rather than a capitalistic way, "so that people would buy into the notion that we are the stewards of the garden" and see "the power of collectivity." Considering the present, Jeremy and Qadira agreed that the garden was currently a place for the Environmental Program youth to engage residents in community caretaking. Qadira noted that the young people ran a green market every Wednesday between Mother's Day and Thanksgiving and that, with the support of staff, they sold fresh, organic produce and, as Sean emphasized, at wholesale prices.

By 2020–2021, Academe had greatly amplified its early commitment to creating liberated space. For example, Sean said that the summer playstreet had become a year-round 6,000-square-foot plaza "with seating areas that're used for various kinds of community events and gatherings." Jeremy recalled the process of developing the plaza, explaining that Academe "started to create events on that street" and then engaged the Department of Transportation, police precinct, community board, city council representative, and an environmental justice group "to let them understand that this is a street where people have had accidents." Jeremy said that closing the street not only created space for outdoor programming, but it also improved safety, citing annual data showing that fifteen to twenty car accidents had reduced to zero.

Academe had also greatly amplified its political voice, especially relative to police reform. Jeremy explained that, unlike schools in more affluent communities, the ones serving its constituency were filled with security guards and police who made the students feel like criminals. He said: "We don't want police in schools. We want more counselors and more social workers." Qadira said that recently, Academe had been working with a coalition "to force New York City and State to increase the budget for our schools so as to be able to hire student support staff," including therapists, nurses, guidance counselors, and career counselors, "and also to stop hiring more school police. And since last year to have no police in schools, period." Jeremy reported that Academe was continuing its battle against over-policing and was educating the young people on how to handle themselves "in the streets when they're being faced with those issues." Sean said that, after George Floyd's murder, "our staff and our members were in the streets a lot protesting," explaining that they were part of a Black Lives Matter march that went from Washington Heights through Central Harlem and into East Harlem, adding that "one of our members spoke at the rally and performed a poem."

In addition, Jeremy said that the young people were raising awareness of the marijuana felony that was "put in place to criminalize people of color in our community," and Qadira added that they were working to close Rikers "cause 80-something percent of people in Rikers haven't been tried." Sean added that the young people were "engaging local politicians, whether that be city council representatives or state representatives, engaging them in conversations around the needs of young people in schools." He believed that the young people were getting a good response because the work they were "doing around police reform, around marijuana legislation, around educational reform—these are all issues that will affect the entire city. And in the marijuana legalization, it's the entire state." Qadira summed up by saying that Academe's "organizing work is around creating better communities for young people of color in New York City."

To these community improvement and advocacy activities, Qadira added that, pre-pandemic, "people would just walk in with like whatever kind of requests, knowing that we could probably support it. So, it would be the random like: 'Hey, can I just print this out because I'm going to a job interview. I don't work here. I'm not a young person, but I need . . . support with a job application.'" Qadira confirmed, as Sean had in 2004–2005, that Academe was not just about youth development; it was a community center.

## Giving Back during the Pandemic

Qadira explained that "early in the pandemic, it was clear that young people were struggling to get food and people in our communities are struggling to get food." So, according to Diego, the leadership "took the proactive step to create a new line item in the budget for a food pantry." At the time of the interviews, Sean said that "we're up to, I think it's like 400,000 meals that we've provided in terms of groceries, fresh produce, shelf-stable items that we're distributing to the community on a weekly basis." Diego beamed as he explained that:

> Every Wednesday, Academe facilitates a food pantry where we feed roughly, I don't know, 200, 250 families and people come to receive quality products. I mean, honestly, like I've gone with members in the past to other food pantries and there's nothing in comparison to what we're providing members in terms of quality. So I'm really proud of that, you know, honestly. I'm one of the staff that facilitate and unload the truck (Diego).

He said that Academe was not only providing food, but that it was also providing the technological resources, such as laptops and internet access, that
families needed for homeschooling and even "providing financial support
whether it's rent or Con Ed on a case-by-case basis." Most heartening to Diego was that alumni were returning with "young arms to pick up these boxes
and bring them in and break them down and load up the bags." He said that
"it continues that sense of like family and purpose and community. Like guys
that I've mentored, you know, ten years ago, they'll come in and just give their
time to give back to the community."

## Future Visions

### Becoming More Refined and Less Radical

Study participants agreed that, though much has changed since Academe's
founding, the organization has maintained continuity largely because 75 percent
of its staff are alumni. As Qadira put it: "What we do and how we do it have remained the same or gotten better with time." Diego counted among Academe's
refinements being more measured in its approach and being more precise in
articulating its values as the leadership networked with youth development professionals, noting that "you start to pick up certain cadences; you start to like
figure things out as you go along. And . . . that helps to kind of leverage certain
things that benefit the organization." But Sean expressed some regret that Academe had lost its youthful edge, noting that the organization had not undertaken an illegal activity after its defiant entry into the vacant school.

> There's a little less radicalism in that regard right now, although I'd
> like to see that change. I'd like to see the young folks take more risks
> in that kind of way personally. I also would like to do that with them.
> You know, I think at times you have to engage in civil disobedience
> in order to really push what you want to see changed (Sean).

In contrast to her employer, Qadira indicated that she cautioned the Freedom Program members against engaging in behaviors that would put them at
risk for arrest "because you still have to graduate, even if I can say that our
schools are bad—are really bad—like it doesn't mean you don't need to graduate." Despite her conservative view, Qadira maintained that Academe's cultural
pieces were intact, "like how we show love, how we still care, how we care for the
whole child, the kind of support we are willing to do." Acknowledging that, while
the organization's increased resources made the job easier, "the lengths to which
we will go to support young people has stayed the same."

## Scaffolding the Next Generation of Leaders

According to Sean, Academe saw the youth being leaders no matter whether they choose to become community organizers, teachers, artists, public servants, or whatever, explaining that:

> Our objective is to help young people to be critical thinkers—to understand the realities that have faced their lives, to make wise decisions, to be able to weigh evidence. And we feel that folks who can do that, who can make wise decisions and guide their own lives, who have the agency to be able to navigate this world are leaders and can be examples for other folks (Sean).

Qadira added that it was on the youth to figure out and construct a life "that you are proud of, and you have to set your own standards and your own tone, because everything else is literally questionable and created without your mind." Diego supported her outlook, saying that "the core tenet of Academe is critical thinking—think for yourself. Even to this day, I tell guys like, 'don't take my word for it; do your homework.'" Echoing Qadira, he said that it was on the youth to be politically engaged and not "be bystanders" and know the difference between fact and fiction. Diego believed that the young people would become leaders by "being truthtellers and not being afraid of standing in your truth and walking in your truth." Sean affirmed the views of his staff, framing investment in the mind as key to the young people's leadership because "whatever it is they're pursuing in their own lives, they're going to be an example—they're going to be an example for their children; they're going to be an example for their families; they're going to be an example for their community." Qadira was insistent in rejecting:

> The standards for success set by dominant culture. Like it's not just about, did they graduate high school or are they not a teenage mom or are they not a drug abuser? . . . Have they been arrested? Like it's about, are they a good person? Do they feel heard, and do they see themselves in this role? Do they see a path for them moving ahead? Do they feel as though they're making the world what they want it to be? (Qadira)

Diego, Sean, and Qadira all talked about helping young people become their better selves by creating employment opportunities within the organization. For example, Diego said that, during Pathway chapter retreats, "we like to bring back our alumni and give them roles to kind of be like the buffer or the intermediary between the chapter leaders and the members." He explained that the alumni were able to "facilitate workshops and develop those relation-ships with the guys and then potentially, you know, maybe that manifests it-self into a permanent position." Noting that this kind of a ladder would also benefit the organization, he said that Sean was developing "a real coherent strategy around bringing in quality chapter leaders that know about the work. They know it viscerally because they've been a part of it, but they just need . . . the training to kind of hold those spaces in a professional way."

Qadira pointed to the difficulty that young people have in getting their first job without experience and before they graduate college. She felt strongly that Academe should "spread the wealth" and make space for the young people "internally so that they can get that external position." Qadira also believed that having near peers on her facilitation team benefited the members because someone who had recently graduated high school could "more completely un-derstand what this young person experienced than I can." Both Qadira and Diego talked about passing the baton to the younger generation. Qadira spoke of the need for "intergenerational compensation" so that younger people can keep older people abreast of changes in the world, while Diego explained why he was slowly phasing out of his role as the Pathways Program coordinator and chapter coleader. He said that, once his current group "matriculates, either into higher education or the workforce, that would be it for me in terms of on-the-ground youth development work. So it is bittersweet, but it's necessary. You have to be relevant in this work."

In thinking about Academe's next generation of leaders, Diego revisited the issue of authenticity, saying that its continuing challenge was to maintain "a foundation of integrity" in engaging with neglected communities "because they're going to call you out quick. You won't last." He clarified that he was referring to a "foundation of core tenets that you won't deviate from no matter the outside influence, the money." With this foundation and a commitment to community, Diego said that the next generation could pick up technical skills like facilitation. He also warned against being seduced by hollow cha-risma: "You know, like a lot of these for-profit preachers out here making money for the church, like they got a lot of charisma. They're not doing it for the right reason." Diego said that the next generation needed to balance charisma with commitment, sincerity, and authenticity because "if you can move people and mean what you say and like follow through, then people will respect you because you show up; you don't just sound good." He ended by saying that the cofounders were as committed to the youth at forty-seven as he was at forty and as the person that they would hopefully bring in who was twenty-five. "If you not about that, you don't belong here."

# Theorizing the Narratives

In this section, I first theorize Academe's curriculum as mind-centric critical pedagogy, and then I ground it as the intellectual realm of place-based activism occurring within Harlem and beyond. To do that, I principally draw upon African American concepts of education and community as a means for realizing democratic ideals, especially ideas put forward by Dr. Martin Luther King Jr. and by Jane Jacobs. Figure 6 offers a visualization of the relationship between mind-centric critical pedagogy and the intellectual realm of place-based activism.

## Critical Inquiry as Mind-Centric Critical Pedagogy

A belief in the transformative power of education was central to African American revolutionary thought, shaping the early practices of teachers in the apartheid South. For them, education was fundamentally a risky political commitment "to resist every strategy of white racist colonization."[23] Until the 1954 Brown v. Board of Education decision that ruled "separate but equal" unconstitutional, teachers in segregated classrooms "saw education not simply as a technical transmission of knowledge but rather as a calling" to develop the full potential of their students. Like W. E. B. DuBois, who argued that schools should train "deft hands, quick eyes and ears, and above all the broader, deeper, higher culture of gifted minds and pure hearts,"[24] these teachers—my ancestors among them—insisted upon academic excellence and viewed education as a community endeavor aimed at students' total development.[25]

A decade after the Brown decision, the Mississippi Freedom Schools pushed further, adopting an explicitly political approach to educating students as

## Harlem, New York
## Intellectual Realm of Place-Based Activism

| Place Awareness<br>Cognitive | Place Agency<br>Attitudinal | Critical Placemaking<br>Behavioral |
|---|---|---|
| Being Intellectuals<br>in the Commons | | |

**Academe**
**Mind-Centric Critical Pedagogy**

Critical Awareness
Cognitive

Collective Action
Behavioral

Collective Agency
Attitudinal

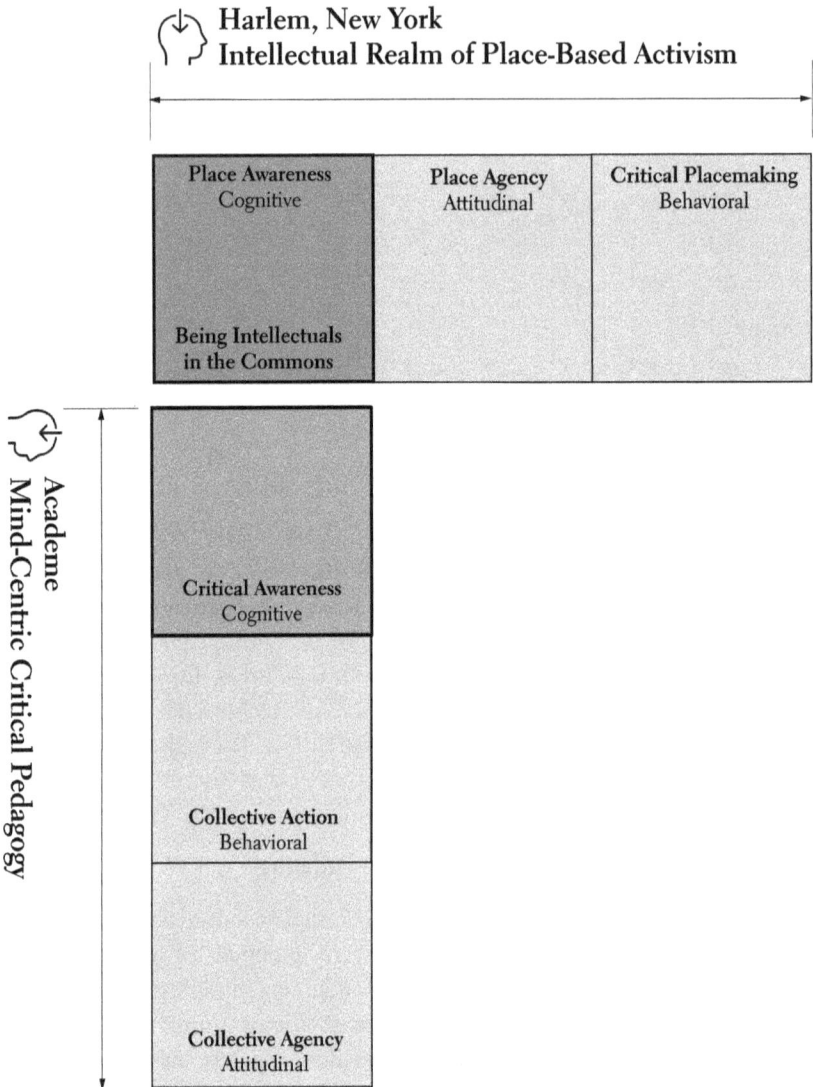

Figure 6. Mind-Centric Critical Pedagogy and the Intellectual Realm of Place-Based Activism
Image credit: Sharon Egretta Sutton, 2023

change agents. Organized by the Student Nonviolent Coordinating Committee during the summer of 1964, these schools had mostly college-age volunteer teachers who exposed thousands of children and adults "to radical and progressive educational ideas and practices."[26] A cadre of movement activists formed as students learned about their ancestors' hidden contributions to the nation and world. Some went on to become teachers, social workers, lawyers, or lifelong activists, and everyone likely experienced a degree of intellectual and cultural liberation. Today, thousands of Freedom Schools exist nationwide[27] and utilize their founding principles of near-peer mentoring and a culturally responsive curriculum.[28]

As students of Africana history, Lucas and Sean were schooled in this legacy and drew upon it to fashion an approach to critical pedagogy that targeted students' total development and sociopolitical transformation and even named one of Academe's summer programs "the Freedom School." At first serving as near-peer mentors themselves, they brought in younger alumni as they aged to deliver a culturally responsive curriculum. Academe's continuously regenerating staff introduced the writings and speeches of the African American intelligentsia of the Black Power Movement, most notably James Baldwin, Angela Davis, and Malcolm X. From 1954 until 1975, this group had "advocated the radical transformation of American society," merging activism with intellectual pursuits and arguing that transformation required a critically informed, politically engaged community of African American scholar activists.[29] Academe's pedagogy adopted this ethos, positioning the Freedom Program members as public intellectuals who had the knowledge and political savvy to assume leadership in the commons of their community.[30]

While technical knowledge insures students' productivity within the existing social order and practical knowledge helps them establish their interactions with society without problematizing inequitable power relations, Academe employed critical pedagogy to advance transformative knowledge.[31] This methodology involves a reiterative process of developing critical awareness of the root causes of unjust conditions, achieving a sense of collective agency and confidence to change those conditions, and then taking action together with others, which Freire referred to as "praxis: reflection and action upon the world in order to transform it."[32] Praxis helps young people learn to perceive injustice not as fixed, but as a constraint that they can transform.[33] Scholars believe that as youth engage in the process, they become increasingly able to connect their lived experiences to community problems and develop the capacity to advocate for change both within themselves and within their community. For example, studies of marginalized African American youth suggest that, as they become more critically conscious of their circumstances and engage more in emancipatory activities, they develop heightened aspirations for their future careers.[34] Academe staff guided its members through the process, emphasizing intellectual development and academic excellence throughout.

Acutely aware of the history of student participation in social and political transformation, Lucas and Sean created spaces within the program and city at large where the youth could "critique and respond to the culture of systemic violence as it manifests itself" in New York City's public schools. In these spaces, they developed "a language to name how white supremacy and state-sanctioned violence function,"[35] while also acquiring the habits of critical thinking and creativity that the struggle for educational equity required. Drawing upon mixed media, including physical activity, the staff helped the young people challenge dominant social structures and power relations "as well as other forms of oppression." In particular, they involved the youth in a critical analysis of the injustices that they experienced in schools where armed police officers were ever present, which gave them language to analyze their limited access to resources and opportunities.[36]

Through a multi-year on-call commitment, Pathways Program coleaders supported the members in developing the confidence to believe that they could rise above low societal expectations and achieve their life goals. Through mentoring, staff showed the members how they could resist being "indoctrinated to support imperialist white-supremacist capitalist patriarchy," while disrupting teachers' low expectations by learning "to open their minds, to engage in rigorous study, and to think critically."[37] They not only provided space for the youth to share their personal experiences, they also set the stage for them to develop solidarity through wilderness retreats and travel locally and abroad, where they lived together and practiced interdependence. By expanding their horizons, the youth were able to situate their experiences in Harlem in relation to injustice globally.

In addition, Academe staff helped the youth achieve a sense of collective agency by providing the space and support for them "to reflect upon and challenge social inequity—engendering a motivation to change unjust social conditions."[38] They motivated the youth by giving them a voice in the organization, by disseminating their writing to the larger community, by helping them refine their analyses of social injustices, and by providing them with opportunities to serve as ambassadors for the organization. Academe staff motivated the youth through love, financial support, and intergenerational relationships, modeling a family and community that support their members, further contributing to the young peoples' solidarity and providing a form of social capital that enabled collective action.[39] Above all, they modeled an intergenerational ladder of commitment, sincerity, and authenticity, prompting the youth to be responsible contributors to their families and community, whether or not they chose to be revolutionary change agents. Academe members acquired a sense of collective agency by using rigorous, culturally relevant knowledge to advance their schoolwork, navigate the challenges of racism, and develop confidence in their capacity to change their circumstances.[40]

Finally, staff engaged the youth in taking collective action, the hoped-for outcome of critical pedagogy. Becoming aware of injustice and understanding how to make a difference does not necessarily translate into action, but it did at Academe.[41] Members in the youth-led Freedom Program identified a problem, researched it, and then organized their peers to address it. This snowball process involved them in numerous campaigns—for rent stabilization, for student support staff in schools instead of police officers, and against police brutality and marijuana felony laws. The youth also took on neighborhood improvement activities such as getting out the vote on election night, interviewing older people, and mapping physical infrastructure, and they worked over many years to organize a coalition of resident advocates for redeveloping a condemned school. Through the Environmental Program, they worked year-round to provide fresh produce in a food dessert. Despite having spent much longer in the Pathways Program, the youth study participants were the most enthusiastic about the Freedom Program, which allowed them to use their knowledge and political savvy to assume leadership as public intellectuals who could advance change.[42]

## Illustrating Place-Based Activism's Intellectual Realm

I hooked the previous section around African Americans' belief in the transformative power of education to demonstrate Academe's reinterpretation of critical pedagogy. Here, I ground that pedagogy in their concept of collectivity to demonstrate its linking of youth development and community revitalization. Like other community-based organizations, Academe was committed to community building and leadership development. However, as a youth-serving organization, its central role was to provide out-of-school educational experiences to youth while positioning them to improve the livability of their surroundings. Scholars argue that such programs foster young people's positive self-identities and capacity to address complex social issues by foregrounding their potential, emphasizing self-exploration, and encouraging community engagement.[43]

Academe excelled in this role but, as an autonomous youth organization that was unaffiliated with a parent nonprofit (as is true for many youth programs), it had a remarkably strong revitalization component and in fact functioned as a miniature community development corporation (CDC). The federal government established these corporations in 1966 to underwrite community-controlled economic development, housing and community development, and job training in low-income neighborhoods.[44] When Gretchen described Academe as a place "where adults, facilitators, and youth come together to improve the physical, political, social, cultural, and economic infrastructure of our neighborhood," she in fact described a CDC, summoning up the ethos of the women activists who sought to rescue Harlem from abandonment in the 1960s and 1970s. Though operating on a small scale, Academe used its land holdings to advance community revitalization, while engaging the youth and community in co-creating a commons—or what I later conceptualize as Dr. King's "beloved community"— where they could resist capitalist social relations.

## Place Awareness: Developing a New Intelligentsia

In 2004–2005, the nation's most iconic African American neighborhood beckoned Academe's members to join the intelligentsia it had birthed. Its restored freestanding brownstone, located between two factions of drug dealers, stood out. At first scrutinized by neighbors and targeted by the police, the property soon became a stage for reenacting Harlem's legacy of political activism, cultural expressiveness, and community control. Through history workshops and a rich array of resources, Academe's members began to author their own story within Harlem's storied history.

They learned to situate themselves not only within the neighborhood's tumultuous cycle of growth, decline, and rebirth but also within the residents' struggle to resist political marginalization through new literary and artistic forms. They zoomed backward to learn about their counterparts in the Black Power movement, and then they scrutinized the new development forces that were resulting in displacement and dispossession internationally. But Academe's members were not passive scribes; they added to their story as they went along, roaming the neighborhood to interview residents and map its infrastructure, using spoken word to express their visions of justice, and traveling abroad to share ideas on the radio and at public gatherings and workshops. Over time, Academe's members constructed a shared story—an intellectual commons—that contained collective lived experiences past and present, local and global. With an extended family that eventually embraced multiple generations, this story was handed down from person to person and, in at least one instance, helped forestall the capitalist extraction of a cherished neighborhood landmark.

Their story disrupted an old narrative that featured armed police officers, racist teachers, and greedy industrialists, replacing it with one that featured Academe's mutigenerational staff who demonstrated integrity and remained uncompromised by capitalist rewards, contributing mightily to youth and community revitalization.

## Place Agency: Modeling an Authentic Beloved Community

The early practices of African American teachers reflected a notion of "communitarian unselfishness" where the community's development was at least as important as that of the individual, which is in stark contrast to the individualistic mindset in U.S. society. Dr. King elaborated this collectivist ideal in his concept of a beloved community where all persons are interconnected, respected, and bound by the transformative power of love. To achieve the beloved community, he called for a total revolution of the capitalist values that had created a society devoid of connectedness,[45] envisioning instead the architectural pattern of a "great world house" where people who are "unduly separated in ideas, culture, and interest" somehow learn to live with each other as a family "because we can never again live apart."[46] In this revolutionary place, individuals "would recognize a 'geographical oneness' with those in the less developed world" whose cultural wealth was being stolen by U.S. corporations. Instead of allowing the forces of global capitalism to eradicate their differences, individuals would claim "the identities and cultural legacies that shape who we are and how we live in the world."[47]

In identifying the intellectual network underpinning Academe's curriculum, none of the study participants mentioned Dr. King except that Diego said he wanted the youth to know that "Martin Luther King is not it." Yet the organization had three tell-tale fingerprints of a beloved community—namely, love, geographical oneness, and embrace of cultural identity and history. In both studies, study participants frequently talked about love, the beloved community's key ingredient. For example, Sean described Harlem as giving a lot of love, Vanessa said that the youth grew to love one another, Deepa said that they learned the love of human beings, Lucas said that the organization provided love for their dreams, Diego spoke of unconditional love, Qadira referred to holistic love and the extent to which staff went to show it, and Sean wanted the young people to experience what real love feels like. Surely this is the love that Dr. King envisioned as a counterforce to a market-driven society at war for the life-sustaining resources that a powerful few control as scarce commodities.

Both sets of study participants also called out international travel as a life-changing exposure that expanded the young people's understanding of the world and their place within it. In particular, they noted having a geographic oneness with Africa that countered America's individualism and exposed the youth to a collective understanding of community. Capping Academe's ideological connection to Dr. King's beloved community was an investment in helping the young people claim their identities and cultural legacies. Its curriculum immersed them in their history from the slave forts of Ghana to the brownstones of Sugar Hill, from hip hop in different countries to social movements around the world. At the same time, it supported them in finding their own voice, politically and artistically, helping them speak out on injustice, while using their talents in drawing, painting, graphic arts, and fashion design. Unquestionably, Academe's modeling of a beloved community offered a powerful source of agency in the intellectual commons it created.

In addition, Academe modeled loyalty—to self, to one another, to the organization, and to the community. Urban activist Jane Jacobs identified loyalty as a key value underpinning what she referred to as "guardian enterprises" that satisfy human needs by protecting what they have as opposed to "commercial enterprises" that trade for what they want. Of this value, Jacobs wrote:

> Loyalty embodies a mystique transcending obedience—the mystic of unbreakable fraternity, unconditional comradeship. Bonds of loyalty thrive on shared adventure and success, but they also make fear and risk tolerable, and disappointment and tragedy endurable.[48]

Academe's cofounders modeled this value, demonstrating what Diego referred to as authenticity through their own behavior—and encouraging the staff and the youth to keep their word and follow through on their promises to themselves, to each other, and to the community. They modeled this value by insisting that the staff be available to the chapter members 24/7, by engaging the youth in spelling out their moral convictions and holding them to those convictions, by using simulations that demonstrated the power of unity and comradeship, by making a space for alumni so that someone who began a program as a middle or high school student could eventually direct it, and by following through on promises to the community so people know "you mean what you're saying, and you say what you mean." The key ingredients in the intellectual commons that Academe supported the youth in creating were an abundance of real love and loyalty. In this commons, culture was not the market-dependent private possession of a powerful elite engaged in "ruthless competitiveness [and] an almost rabid individualism";[49] rather, it was the collective hope, vision, energy, and passion of many unique identities bridging across time and space to create a beloved community.

## Critical Placemaking: Activating an Enlarged Commons

Between the two studies, this miniature youth-led CDC greatly enlarged its portfolio through a combination of youth organizing and infrastructure improvements. By adding programs, the organization tripled the number of youth it served and expanded its geographic boundaries to include all New York City public school students of color. With an enlarged membership, the Freedom Program became a political force in the city, advocating not just for its own interests but on behalf of those youth who were unable to speak for themselves. To increase their political influence, the youth organized or joined huge coalitions to advance neighborhood initiatives like the community center as well as city- and state-wide ones related to the education and criminal justice systems.

Academe's infrastructure improvements similarly radiated out to affect a larger area. In 2004–2005, they consisted of the adaptive reuse of an abandoned rooming house, stewardship of a community garden where seven youth had built a gazebo and storage shed, and closure of a playstreet during the summer. By 2020–2021, the brownstone had been demolished to make way for a much larger building. The community garden had a greenhouse and aquaponics system where fifty youth grew and sold produce in a weekly green market, an operation that staff converted into a food bank for hundreds of families affected by the pandemic. The playstreet had become a landscaped plaza with seating that accommodated community activities year-round, and a block of storefronts that Academe had rehabilitated as a temporary home would possibly be used for social enterprises after its new building opened. In addition to this local work, Academe was sharing its expertise as a youth-led CDC with organizations internationally so that they could create similar entities in their own neighborhoods.

Though Academe engaged in all three dimensions of critical pedagogy, it excelled in the cognitive dimension, engaging young people as scholars who could name and analyze problems, plan policy interventions, and organize others to join them. Its culturally responsive curriculum built the habits of mind that the youth needed to decide how they wanted to live and then work responsibly to achieve their goals. Grounded in literature and movement history, they became public intellectuals who were adding a new story in the storied history of a beloved community by recording and making public its long struggle for justice and by engaging in campaigns and community service to advance the struggle. As an organization that was equally passionate about young people and about community, Academe exemplified the intellectual realm of place-based youth activism, helping the youth recognize their capacity for self-determination and acquire the courage "to be the exception, not the rule." The youth were charged with using their minds to figure out and construct lives that they could be proud of—to stand in their own truths and deliver on their promises. Their critically informed activism reflected collectivity in balancing individual and community well-being, which has profound relevance "for achieving the ideals of a participative, democratic society."[50] As Sanjiv put it: "As we change ourselves and grow up, tomorrow we can make the world a better place."

## Conclusions: Exemplifying the Intellectual Realm of Place-Based Activism

Rising residential and commercial rents in Harlem have displaced longtime residents and businesses, fundamentally altering the character of the nation's famed African American mecca.[51] Academe has become a counterforce in pushing back against commodification of the neighborhood commons through a youth-focused form of revitalization. Reaching its quarter-century mark in 2020, the organization has enhanced its members' academic performance while helping them become socially critical thinkers who exemplified responsible behavior within their families and community. Recognized for its justice-oriented youth programming, Academe's expertise is sought out by organizations around the world, and I would also argue that its achievements point the way toward a new kind of democratic commons.

Academe exemplifies the concept of place-based activism that I am proposing by privileging young people's internal experiences of loyalty and love over those external demographic forces that make them into second-class citizens, helping them use those experiences as "a foundation to combat everything that inevitably will come their way." The organization strengthened the young people's internal foundation through activities that developed them as whole persons, intellectually, artistically, socially, physically, and spiritually. It prepared them with "deft hands, quick eyes and ears" and above all "gifted minds and pure hearts,"[52] nurturing socially critical thinkers who were loyal to their own moral convictions, to one another, to the organization, and to their families and community and who grew to love one another. Upon this foundation, Academe erected an intergenerational scaffold, linking youth and adults through mutual learning and comradeship. With the framing of a great world house in place, Academe opened its doors so the young people could share what they had learned about democratic life with the community. Then they began working to build that community, using whatever tools were appropriate to the task at hand—political, intellectual, manual, artistic—and to enact Grace Lee Boggs's vision of community-building activism.

## Notes

1. Using a pseudonym is required by the participating institutional review boards that established the terms of conducting the research.

2. Themis Chronopoulos, "Race, Class, and Gentrification," in *Race Capital? Harlem as Setting and Symbol*, ed. Andrew M. Fearnley and Daniel Matlinn (New York: Columbia University Press, 2018), 213, http://www.jstor.com/stable /10.7312/fear18322.16.

3. Three GRAs administered a structured survey and fourteen open-ended interviews via telephone and were supervised by Susan Saegert. The transcript that I constructed from their much longer verbatim documentation contains only the responses that inform my theoretical framework. Per contracts with the Human Subjects Review Boards of each of the three participating academic institutions, the names that appear in the narratives are pseudonyms.

4. Staff study participants included: Lucas, thirty-one, African American, and cofounder (completed the initial survey and an interview); Sean, thirty-one, African American, and cofounder; Gretchen, forty, African American, and codirector; Camila, under thirty-five, Puerto Rican, and coordinator of the After-School Program; Darnell, under thirty-five, and African American; and Josephina, under thirty-five, and Caribbean.

Youth study participants included: Sanjiv, twenty, and in his sixth year; Demetrius, sixteen, and in his fifth year; Jennifer, sixteen, and in her fourth year; Morgan, sixteen, and in her third year; and Vanessa, seventeen, and in her fourth month. They were all African American except for Sanjiv (who was South Asian) and Vanessa (who was Dominican).

Parent study participants included: Kendra, forty-seven, African American, and mother of Jennifer; Deepa, thirty-five, Pakistani, and mother of Sanjiv and two other sons who attended. The volunteer was: Clarence, thirty-five, African American, and working on marketing and outreach.

5. Drawing from the literature, I define "critical awareness" as young people sharing their personal experiences with peers in order to understand the societal systems that perpetuate the injustices in their lives; "collective agency" as young people perceiving a common purpose and becoming confident that they can work together to change their circumstances; and "collective action" as young people working together to change unjust conditions. See the section on critical pedagogy in the Introduction for more information on how I have used this educational philosophy in framing the book.

6. My RA administered these interviews via Zoom and transcribed them using Temi. Study participants included: Sean, forty-seven, African American, and cofounder and associate executive director overseeing all programming; Qadira, thirty-two, Haitian American, and youth participant beginning in 2004, part-time staff beginning in 2007, and coordinator of the Freedom Program beginning in 2016; Diego, forty, Dominican, and founding member in 1994, full-time staff beginning in 2004, and coordinator of the Pathways Program; and Jeremy, youth participant beginning in 2004, and coordinator of the Environmental Program beginning in 2005.

7. The refocused dimensions of critical pedagogy are: "place awareness" (or helping youth understand the systemic causes of injustices in their neighborhoods); "place agency" (or equipping them with the capacity to transform these injustices); and "critical placemaking" (or engaging them in a participatory process of transforming their neighborhoods).

8. Kenneth T. Jackson, Lisa Keller, and Nancy V. Flood, eds., "Harlem," in *The Encyclopedia of New York City*, 2nd ed. (New Haven, Conn.: Yale University Press, 2010), 573–75, http://www.jstor.org/stable/j.ctt5vm1cb.13.

9. Sidney H. Bremer, "Home in Harlem, New York: Lessons from the Harlem Renaissance Writers," *PMLA* 105, no. 1 (January 1990), http://www.jstor.org/stable/462342.

10. Cornelius L. Bynum, "The New Negro and Social Democracy during the Harlem Renaissance, 1917–37," *Journal of the Gilded Age and Progressive Era* 10, no. 1 (January 2011): 89–112, http://www.jstor.org/stable/23046624.

11. Daniel Matlin, "Who Speaks for Harlem? Kenneth B. Clark, Albert Murray, and the Controversies of Black Urban Life," *Journal of American Studies* 46, no. 4 (November 2012), http://www.jstor.org/.

12. Stephen Robertson et al., "This Harlem Life: Black Families and Everyday Life in the 1920s and 1930s," *Journal of Social History* 44, no. 1 (Fall 2010), http://www.jstor.org/stable/40802110.

13. Matlin, "Who Speaks for Harlem?"

14. Dennis A. Doyle, "The Limits of Racial Liberalism: Harlem Hospital and the Black Community, 1963–68," in *Psychiatry and Racial Liberalism in Harlem, 1936–1968* (Rochester, N.Y.: University of Rochester Press, 2016), 136–55, http://www.jstor.org/stable/10.7722/j.ctt1wx918z.11.

15. Doyle, "Limits of Racial Liberalism," 145.

16. Sheila Rule, "Some Ex-Residents Keep Coming Home to Harlem: Harlem Is an Attitude," *New York Times*, ProQuest Historical Newspapers: The *New York Times*, December 7, 1980: 82.

17. Brian D. Goldstein, *The Roots of Urban Renaissance: Gentrification and the Struggle Over Harlem* (Cambridge, Mass.: Harvard University Press, 2017).

18. Goldstein, *Roots of Urban Renaissance*.

19. Themis Chronopoulos, "Race, Class, and Gentrification," in *Race Capital? Harlem as Setting and Symbol*, ed. Andrew M. Fearnley and Daniel Matlinn (New York: Columbia University Press, 2018), http://www.jstor.com/stable/10.7312/fear18322.16.

20. Chronopoulos, "Race, Class, and Gentrification."

21. Chronopoulos, "Race, Class, and Gentrification."

22. Chronopoulos, "Race, Class, and Gentrification."

23. bell hooks, *Teaching to Transgress: Education as the Practice of Freedom* (New York and London: Routledge, 1994), 2.

24. W. E. B. DuBois, *The Souls of Black Folk*, Original Classic Edition, Kindle ed. (Gildan Media LLC, 2019), 22. First published in 1903.

25. hooks, *Teaching to Transgress*.

26. William Sturkey, "'I Want to Become a Part of History': Freedom Summer, Freedom Schools, and the Freedom News," *Journal of African American History* 95, no. 3–4 (Summer–Fall 2010): 350, https://www.jstor.org/stable/10.5323/jafriamerhist.95.3-4.0348.

27. William Sturkey, "The 1964 Mississippi Freedom Schools," *Mississippi History Now*, Feature Story, May 2016, http://www.mshistorynow.mdah.ms.gov /articles/403/The-1964-Mississippi-Freedom-Schools.

28. Tambra O. Jackson and Tyrone C. Howard, "The Continuing Legacy of Freedom Schools as Sites of Possibility for Equity and Social Justice for Black Students," *Western Journal of Black Studies* 38, no. 3 (2014): 155–62.

29. Peniel E. Joseph, "Black Liberation without Apology: Reconceptualizing the Black Power Movement," *Black Scholar* 31, no. 3/4 (Fall/Winter 2001): 2–19, https:// www.jstor.org/stable/41069810.

30. Tyson E. J. Marsh, "Critical Pedagogy for Black Youth Resistance," *Black History Bulletin* 79, no. 1 (Spring 2016): 14–23, https://www.jstor.org/stable/10.5323 /blachistbull.79.1.0014.

31. Marsh, "Critical Pedagogy for Black Youth Resistance."

32. Julio Cammarota, "A Map for Social Change: Latino Students Engage a Praxis of Ethnography," *Children, Youth, and Environments* 17, no. 2 (2007): 345, quoting Paolo Freire, *Pedagogy of the Oppressed* (New York: Continuum Press, 1993), 33, https://www.jstor.org/stable/10.7721/chilyoutenvi.17.2.0341.

33. Soo Ah Kwon, "Moving from Complaints to Action: Oppositional Consciousness and Collective Action in a Political Community," *Anthropology and Education Quarterly* 39, no. 1 (March 2008): 59–76, https://www.jstor.org/stable /25166648, referring to Freire, *Pedagogy of the Oppressed* (New York: Continuum Press, 1996).

34. Brian D. Christens, Lawrence T. Winn, and Adrienne M. Duke, "Empowerment and Critical Consciousness: A Conceptual Cross-Fertilization," *Adolescent Res Rev* 1 (2016): 15–27.

35. Marsh, "Critical Pedagogy for Black Youth Resistance," 14–15.

36. Christens, Winn, and Duke, "Empowerment and Critical Consciousness."

37. bell hooks, *Teaching Community: A Pedagogy of Hope* (New York: Routledge, 2003), xiii.

38. Matthew A. Diemer and Cheng-Hsien Li, "Critical Consciousness Development and Political Participation among Marginalized Youth," *Child Development* 82, no. 6 (November/December 2011): 1,816, https://www.jstor.org /stable/41289885.

39. Marion Coddou, "An Institutional Approach to Collective Action: Evidence from Faith-Based Latino Mobilization in the 2006 Immigrant Rights Protests," *Social Problems* 63, no. 1 (February 2016): 127–50, https://www.jstor.org/stable /44014898

40. Christens, Winn, and Duke, "Empowerment and Critical Consciousness."

41. Alexis Jemal, "Critical Consciousness: A Critique and Critical Analysis of the Literature," *Urban Rev* 49 (2017): 602–26.

42. Marsh, "Critical Pedagogy for Black Youth Resistance."

43. Julie Anne Paul Poncelet, *A Community-Based Grassroots Organization in the South Bronx as a Catalyst for Youth Organizing and Activism: Analyzing the*

*Dynamics of a Transformative Youth Program* (Ann Arbor, Mich.: ProQuest Dissertations Publishing, 2013), referring to Dorothy Stoneman, "The Role of Youth Programming in the Development of Civic Engagement," *Applied Developmental Science* 6, no. (2002): 221–26.

44. Kimberley Johnson, "Community Development Corporations, Participation, and Accountability: The Harlem Urban Development Corporation and the Bedford-Stuyvesant Restoration Corporation," *Annals of the American Academy of Political and Social Science* 594 (July 2004): 109–24, https://www.jstor.org/stable /4127697.

45. Joshua F. J. Inwood, "Searching for the Promised Land: Examining Dr Martin Luther King's Concept of the Beloved Community," *Antipode* 41, no. 3 (2009): 487–508.

46. Martin Luther King Jr., *Where Do We Go from Here: Chaos or Community?* Kindle ed. (1968; Boston: Beacon Press, 2010), 177.

47. Inwood, "Searching for the Promised Land," quoting bell hooks, *Killing Rage* (New York: Owl Books, 1995), 265.

48. Jane Jacobs, *Systems of Survival: A Dialogue on the Moral Foundations of Commerce and Politics* (New York: Vintage Books, 1994), 68.

49. Henry A. Giroux, "Introduction," in *On Critical Pedagogy* (New York: Bloomsbury Publishing, 2020), 8, ProQuest E-book Central, http://ebookcentral .proquest.com/lib/washington/detail.action?docID=5997010.

50. Sharon E. Sutton and Susan P. Kemp, "Introduction: Place as Marginality and Possibility," in *The Paradox of Urban Space: Inequality and Transformation in Marginalized Communities*, ed. Sharon E. Sutton and Susan P. Kemp (New York: Palgrave Macmillan, 2011), 2.

51. Emma G. Fitsimmons, "In a Crowded New York City, Should Newcomers 'Go Back to Iowa'?," *New York Times*, January 21, 2020.

52. DuBois, *The Souls of Black Folk*, 22.

# Conclusions

*Pedagogy of a Beloved Community*

I set out to explore an aspirational framework that would help young people take hands-on action within the commons of low-income neighborhoods where they "witness daily symbolic reminders of their abandonment and marginal status."[1] I began by proposing that the emotional, physical, and intellectual realms of place-based critical pedagogy could help them ameliorate disinvestment in community infrastructure and amplify their political voice. In this concluding chapter, I synthesize the lessons learned from three youth-serving exemplar organizations into the book's moniker, "pedagogy of a beloved community." I build this synthesis sequentially, beginning with an analysis of the organizations themselves, and then I refine my initial definition of the commons and summarize the organizations' contributions to it. After reviewing how each organization foregrounded one of the three realms of place-based critical pedagogy, I suggest that a coalition of organizations could offer a pedagogy that integrates all three realms and simultaneously engages the hearts, bodies, and minds of young people. Given the downturn of one of the exemplars, I speculate about the factors that helped the other two sustain themselves. Then, I consider whether the place-based activism of these organizations has cultivated citizens who can alter the injustices spelled out in the introduction and offer a synthesis of the critical placemaking strategies they employed to help enhance the commons of both their organizations and neighborhoods. I end the chapter by calling for a radical restructuring of individualistic relationships within a beloved community that supports young people in pursuing democracy's promise.

## Pushing the Boundaries of Community Revitalization

Academe and Hoʻoulu ʻŌpio Farms are part of a genre of organizations that advance community revitalization in low-income neighborhoods—namely, community development corporations (CDCs) and their smaller counterpart, community-based organizations (CBOs). CDCs and CBOs have similar roles and share the principles that Senator Robert F. Kennedy drew upon in conceiving the Bedford-Stuyvesant Restoration Corporation (BRC) in 1966. Skating in between conservative white voters who had wearied of addressing economic inequality and liberal poor ones who had wearied of living in poverty, Kennedy proposed an organizational structure that he hoped would appease both. It would give ghetto residents a degree of control over their own destiny, but it would also curb the political radicalism of urban youth by elevating moderate African American leaders, and it would invite U.S. businesses to share the public burden of revitalizing the nation's slums.[2] Since BRC formed, its look-alike neighborhood CDCs and CBOs have multiplied exponentially and include many formerly radical and political groups that became 501(c)(3) nonprofit organizations in order to secure funding.[3] They are rooted within a particular geographic place and aim to broker increased public and private resources while building relationships among community constituents. However, because of their dependence upon government funding and private capital, these organizations are, as Kennedy hoped, typically less oppositional than protest movements.[4]

In the shift from a welfare state to a neoliberal one that began in the Reagan era, individuals and communities became increasingly responsible for their own economic and social well-being as governments devolved their role to the private sector.[5] Faced with worsening disinvestment, CDCs and CBOs became the primary dispensers of public services,[6] and—because of the obsession in public schools with testing procedures that "prepare students for a role in the global economy rather than a democracy"—they also became the primary dispensers of citizenship education for low-income youth.[7] Accordingly, many nonprofit organizations that are fighting for affordable housing, educational justice, environmental justice, more jobs for youth and community residents, and increased social services have also created out-of-school youth programs. These programs engage young people as civic participants and sometimes even offer them stipends to take the lead in addressing community problems that concern the parent organizations. Indeed, since the 1990s, nonprofit organizations have supported poor, urban teenage youth of color in resisting the "injustices they encounter in their everyday lives" related to racial, educational, and criminal justice inequities.[8] The few studies that look at this population find that these organizations can engage youth "in informed analysis and discussion regarding social, political, and economic structures."[9] By helping them address the root causes of problems, they can prepare citizens who have the individual and collective capacity to improve themselves and their communities.[10]

Academe and Hoʻoulu ʻŌpio accomplished all this but pushed the traditions of nonprofit community development to an unseen level of youth-led community change. Both centered youth development in organizations that advanced community revitalization, though each arrived at a unique balance of these two enterprises via different routes. Hoʻoulu ʻŌpio began as a CDC (and remains so legally), but the social enterprise of growing food to grow youth took over, making youth development the center of community empowerment. Hoʻoulu ʻŌpio linked economic development with education by helping the young people advance academically and in chosen careers while growing the produce (and eventually building the housing) that contributes to individual and community health. On the other hand, Academe began as a youth development organization, but the cofounders' commitment "to liberating the community, controlling the resources, giving more power to the people" took over, making community empowerment the center of youth development. Academe linked systems reform with education by helping its members advance academically and in chosen careers while engaging them in community service and organizing.

By equally attending to the personal benefits that derive from youth development and the public ones that derive from community revitalization, Hoʻoulu ʻŌpio and Academe were able to create the relationships that helped young people build their capacities as change agents while improving the sociospatial infrastructure of their host communities. They both engaged in multi-layered community-building processes, forming coalitions and acquiring land that they placed in the hands of the communities they served. These characteristics set the two organizations apart from Storyhouse Theatre Company, though, as I argue in the next section, I can easily imagine the latter becoming more community embedded. In reality, all three organizations balanced developing young people's internal compass with developing their skills to address real-world problems through political, intellectual, manual, and artistic means that achieved practical results. In addition, all three organizations embraced intergenerational collaboration, not only to build the young people's agency and power but also to connect the adults to present-day realities. Everyone pitched in to address high-stakes problems hands-on, given their expertise, interests, and skills, and the adults excelled in taking the young people seriously as "thinkers and actors engaged in collective action alongside older people."[11]

In an ideal approach to place-based activism, youth-serving organizations would erect a multiage scaffold of youth and adults in order to balance goals for enhancing the "infrastructure" of their communities—a concept I elaborate in the next section—with goals for enhancing young people's understanding of, and capacity to tackle, the problems in those communities. Young people's citizenship development is key to genuine community revitalization and vice versa; young people's active engagement in community revitalization is key to their becoming citizens who can pursue the promise of democracy. Also key is following Hoʻoulu ʻŌpio's lead in securing funding while engaging in the oppositional protest that many funders of nonprofit organizations, especially governments and corporations, seek to tamp down through stringent grant requirements.[12]

## Contributing to the Commons

In the Introduction, I defined "the commons" as a public domain where people simultaneously experience communal existence and participate in self-determining the quality of that existence. I embraced the notion that active engagement in democratic governance can turn inert public space into a commons where such experience occurs.[13] In particular, I drew upon John Dewey's notion of deliberative democracy to conceptualize it as a space that contains life-sustaining infrastructure—both tangible (e.g., housing, schools, and food) and intangible (e.g., safety, culture, and beauty)—and as the space where people come together to negotiate human and ecological relationships.[14] I also acknowledged Dr. Martin Luther King Jr.'s vision of a "beloved community" where people of differing outlooks come together and learn to share the earth's finite resources.[15] Finally, I argued that democratic participation in the commons has been vanishing in the onslaught of rampant economic inequality that amplifies the voices of the rich and powerful and silences those of the poor and disenfranchised.

I proposed to refine these initial conjectures by analyzing how my exemplar organizations experienced and participated in the commons of their communities. This exercise led me to make a distinction between the commons as a psychic (imagined/envisioned) space and a physical (actual/experienced) space, each of which offers a unique stage for activism, and to recognize that actions (doing/acting) as well as ideas (values/propositions) can transform the infrastructure of either space. These distinctions add nuance to the varied ways that youth can engage in activism, which I initially had conceived as residing in clear either-or categories. Indeed, my research revealed that place-based activism is a both-and affair; youth can engage in a deep critique of existing systems, places, and mindsets (i.e., oppositional activism), and they can also work proactively to change what exists (i.e., community-building activism), and many variations can and do occur along a continuum of critical placemaking. Figure 7 visualizes the actions and ideas that can transform the physical or psychic space of the commons and indicates the arena where each organization excelled.

Applying this refined definition to the exemplars, Storyhouse's activism occurred in the psychic space of theatre where the performers and audiences reenacted community problems in order to reconceive an unjust world. This illusory commons helped participants take the risk of naming what seemed to be personal failings on a public stage in order to reveal their systemic roots. It had the potential to be anywhere in the city and helped the performers and audiences act out new endings for familiar problems within the safety of dramatic form. Further, as Kordell noted, this psychic space was most effective when it provided a stage for performers and audiences to engage outdoors within a specific locality of the city. Though Storyhouse's psychic space of activism had diminished by its twenty-ninth year as a result of narrowly centered neoliberal values, this mindset could easily change and support a provocative approach to transforming the commons.

For example, the new executive director might deepen the organization's social justice roots by assembling leadership boards (directors, advisory) that include representatives of Southwest Detroit's poor and disenfranchised ethnic population. With a community-embedded support system in place, her funding rationale might become more radical. Instead of marketing the utilitarian purposes of theatre (e.g., to improve reading), she might exaggerate its unique potential for examining "what it is to be human in all its variety: politically, socially, philosophically, physically, and poetically."[16] She might enliven Storyhouse's well-worn agenda of scripting plays, considering fresh possibilities such as developing talkbacks to use in negotiating consensus at confrontational community meetings or undertaking research to assess the influence of its performances on public opinion. She might also extend the locales for performances, for example to neighborhood parks, municipal building plazas, urban farms and farmers' markets, hospital and supermarket parking lots, and Detroit's public access TV channel. The possibilities seem limitless for Storyhouse performers to engage Detroit audiences in envisioning a revitalized commons.

In contrast, Ho'oulu 'Ōpio's activism primarily occurred in the physical spaces the organization occupied, where the young people worked hands-on

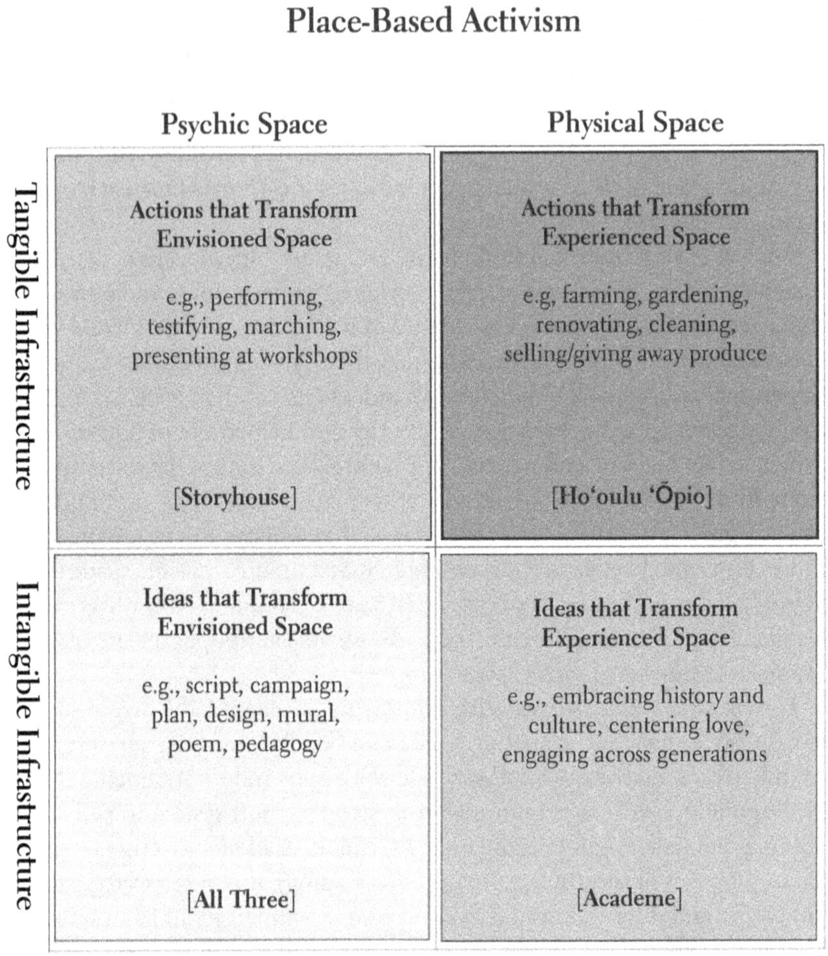

## Place-Based Activism

|  | Psychic Space | Physical Space |
|---|---|---|
| **Tangible Infrastructure** | Actions that Transform Envisioned Space<br><br>e.g., performing, testifying, marching, presenting at workshops<br><br>[Storyhouse] | Actions that Transform Experienced Space<br><br>e.g, farming, gardening, renovating, cleaning, selling/giving away produce<br><br>[Ho'oulu 'Ōpio] |
| **Intangible Infrastructure** | Ideas that Transform Envisioned Space<br><br>e.g., script, campaign, plan, design, mural, poem, pedagogy<br><br>[All Three] | Ideas that Transform Experienced Space<br><br>e.g., embracing history and culture, centering love, engaging across generations<br><br>[Academe] |

Figure 7. Transforming the Commons through Actions and Ideas
Image credit: Sharon Egretta Sutton, 2023

to transform its tangible infrastructure, including a five-acre farm that grew to 281 acres, an ever-growing network of distribution sites (farmers' markets and clinics), and the gardens at Wai'anae's middle and high schools. The young people also embraced Hawaiian values in order to transform its intangible infrastructure, including experiencing *aloha* (love) and *ohana* (family), being grounded in *'āina* (the land), and engaging across generations, among others. This ever-expanding commons helped the young people develop the skills and sense of responsibility to prepare soil, plant, weed, thin, nurture to maturity, harvest, and begin the process over again so their families could eat well. On land abounding in mosquitos, involvement in Hoʻoulu ʻŌpio required back-breaking, ill-compensated labor in mud that ruined manicured nails, but the farm was collectively owned by the community and connected to a psychic space where youth confronted teachers at public hearings, challenging negative stereotypes of themselves and accessing their Hawaiian-ness through *malama ʻāina* (caring for the land). By its twentieth year, Hoʻoulu ʻŌpio had grown to offer Waiʻanae's predominately Native Hawaiian population a more just and inclusive commons, and it is on track to continue doing so.

The farm's increased acreage means that the young people can help reclaim Waiʻanae's magical ecology by rebuilding the forestry and water systems that colonizers destroyed. Its increased acreage also means that more crops, and more diverse crops, can be grown, which will support more youth education and employment. Growing more youth means that the cohort of alumni who are, as Aulani said, "in this space of whatever—food justice, education justice, social justice, environmental justice"—will continue to grow Waiʻanae's intangible infrastructure of self-sufficiency, health, and well-being. Then too, increased acreage means that Hoʻoulu ʻŌpio must bring more capital to the table by broadening its appeal to foundations, governments, and even the U.S. military, thereby making its commons even more inclusive. Further, this CDC is sharing its economic development model with other local organizations, showing them how a triple bottom line of people, planet, and profit can generate the income to enhance Waiʻanae's infrastructure.

Academe's activism also primarily occurred within its physical spaces, where the young people adopted ideas—such as embracing history and culture, being loyal and loving, and engaging across generations—that transformed the intangible infrastructure of the "liberated land" (buildings and adjoining public spaces) that "belonged" to the community. Academe's intellectual commons helped the members demonstrate their prowess as public scholars and activists who could conduct research and then use their knowledge to organize others in advocating for policy change. It offered a safe space where the adults, facilitators, and youth could work collectively to improve the neighborhood's tangible infrastructure—for example, by gardening or campaigning for the adaptive reuse of an abandoned school. By engaging in the physical space of local and global communities, Academe's members acquired a sense of loyalty—to self, to one another, to the organization, and to the community. By its twenty-fifth year, the organization had grown to strengthen an intellectual commons where African American and Latino/a youth can thrive as public intellectuals, and its trajectory is unstoppable.

Academe has tripled the number of youth who attend an increased number of programs, and it has expanded its community beyond the immediate

Harlem neighborhood to include all New York City public school students of color. With this expanded population, the scope of Academe's organizing has also enlarged to include advocacy on citywide and even statewide issues, though it remains dedicated to enhancing its immediate surroundings, especially through a community garden and green market that provide healthy, affordable produce in a food desert. An expanded population means that more youth of color will have a pathway to college and to possible employment in an organization that is committed to supporting its alumni. Like Hoʻoulu ʻŌpio, Academe is sharing its evidence-based youth development model with other organizations, showing them how to enhance the public domain through research and policy making while increasing the academic success and political efficacy of its members.

In short, the commons can be a psychic or physical space that holds the tangible and intangible infrastructure of a community; ideally, it belongs to residents and engages them in learning how to live together as a beloved community. I applaud Hoʻoulu ʻŌpio and Academe for having greatly improved the commons of their disenfranchised communities, and I applaud all three organizations for uniting generations through hands-on engagement in their immediate surroundings, which simultaneously enriched youth development and community revitalization. The exemplar organizations' actions and ideas can inspire innovation and resonate with readers' dreams of a more just future.[17] They illustrate what Boggs referred to as "community-building activism," which she envisioned as "more participatory, empowering, and horizontal" than that of the male-dominated Civil Rights Movement, one that offers love, caring, and listening as tools for constructing "a spiritual framework for our everyday lives"—an apt characterization for the commons I set out to reimagine.[18]

## Contributing to the Pedagogy of a Beloved Community

In the Introduction, I suggested that, though the exemplar organizations tapped into all three dimensions of place-based critical pedagogy (cognitive, attitudinal, and behavioral), they unsurprisingly foregrounded the dimension that aligned with their particular mission. For example, Storyhouse excelled in its attitudinal dimension and within an emotional realm, utilizing theatre to help the youth develop place agency. On stage, they gained literacy and communication skills, were mentored by professional artists, had fun working together and with others toward a common goal, and were successful in an illusory world that they had created. Storyhouse's measure of success was the public appeal of its programming, the size of its audiences, and its recognition through awards for creative excellence, reflecting its heart-centric mission.

On the other hand, Hoʻoulu ʻŌpio excelled in its behavioral dimension and within a physical realm, utilizing organic farming to help the youth engage in critical placemaking. In the field, the interns learned to reclaim fallow agricultural land, restore and protect natural resources, prepare and eat simply cooked meals, and promote healthy eating habits in their families and community. Hoʻoulu ʻŌpio's measure of success was the tons of produce grown and marketed to support internships that yielded academic credentials and employment, reflecting its body-centric mission. Then too, Academe excelled in its cognitive dimension and within an intellectual realm, emphasizing critical inquiry to help its members develop place awareness. In discussions and fieldwork, the youth learned to use their minds to establish life goals, conducted primary and secondary research, acquired an understanding of history, culture, and politics and taught others what they had learned. Academe's measure of success was the percentage of alumni who had received high school diplomas and were enrolled in college or working full-time, reflecting its mind-centric mission.

Foregrounding the dimension of place-based critical pedagogy that aligned with a particular mission helped each exemplar organization evolve a unique form of activism. As beneficial as that is, young people would also benefit from a pedagogy that calls forth their full humanity: heart, body, and mind. I refer to the simultaneous enactment of all three dimensions of place-based critical pedagogy as the pedagogy of a beloved community—perhaps offered through a coalition of community-based organizations—because I believe that a whole-person approach offers the best possibility for learning to resist capitalist values. I envision this idea in Figure 8 and reinforce it later in the chapter by collapsing outcomes across organizations to show their collective contribution to advancing democracy.

## Contributing to Organizational Stability

Without question, the exemplar organizations modeled unique aspects of place-based activism. Here I consider three factors—cofounder credentials and networks, total budget, and leadership succession strategy—to speculate about what influenced their respective trajectories. The oldest of the three organizations, Storyhouse, was cofounded by a couple in their late thirties, both in theatre, who had just moved cross-country to Detroit. An initial survey reported that the organization relied "a lot" upon partnerships and social networks (which the survey did not specify), and the 2004–2005 interviews revealed only one mother-daughter relationship between a staff member and youth participant. Thus, despite the give-and-take between the company and the surrounding

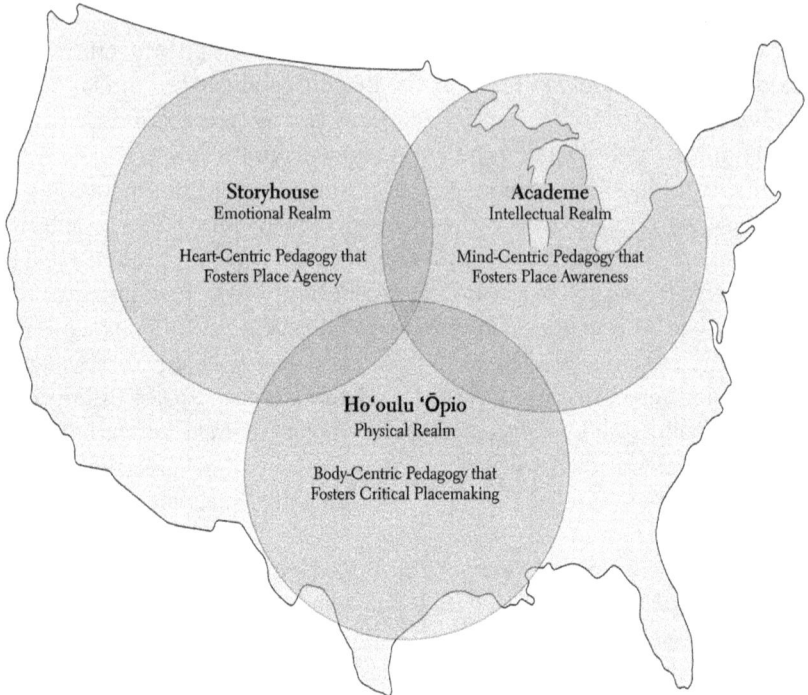

**A Whole-Person Approach to Resisting Capitalist Values**

Figure 8. Pedagogy of a Beloved Community
Image credit: Sharon Egretta Sutton, 2023

community that study participants noted, Storyhouse lacked the deep local roots that distinguished the other two organizations. In its thirteenth year at the time of the 2004–2005 study, one of the cofounders was running the organization while the other had become a high school teacher and was only involved part time.

Storyhouse's total 2004–2005 budget of $175K was cobbled together year to year and even quarter to quarter and frequently required stop-gap infusions from the cofounders to keep programs running. By 2020, its total budget had declined to $162K (or .93 times the 2004–2005 budget, not considering changes in dollar value). Storyhouse's low salaries resulted in frequent staff turnover, which meant that it did not build in-house talent and thus experienced a nearly fatal leadership crisis when the managing cofounder suddenly resigned. The lack of a leadership development strategy, combined with narrow credentials and weak community roots, likely contributed to Storyhouse's declining financial stability and narrowed focus.

Hoʻoulu ʻŌpio was the polar opposite of Storyhouse. The youngest of the three organizations, it was cofounded by a couple in their mid-thirties whose parents and grandparents were farmers; one had a background in banking, the other in Hawaiian culture and education. They organized a group of community members to conceive the organization, involving a sister credentialed in retail management and a board member/mentor credentialed in agriculture. The cofounding partners and their advisory board all had deep Waiʻanae roots. The initial survey reported that the organization relied "a lot" upon partnerships and social networks and listed as collaborators the public schools, a community college, a research university, a private school for children of Hawaiian descent, two health clinics, and local businesses. Further, both studies revealed a web of interpersonal relationships and emphasized the mentoring and expertise that the board of directors, advisory board, and various other supporters contributed to the organization. In its fourth year at the time of the initial study, its beginning budget of $275K had skyrocketed to $475K, most coming from federal, state, and city governments rather than foundations and individuals. In 2020, its total budget had increased to $5,165K (or eleven times the 2004–2005 budget, not considering dollar value changes), and foundations had surpassed governments in contributing a slightly larger share of the total.

Hoʻoulu ʻŌpio's operational strategy insured in-house talent development. At the time of the 2004–2005 study, interns were being mentored by alumni; by the 2020–2021 study, members of that cohort had worked their way up to become a strong second line of leadership that was steeped in Hoʻoulu ʻŌpio's operations and ethos.[19] Its strong leadership succession strategy, combined with broad credentials and deep community roots, likely contributed to its increasing financial stability and expanded operations.

Academe clearly benefitted from the youthfulness of its twenty-one-year-old cofounders, who had grown up in Harlem and closely identified with the young men living there. Having piloted the program in college that became the centerpiece of the organization, the cofounders grew the breadth of their own expertise over time; one began with a BA degree in Africana Studies and later earned a law degree, the other had nonprofit experience and later developed expertise in permaculture and community organizing, and both had hands-on experience working with youth. And in their fourth year, the pair expanded the organization's credentials by bringing in an education consultant. The initial survey, conducted in its ninth year, revealed that Academe relied "a lot" upon partnerships and social networks (which the survey did not specify), and that an annual budget of about $750K was patched together with significant contributions from volunteers, fundraisers, and individuals, including from the parents and even the youth. The interviews further revealed that

the staff had worked unpaid for three months during the previous year. However, its connection to a community that "gave a lot of love" allowed Academe
to expand its homespun startup three-fold while undertaking a successful capital
campaign for a new building. Its 2020 budget was $10,674K (or twelve times the
2004–2005 amount), with the lion's share coming from foundations.

Academe has grown in-house leaders who make up 75 percent of its staff, including one person who was a member of the inaugural class and another who
was in the second class. Its strong leadership succession strategy mirrored the
cofounders' own work-and-study career development strategy and likely contributed to the organization's increasing financial stability and expanded influence.

The profiles of these three organizations suggest that the breadth of credentials on the leadership team is an important factor in their long-range health and
stability. Storyhouse's credentials were the thinnest, limited to mid-career experience as contract artists in professional theatre. Hoʻoulu ʻŌpio's was the deepest,
spanning mid-career experience in business (banking and retail), education, and
agriculture. Reflecting its youthfulness, Academe's was on the thin side, spanning entry-level Africana Studies and nonprofit and youth work, but it soon
deepened to include education and then, as the cofounders matured in their
own careers, to include law, permaculture, and community organizing.

On the other hand, the relevance of the organizations' total budget is more
difficult to unravel. Storyhouse's was the smallest at the time of both studies
($175K and $161K) and was likely insufficient to allow stability; even without a
leadership crisis, it was operating in survival mode. However, the other two
organizations switch places in fundraising prowess, with the less credentialed
Academe having the largest annual budget ($750K and $9,674K) and the more
credentialed Hoʻoulu ʻŌpio having a much smaller one ($475K and $5,165).
Academe's consistently larger budget is undoubtedly because of the larger reach
of its enterprise—it has served "thousands of young people" while Hoʻoulu
ʻŌpio's more labor-intensive one has supported just 1,022 internships—a difference in scale that possibly reflects the influence of its foundation support.
Annual budget aside, what marks both these organizations for future success
is the degree to which they have nurtured in-house leadership.

## Cultivating Citizens to Pursue Democracy's Promise

In the Introduction, I observed a serious disruption in the trajectory of American democracy as a result of economic inequality, environmental injustice,
and intolerance and promised to deliver a pedagogy that could help reboot the
nation's progress toward achieving its "founding creed to embrace all, and not
just some."[20] I suggested that this pedagogy would cultivate citizens who have

the critical skills to challenge injustice, who can hold the rich and powerful accountable, and who are committed to advance not just their own self-interest but also the health of their community and the earth's ecosystems.[21] I borrowed from Boggs to argue that the hands-on activism of young people within a geographically bounded locality—or place-based activism—would help build these habits of mind and address real problems therein. And, as noted earlier, I also tapped into Dr. King's vision of a beloved community where all persons are interconnected, respected, and bound by the transformative power of love.

Here I look at whether the pedagogy I have proposed and the organizations I have chosen to exemplify it live up to my opening claims. I do not proceed organization by organization, but rather view their combined contributions to helping young people acquire the practical skills and values to counter the forces of global capitalism.

## Challenging Injustice

Collectively, the young people who populate the pages of this book inhabited places that threatened their physical well-being and undermined their sense of self-worth. In schools, where teachers should have helped them rise above their surroundings, they were more often treated as failures, deserving of punishment and an imprisoning educational environment. This would have been a tough reality for anyone to go up against, especially developing beings whose identity is influx. And yet, the exemplar organizations found ways to arm these young people with the courage to resist the marginalization they encountered in their schools and neighborhoods. They used varied ideation tools—literature, creative writing, chanting, travel, physical labor, and so forth—to help their charges think in new ways about themselves and their relationship to one another and nature. The youth learned to ask questions about their consignment to poor schools and poor health, about what caused violence and who the villains and victims were, about why fathers were absent and mothers were impatient, and about their own struggles to be someone that their parents and neighbors could love. They learned to turn what they thought they knew inside out, to see impoverishment as abundance, to see boulders as sculptures, to see common cause with gang members.

Because the organizations' endeavors were grounded within the specificity of place, the youth were able to go beyond asking questions to generate concrete proof of their new reality. The proof was as varied as the tools that generated it, ranging from actors who memorized the lines of a play to poets who recited their creations at rallies to farmers who grew lettuce that was so good it did not need dressing to organizations led by people of color that assisted residents in ways that politicians had not. By helping the youth resist their own marginalization, the organizations produced outcomes that could change the hearts and minds of conservative voters and policy makers, including tons of produce, degrees earned, jobs held, and awards won, all without the "rote learning, memorization, and high-stakes testing" that neoliberal education requires.[22] More importantly, the organizations cultivated the skills of democratic citizenship, providing safe spaces—for listening and learning to embrace the disagreements that occur when people have different opinions and for learning to embrace challenge while challenging others to become their truest selves. I would argue that these organizations support my proposition that, when young people refuse to accept the limitations in their immediate surroundings, they become engaged citizens, capable of advancing the nation's founding principles.

## Speaking Truth to Power

Collectively, the exemplar organizations helped the young people who populated the pages of this book find the courage to upend negative stereotypes and demonstrate that they could perform quite well within normative society. However, they went beyond that to shatter its norms. With the familial love and support that the organizations provided, especially through peer and near-peer mentoring and intergenerational relationships, the young people showed up in places that they were not supposed to be, invading the public domain that corporate capital had privatized. They refused to be backed down by teachers who demeaned them, speaking their minds in a clear and emotional way about their needs. They had the chutzpah to try buying land when they had no money and to investigate the legality of landlords charging exorbitant rents. They scared people with their determination to get answers to problems, and they entertained them with their own answers. With the support of youth-serving organizations that were equally dedicated to community revitalization, they learned how systems worked and then organized others to change those systems. I would argue that, when young people act with authority to challenge power and reimagine it "working in the interest of justice, equality, and freedom," they become socially responsible citizens, capable of advancing the nation's founding principles.[23]

## Advancing the Common Good

Henry A. Giroux, a mentee and colleague of Paulo Freire and founding theorist of critical pedagogy, wrote that "neoliberal ideology emphasizes winning at all costs, even if it means a ruthless competitiveness, an almost rabid individualism, and a notion of agency largely constructed within a market-driven rationality."[24] The consensus among persons concerned with democracy's downward trajectory is that the embrace of market values in public and higher education is producing an alienated and uninformed citizenry, acquisitive, narcissistic, and unable to engage in civil discourse; they say that it is "replacing concern for community with narrow self-interest."[25]

In contrast to this ethos of individualism was one of community and responsibility to others that the exemplar organizations embraced. On stage, the young people learned that they had to trust others when a scene did not go as planned, that they could have fun hanging out with a bunch of people and working toward a common goal, and that it was less scary to perform if they bonded with each other. On the farm, they learned that *laulima* (many hands working together) could get a hard job done, that they had to complete their assigned *kuleana* (responsibility) or their family would not have food, and that they should respect each other's different styles of getting a job done. On field trips, they learned that they all had to pitch in when one person was suffering, that people in Africa lived as a collective, and that enslavement to money could lead them to harm their community, the environment, and even their own family. The sense of communal responsibility meant that, in good times and bad, the young people were willing to give back to the community and the organization—through work, money, or other means. I would argue that when young people learn the language of solidarity and collectivity, they become "capable of defending the public good and the symbolic and institutional power relations necessary for a sustainable democracy."[26]

I believe that the exemplar organizations have more than allowed me to deliver on my promise to show how a critical pedagogy that occurs in relation to a particular place—or place-based activism—can help reboot the nation's progress toward its democratic ideals. Now I synthesize the strategies that can guide other youth-serving organizations in similarly helping young people inhabit and exercise agency in their communities.

## Reclaiming the Commons through Critical Placemaking

In the previous section, I demonstrated how place-based activism can cultivate democratic citizenship. Here I turn the frame around and look at how it can contribute to a just and politically engaged commons. In particular, I look at the notion of "critical placemaking" and how it can help young people become active change agents in securing life-sustaining resources in their surroundings while simultaneously elevating their fundamental right to participate in the public domain. In general, "placemaking is the participatory act of imagining and creating places with other people,"[27] but I am specifically interested in the strategies that disrupt inequality and create "more inclusive, participatory, and democratic communities."[28] Instead of presenting each organization's contributions to the commons, as I did earlier, in this penultimate section of the book I present a thematic analysis of their combined critical placemaking strategies, which generalizes what has been a very specific representation of these exemplars. To push this synthesis even further, I have taken the liberty of dipping into the thematic analysis that my research team conducted of the interviews with constituents of all six Ford study organizations, including the three that I elected not to include in this book. My research team's analysis yielded twenty-five categories, five of which align with my own analysis of the exemplar organizations.[29] Thus, I include the data from the Ford study as well as the ones reported herein for a robust presentation of the critical placemaking strategies that other organizations can draw upon.

Several interesting surprises came from this exercise. First, my initial theoretical framework for place-based activism envisioned a neat division in which place awareness and place agency would occur within the organization and critical placemaking would occur within the commons of a community (see Figure 2 in the Introduction). In reality, critical placemaking also occurs within the organization, which has its own commons, and is essential to being effective in the community. As Sanjiv put it: "We help the community inside Academe first, and then Academe can help the community all around," so organizations must strive to disrupt their own unjust practices and be the change they want to create. Second, the strategies are twofold, including ones that are the purview of the organizations and ones that are the purview of the youth. Thus, this form of activism requires an institutional context that centers communal outcomes, which means that organizations need to circumvent funders that emphasize individual development rather than community change and expect such measurable outcomes as better grades, job skills, and motivation to learn and advance.[30] Third, as noted previously, a careful look at strategies revealed that place-based activism is a both-and affair in which youth can engage in a continuum of activities from protest and political activism to volunteerism and community service—and from advancing ideas to taking concrete actions. Finally, I should clarify that the combined analysis includes strategies that the exemplar organizations did not employ.

In the next section, I shift into the present tense in order to share with readers a theoretical framing of the remarkable critical placemaking activities this study unearthed, the book's key contribution to the fields of youth and community development. I hope that it will be useful in your own journey toward the promise of democracy. Just as a reminder, critical placemaking involves hands-on engagement in the commons combined with active participation in its governance.

## Practicing the Change You Want to Create

Critical placemaking begins within an organization and creates a laboratory for experimenting with the transformation it envisions in the larger community—experiments that strengthen its own infrastructure and engage its youth in practicing inclusive citizenship.

### Strengthening Intangible Infrastructure

Because critical placemaking encourages social interdependence, it can strengthen an organization's intangible infrastructure. Its hands-on, personally meaningful projects lend themselves to family-like, intergenerational relationships with significant others; they allow youth to experience how a group of people with differing outlooks can work together toward a common goal; show them what it means to be caring, loyal, responsible, and loved; and help staff learn to scaffold wide-ranging skillsets. In addition, critical placemaking has the potential to create social enterprises or other community development financial models that can insure an organization's stability. Not-for-profit business structures go well beyond the idea of in-kind contributions to support the social mission of an organization; they provide a venue for marketing its goods and services and offer some degree of independence from the vagaries of fundraising and its ever shifting and depoliticizing priorities. Its activities also help expand an organization's programming and space to attract a broader base of support without deviating from its founding values. Finally, critical placemaking can help ensure an organization's leadership succession, offering a meaningful context for building in-house talent and scaffolding youth from unpaid staff positions into managerial ones.

### Cultivating Inclusive Citizenship

Critical placemaking involves youth in making decisions about an organization's day-to-day and long-range programming; hands-on projects—especially ones that are youth-led—offer an ideal venue for such involvement. Because critical placemaking taps the creative energy of both youth and staff, it can promote power sharing across age and experience and encourage synergistic youth/adult partnerships; its activities help young people gain a sense of ownership of an organization and increase their buy-in to it, as the exemplars in this book demonstrated. At the same time, youth can amplify their own voice by recruiting siblings and friends to help out with projects while pushing for participatory parity. In addition to democratizing governance, critical placemaking can help an organization promote inclusivity because project-based work creates safe spaces for youth to listen to one another, openly embrace diverse populations and concerns, and acquire tolerance for difference, and its projects can be the subject of diversity workshops for both staff and youth. Yet, the notion of inclusivity gives me pause in organizations that serve specific cultural groups as I wonder how youth will learn "to be tolerant, to work things through, to compromise"[31] if they are isolated from their white or more affluent counterparts. I wonder how the latter group will develop geographical oneness with impoverished youth of color and be prepared to share their privileges. And I wonder how both groups will learn to live together as a family in a great world house. Though many organizations in my study were identity-based, being inclusive across race and class lines is top on my list of the critical placemaking strategies that I envision in a deliberative democracy.

Table 1 lists the critical placemaking activities that this study revealed related to improving an organization's infrastructure and engaging in its governance.

## Moving Toward the Beloved Community

Critical placemaking within a locality allows an organization to build a sense of community, cultivate active engagement in that community, educate residents, and strengthen its infrastructure.

### Building Community

Critical placemaking builds a sense of community—an arena where youth excel—by proving that the negative stereotypes of a locality are false. As study participants demonstrated, young people have the innate curiosity, physical energy, and stamina to be critically conscious community researchers who are unstoppable in digging up the facts. They can produce spatial knowledge, for example by conducting needs assessments, inventorying environmental resources, and mapping community assets and patterns of displacement. They can produce cultural knowledge, for example by recording oral histories, sharing stories of their own experiences, dipping into the archives of neighborhood history, and identifying unsung local artists. Surveying spatial and cultural conditions lies at the heart of critical placemaking because it identifies a community's strengths, weaknesses, opportunities, and threats—findings that young

Table 1. Critical Placemaking within an Organization

| Cultivating Participatory Citizenship | |
|---|---|
| | **Creating a Democratically Governed Organization** |
| Organizations | Creating youth-led programs \| including youth and alumni in governance \| instituting collective decision making and power sharing \| training staff in participatory governance. |
| Youth | Recruiting siblings and friends. |
| | **Creating an Inclusive Organization** |
| Organizations | Creating safe spaces for listening \| embracing diverse populations and concerns \| offering diversity workshops for youth and staff \| practicing tolerance. |
| **Strengthening Intangible Infrastructure** | |
| | **Modeling Social Interdependence** |
| Organizations | Creating a sense of family (caring, love, loyalty, responsibility) \| creating intergenerational spaces \| supporting staff development. |
| | **Insuring Stability and Succession** |
| Organizations | Building a social enterprise (for revenue stability) \| building in-house talent \| expanding programming \| expanding space \| expanding the base of support. |

Text credit: Sharon Egretta Sutton, 2023

people can share with residents and stakeholders as the basis for configuring a variety of community development projects and seeking funding for them. The research that young people conduct within a locality can help disrupt blind negativity and build a sense of community. And it creates concrete evidence of their creativity, which an organization can share with school staff, politicians, and residents who too often ignore their talents.

### Cultivating Inclusive Citizenship

Because critical placemaking intentionally engages a community in deliberating the collective ideas and ideals it wishes to embrace, it "fosters civic competence and extends the idea of citizenship."[32] Young people can play starring roles in the deliberative process by creating a smorgasbord of interactive venues that invite different types of people to engage with one another. Through talkbacks, exhibitions, workshops, block parties, parades, and other fun events, they can help people debate confounding social issues with fresh eyes. An organization can also play its part by promoting tolerance; for example, it can publish the creative writing of youth so naysayers understand their experiences, advocate for including their voice in school governance, especially in the election or appointment of school officials, and embrace youth who are stigmatized as villains and enemies. But it is the young people themselves who make inclusive citizenship come alive, attending and testifying at community meetings, campaigning door-to-door, doing teach-ins at public schools, holding press conferences, appearing on radio programs, organizing campaigns, and reciting original poems at protests and rallies. With institutional support, they can become an unflappable voice in neighborhood governance, refusing to accept their consignment to the margins of society—or its prisons.

### Educating Youth and Adults

Critical placemaking's project-based nature helps an organization reach out beyond the specific youth who attend its out-of-school programs to educate the larger community. It can provide a basis for sharing technology, compensating for faulty neoliberal schooling, offering continuing education, and so forth, whether the youth and adults are related to program attendees or not. It can also provide a basis for consultations and workshops, allowing an organization to share its expertise with other organizations locally, nationally, and globally. Critical placemaking allows youth to play a vital role in educating the community as well. They too can offer consultations and workshops while serving as role models, mentoring younger peers, and encouraging their verbal and political literacy. These outreach activities can foster critical consciousness in the larger community; for example, an organization can help adults learn to work with and be more respectful of young people. However, it is the critical placemaking activities of youth that can shine the brightest light upon social issues (e.g., prejudice, school segregation, institutional racism, and discrimination against immigrants and LGBTQ+ populations) and the outrage of environmental injustice (e.g., air and water pollution, inadequate access to healthy food, unsafe homes, and inadequate transit). And with their abundant creativity, youth can use every artistic form—performance, film, poetry, music, dance, multimedia—to educate and provoke community members while being entertaining, as the research revealed. Art is what can blur oppositional and community-building activism.

### Strengthening Intangible Infrastructure

Because critical placemaking involves taking action and making change, it is an empowering process that can increase a community's political efficacy. Rather than work independently to advance initiatives, an organization can increase its likelihood of success by networking with other organizations, and youth can join in, registering voters and educating them about the issues that are the focus of initiatives. Working collaboratively, a community can acquire the political clout to change oppressive conditions (e.g., police brutality and the school-to-prison pipeline), not only in their schools and neighborhoods but also further afield in the city and state. Critical placemaking also creates relationships—among people and with place—and thus it encourages the interactions that, as one study participant noted, used to happen naturally before television privatized civic life. For example, to increase the likelihood of successful projects, an organization can build coalitions with local institutions and with parents, school staff, community members, and elected officials. As this research revealed, these relationships are essential to replacing individualistic social structures with communal ones—for example, collective ownership of land, sustainable food systems, and solidarity economies that build community rather than individual wealth. Then too, critical placemaking brings about social interactions in the public domain— at markets, yard sales, block parties, cafés—which can spawn a sense of ownership and belonging while generating the monies to advance community economic development and self-sufficiency. An organization can guarantee an audience for public gatherings by offering free programming (no doubt showcasing its youth talent) and use its political influence to enhance the public safety that civic life requires but without creating a police presence. Youth can join in, designing and implementing safety plans, selling their own and other local goods at markets, and being an ever-present creative voice.

By increasing its political efficacy and reinforcing its social fabric, critical placemaking can help strengthen a community's intangible infrastructure.

### Strengthening Tangible Infrastructure

Finally, critical placemaking strengthens a community's tangible infrastructure—undoubtedly the most remarkable finding in this study. For one, an organization can improve physical space by gaining access to underutilized private or city-owned properties, and then it can steward its takings or give them over to community ownership. Youth can further improve physical space by constructing small structures or entire buildings, rehabilitating or painting old buildings, constructing playgrounds and other recreational facilities, and even designing new student-responsive schools. Notably, they can improve physical space in the public domain by simply asserting their inalienable right to occupy it, whether engaged in performances, parades, protests, and rallies or service and civic activities. Then too, youth can beautify physical space through the kind of projects that Boggs envisioned. They can plant hundreds of flowers and trees; clean up abandoned and fallow land, polluted rivers, and school bathrooms; create huge organic farms and tiny community gardens so they can grow and market fresh produce in food desserts; restore the natural environment with native plants; construct and carry larger-than-life hero puppets through the streets; and make and install their art at every opportunity. After all, the public domain of a democracy should be beautiful.

In addition to improving physical space, critical placemaking can strengthen the tangible infrastructure of a community by providing services to people in need. For example, an organization can provide tons of free nutritious food to residents, contribute resources to support community events, provide access to technology for households that lack it, and respond to emergency needs, whether caused by climate-related or other life-threatening crises. Youth can help out by doing home repairs for the elderly and disabled, giving away their fresh produce and serving it in low-income clinics, nursing homes, and homeless shelters, organizing food and clothing drives, and reading to children. By improving physical space and providing humanitarian services, critical placemaking strengthens a community's tangible infrastructure and, at the same time, foregrounds the energy and creativity of its youth. It contributes to the creation of a democratic loving community that can thwart the neoliberalist trajectory toward a commons of disenfranchisement, exclusion, and impoverishment of the human spirit.[33]

Table 2 lists the critical placemaking activities that this study revealed related to improving a community's infrastructure and engaging in its governance.

Critical placemaking exemplifies the new, more participatory, and place-based concept of citizenship that Boggs envisioned. By undertaking hands-on personally meaningful projects internally and in the larger community, the organizations in this study prepared youth with the mental capacities, manual skills, and emotional sensitivities to wrench themselves and their communities from the dehumanizing grasp of the marketplace. They helped turn neoliberal's "relentless campaign for personal responsibility" on its head, disrupting the "growing sense of insecurity, cynicism, and political retreat" that enslavement to consumer culture has engendered among Americans. They helped reimagine a market-driven conception of responsibility as an obligation to enrich one's family, community, and the earth's ecosystems, which requires a reciprocal obligation to provide the means to do so on the part of governments and industries. In place of "competitive, self-interested individuals vying for their own material and ideological gain,"[34] these organizations envisioned young citizens responsible to themselves, their significant others, and the earth's ecosystems, capable of generating the social relationships and political efficacy to help restore a democracy hollowed out by corporate culture.

Table 2. Critical Placemaking within a Community

## Building Community

### Generating Spatial Knowledge

| Youth | Conducting needs assessments \| inventorying environmental resources \| mapping community assets \| mapping displacement. |

### Generating Cultural Knowledge

| Youth | Conducting oral histories \| sharing stories of their experiences \| researching neighborhood history. |

### Raising Awareness of Community Assets

| Organizations | Exposing school staff to the creativity of youth \| introducing the community to local artists \| publishing young people's creative writing. |
| Youth | Providing information on community strengths, weaknesses, opportunities, and threats. |

## Cultivating Participatory Citizenship

### Encouraging Social Interactions

| Youth | Creating participative venues (talk-backs, block parties, etc.) \| provoking dialogue (through interactive plays, workshops, exhibitions, etc.) \| staging celebrations and rituals. |

### Encouraging Civic Engagement

| Organizations | Advocating for youth engagement in school governance. |

### Being Inclusive

| Organizations | Creating a beloved community of difference \| embracing villains and enemies. |

### Being Engaged

| Youth | Attending/testifying at community meetings \| campaigning door-to-door \| doing teach-ins at public schools \| holding press conferences \| appearing on radio programs \| organizing campaigns \| participating in protests and rallies. |

## Educating the Community

### Educating Neighborhood Youth and Adults

| Organizations | Involving families in programs \| offering classes for adults \| sharing technology with families \| sharing skills/consulting with other organizations. |
| Youth | Doing workshops at other organizations \| mentoring younger youth \| reading to children. |

### Encouraging Critical Consciousness

| Organizations | Helping adults be more respectful of youth. |
| Youth | Raising awareness of environmental toxins \| raising awareness of social injustice (prejudice, school segregation, institutional racism, discrimination against immigrants and LGBTQ+) \| using activist art (performance, film, poetry, music, dance, multimedia) to educate, provoke, and entertain. |

(continued)

Table 2. *(continued)*

### Strengthening Intangible Intrastructure

#### Increasing Political Influence

Organizations  Advancing community economic development | becoming a political force | fighting police brutality.

Youth  Educating and registering voters | getting oppressive policies changed (in schools, neighborhoods, city, state).

#### Establishing Social Relationships

Organizations  Building coalitions with institutions + parents, school staff, community members, and elected officials.

#### Reinforcing the Social Fabric

Organizations  Creating space for social exchange (at markets, yard sales, cafés, block parties, etc.) | enhancing community safety | generating a sense of ownership/belonging | promoting self-sufficiency | offering free community programming.

Youth  Designing and implementing safety plans | engaging in art activities | selling their own and other local goods at markets.

### Strengthening Tangible Infrastructure

#### Creating Space

Youth  Constructing small structures and new buildings | constructing playgrounds and other recreational facilities | designing new student-responsive schools | rehabilitating and painting old buildings.

#### Claiming Space

Organizations  Acquiring land for community ownership | becoming stewards of city-owned land.

Youth  Occupying public space (through performances, parades, protests, rallies, etc) | creating a presence through service and civic activities.

#### Improving Health and Well-Being

Organizations  Providing free nutritrious food.

Youth  Beautifying the public domain by planting flowers and trees | cleaning up abandoned and fallow land | cleaning up polluted rivers | cleaning school bathrooms, creating organic farms and community gardens | growing and marketing produce | making and installing art, restoring the natural environment with native plants.

#### Providing Community Services

Organizations  Contributing resources to community events | providing access to technology | responding to emergency needs.

Youth  Doing home repairs for the elderly and disabled | giving away food | organizing food and clothing drives | serving fresh produce in low-income clinics, nursing homes, and homeless shelters.

Text credit: Sharon Egretta Sutton, 2023

## Architecture of a Beloved Community

In this concluding section, I respond to Dr. King's call for "a radical restructuring of the architecture of American society" whose aging social structures are steadily collapsing under the weight of racism, poverty, and militarism.[35] In light of the lessons learned herein, I specify a new structure that can help young people pursue the promise of democracy. Its foundational principles demand synergy between individual and collective growth so as to create a loving, intergenerational commons where people are interconnected, bound together by struggle, inclusivity, engagement, introspection, and stability. I refer this this radical restructuring of individualistic relationships as the architecture of a beloved community.

### Struggle: Learning to Live Together Despite Differences

Democracy is not fixed but rather is a continuous social process of shaping and reshaping values that are often contradictory and that therefore result in disagreement.[36] Living together requires that young people learn to embrace difference and the conflict that accompanies it. It requires that they learn to negotiate disputes in order to achieve reasonable consensus about the sociospatial infrastructure that is crucial to communal life and livelihood[37] while maintaining their willingness to be oppositional when their values are compromised. Additionally, it requires that young people have the empathy to get into another's shoes and bear witness to the *kaumaha* (grief) that results from the deep racial and social divides that plague the nation because sharing these burdens is the only way to change them. Such social practices make up the ongoing struggle of an unstable but alterable beloved community.

### Inclusivity: Learning across Age, Race, Class, and Culture

With Washington and other seats of government bereft of political imagination, "deadlocked between those determined simply to hang onto power and those seeking modest tweaks,"[38] democracy calls out for all hands on deck to solve the nation's cascading economic, racial, and ecological problems. It calls out for young people who are diverse in age, race, class, and culture (and not just those in a particular social media network)—who can approach problems through *'ewalu mau maka* (eight different eyes). It calls out for them to create narratives that feature the supposed villains as protagonists so that they can inaugurate new ways of seeing and imagine a whole new world. It calls out for young people to

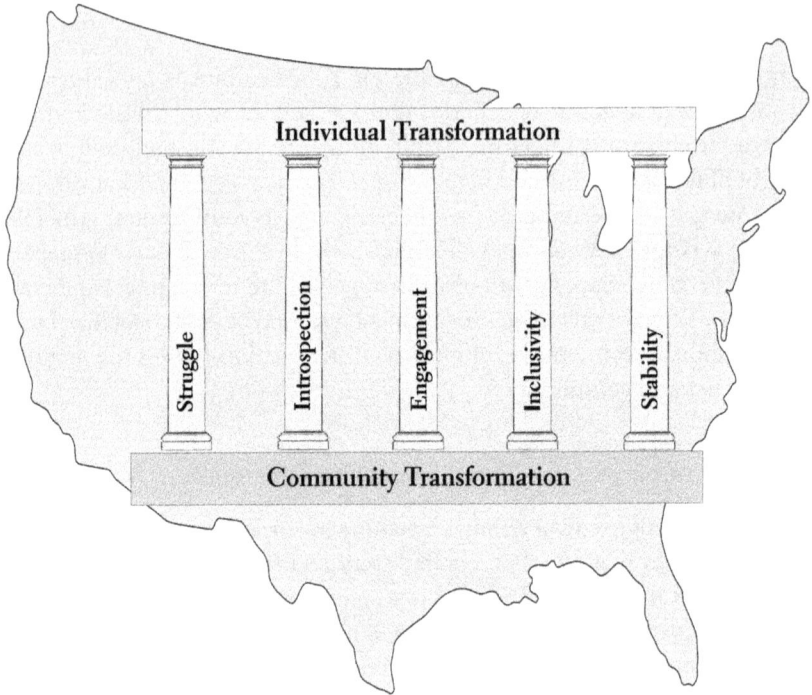

Figure 9. Architecture of a Beloved Community
Image credit: Sharon Egretta Sutton, 2023

ground themselves in their local history and culture while experiencing geographic oneness with other cultures and identities. Finally, it calls out for them to feel a connection with anyone who is suffering or experiencing some kind of pain or need—because it is on everyone to show solidarity. Such social practices push the boundaries of a beloved community toward true inclusivity.

### Engagement: Learning through the Whole Person

Democracy is "a way of life that meets the deep human need to know that our voices count, to shape the decisions that most affect our well-being."[39] A pedagogy for achieving a living democracy engages the whole person emotionally, socially, intellectually, and physically. It helps young people take advantage of wide-ranging subject matter and inspires them to work hard, take care of one other and the earth's ecosystems, and use whatever means appropriate to reimagine and recreate the infrastructure of their community. Additionally, it requires a connectedness, or us-ness, between young people's individual aspirations and their collective commitment to love and improve their locality and its natural and constructed habitats. Such social practices help young people use their voice in spaces where they are typically absent and then take action to achieve equity within a beloved community.

### Introspection: Learning to Love, Honor, and Respect One Another

Democracy calls out for young people who are loving, loyal, respectful, compassionate, and kind, and they acquire such personal characteristics by observing them in others. It calls out for them to have relationships with adults who are not their parents or teachers who appreciate their fearless adventurousness and can help them ideate and move beyond anger to work on policy and strategy in a loving, respectful way. It calls out for young people to experience a sense of family with peers and near-peers so they can mutually challenge one another to be their truest selves. It calls out for them to "hold space" and take the time to be present in the work of healing themselves and their community. Such social practices allow young people to experience, and pay forward to others, the real love of a beloved community.

### Stability: Learning to Sustain the Commons

The end-wall support that mirrors the struggle of negotiating a living and unstable democracy is stability. It requires youth-serving organizations to invest in mentoring alumni into positions of leadership. It requires them to create financial stability by establishing the social enterprises that can generate monies to ward off depoliticizing funders while supporting their mission and keeping the fruits of young people's labor in the community. It requires organizations to invest in the community's infrastructure in a communal, rather than a capitalistic, way so that it belongs to residents who will refuse to let their efforts die. Such social practices allow youth-serving organizations to plant the seeds of a beloved community that will become a *kumu* (tree) that creates even more trees and more fruit.

I have no illusions about the enormous effort that will be needed to reverse the nation's snowballing trajectory toward chaos, but I believe in my heart that young people have been, and are, the foot soldiers who can take on today's economic, racial, and ecological crises and "transform this reluctant nation into its best possible self."[40]

## Notes

1. Erin E. Toolis, "Theorizing Critical Placemaking as a Tool for Reclaiming Public Space," *American Journal of Community Psychology* 59 (2017): 192.

2. Tom Adam Davies, "Black Power in Action: The Bedford-Stuyvesant Restoration Corporation, Robert F. Kennedy, and the Politics of the Urban Crisis," *Journal of American History* (December 2013): 736–60.

3. Soo Ah Kwon, Chapter 2, "Youth Organizing and the Nonprofitization of Activism," in *Uncivil Youth: Race, Activism, and Affirmative Governmentality* (Durham, N.C.: Duke University Press, 2013), 45–72.

4. Nicole P. Marwell, "Privatizing the Welfare State: Nonprofit Community-Based Organizations as Political Actors," *American Sociological Review* 69, no. 2 (April 2004): 265–29, https://www.jstor.org/stable/3593087.

5. Kwon, "Introduction," in *Uncivil Youth*, 1–25.

6. Marwell, "Privatizing the Welfare State."

7. Jessica T. Shiller, "Preparing for Democracy: How Community-Based Organizations Build Civic Engagement among Urban Youth," *Urban Education* 48, no. 1 (2013): 69–91, referring to Arne Duncan, "Back to School: Enhancing U.S. Education and Competitiveness," *Foreign Affairs* (November/December 2010), http://www.foreignaffairs.com/articles/66776/arne-duncan/back-to-school.

8. Kwon, "Introduction," 1.

9. Joel Westheimer and Joseph Kahne, "What Kind of Citizen? The Politics of Educating for Democracy," *American Educational Research Journal* 41, no. 2 (2004): 243.

10. Shiller, "Preparing for Democracy," citing Shawn S. Ginwright and Julio Cammorata, "Youth Activism in the Urban Community: Learning Critical Civic Praxis within Community Organizations," *International Journal of Qualitative Studies in Education* 20, no. 6 (2007): 693–710.

11. Ben Kirshner, "Conclusions," in *Youth Activism in an Era of Education Inequality*, Qualitative Studies in Psychology, Kindle ed. (New York and London: New York University Press, 2015), 132, 163–238.

12. Kwon, "Youth Organizing."

13. David Harvey, Chapter Three, "The Creation of the Urban Commons," in *Rebel Cities: From the Right to the City to the Urban Revolution* (London and New York: Verso, 2013), 67–88.

14. Robert J. Antonio, "Plundering the Commons: The Growth Imperative in Neoliberal Times," *Sociological Review* 61, S2 (2013): 18–42.

15. Martin Luther King Jr., *Where Do We Go from Here: Chaos or Community*, Foreword by Coretta Scott King, Introduction by Thomas Hardin, Kindle ed. (1968; Boston: Beacon Press, 2010), 201.

16. Martin Robinson, "Drama," in *What Should Schools Teach? Disciplines, Subjects and the Pursuit of Truth*, ed. Alka Sehgal Cuthbert and Alex Standish (London: UCL Press, 2021), 94, https://www.jstor.org/stable/j.ctv14t475s.

17. Kirshner, "Conclusions."

18. Grace Lee Boggs and Scott Kurashige, *The Next American Revolution: Sustainable Activism for the Twenty-First Century*, Kindle ed. (Oakland: University of California Press, 2011.

19. For a discussion of the importance of developing in-house talent, see, for example, Prabhir Correa, "Surviving a Leadership Transition, *Times of India*, Business, December 8, 2020, https://timesofindia.indiatimes.com/blogs/developing -contemporary-india/surviving-a-leadership-transition/.

20. "Read the Full Transcript of President Obama's Farewell Speech," *Los Angeles Times*, January 10, 2017, https://www.latimes.com/politics/la-pol-obama -farewell-speech-transcript-20170110-story.html.

21. These dimensions of educating for critically informed citizenship blend two sources: Henry A. Giroux, "Introduction," in *On Critical Pedagogy* (London and New York: Bloomsbury Publishing, 2020), 1–15, http://ebookcentral.proquest.com/lib /washington/detail.action?docID=5997010; and Richard Neumann, "American Democracy at Risk," *Phi Delta Kappan* 89, no. 5 (January 2008): 328–39, https:// www.jstor.org/stable/20442493.

22. Giroux, "Introduction," 8.

23. Giroux, "Introduction," 3.

24. Giroux, "Introduction," 8.

25. Neumann, "American Democracy at Risk," 331, referring to Henry A. Giroux, *America on the Edge: Henry Giroux on Politics, Culture, and Education* (New York: Palgrave Macmillan, 2006).

26. Giroux, "Introduction," 8.

27. Victoria Derr, Louise Chawla, and Mara Mintzer, *Placemaking with Children and Youth: Participatory Practices for Planning Sustainable Communities* (New York: New Village Press, 2018), 2.

28. Toolis, "Theorizing Critical Placemaking as a Tool for Reclaiming Public Space," 184.

29. To generate the placemaking strategies, I overlaid the five themes that emerged from an analysis of forty-two interviews from the combined 2004–2005 and 2020–2021 studies reported in this book with the same themes that emerged from an analysis of eighty-two interviews from the Ford Foundation study. I acknowledge that some of the interviews are in both data sets but emphasize that the analyses were completed in two different contexts and fifteen years apart. The five critical placemaking themes are:

1. Democratic governance: involving youth/parents/adults in decision making, consensus-building, power-sharing, voting, developing agendas or activities, etc.

2. Community participation: involving youth/parents/adults in program activities, staging exhibitions, performances, conference, etc., collaborating on campaigns, creating organizational partnerships, building coalitions, networking, etc.

3. Community education: staff/youth/parents/adults developing greater insights due to program activities, offering workshops, consultations, trainings, etc., creating instructional materials, etc.

4. Community development: documenting/disseminating community needs, engaging in placemaking (making public art, building, gardening, cleaning up, etc.), improving schools/public policy, securing resources, securing investment, marketing goods.

5. Community service: volunteering/helping/addressing needs (serving in soup kitchens, caring for the elderly, mentoring young children, doing tax returns, etc.), organizing others to volunteer/help/address needs.

30. Kwon, "Youth Organizing."

31. William W. Goldsmith, "From the Metropolis to Globalization: The Dialectics of Race and Urban Form," in *Globalizing Cities: A New Spatial Order*, ed. Peter Marcuse and Ronald van Kempen (Oxford: Blackwell, 2000), 41.

32. David W. Orr, *Earth in Mind: On Education, Environment, and the Human Prospect* (Washington, D.C.: Island Press, 1994), 114.

33. King, *Where Do We Go from Here*, 174.

34. Henry A. Giroux, "Neoliberalism and the Politics of Public Pedagogy," in *On Critical Pedagogy*," 153–54.

35. King, *Where Do We Go from Here*, 141.

36. Nan Fairley and Mark Wilson. Chapter One, "From Service to Something Else," in *Living Democracy: Communities as Classrooms, Students as Citizens*, ed. Mindy LaBreck (Dayton, Ohio: Kettering Foundation, 2017), http://ebookcentral .proquest.com/lib/washington/detail.action?docID=5214874.

37. Harvey, "Creation of the Urban Commons."

38. Daniel Immerwahr, "The Death of America's Political Imagination," *New York Times*, Opinion, 4.

39. Frances Moore Lappé and Paul Martin Du Bois, *The Quickening of America: Rebuilding Our Nation, Remaking Our Lives* (San Francisco: Jossey-Bass Publishers, 1994), 3.

40. Vincent Harding, "Introduction." In King, *Where Do We go from Here*, Location 142.

# Epilogue

> *By history, mission, and concept, American universities are uniquely*
> *woven into the fabric of American democracy. There is no comparable*
> *socializing agent with the same ability to train the students in their care*
> *to become civic agents, to give heart and mind to their local communities,*
> *to shape institutions, to debate and develop policies, and to critically*
> *reflect on the future direction of our country and our world.*

I began this book by observing that education has veered away from the idealism articulated in the foregoing quote and is, instead, careening headlong toward a market mandate to prepare productive workers for the global economy. I zoomed in to the low-income youth who attend public schools where they are denied a decent education and treated as criminals in a competitive, market-driven system.[1] In the body of the book, I theorized a place-based critical pedagogy, offered by three community-based organizations, to demonstrate its effectiveness in subsuming the civilizing purpose of education that public schools have abdicated. In this epilogue, I zoom back out and pivot to the nation's universities, where a job-training mentality has similarly usurped the educational agenda. That is, I redirect my focus (hopefully without causing whiplash) from youth and community-based organizations to universities and specifically to students and faculty in the community development fields of architecture, landscape architecture, and urban design and planning, among other disciplines that are—or should be—concerned with the issue that was central in this book—namely, improving the disinvested infrastructure of low-income neighborhoods.

I begin by summarizing the heralded democratizing mission of the university and what its critics see as a shift toward the marketplace. I then argue that, with its exclusionary campuses, hierarchical governance structures, and abusive labor practices, the university has never measured up as a commons where people simultaneously experience life-sustaining infrastructure and engage in determining its quality—the definition of a commons articulated herein. After showing that its biggest leap toward democracy occurred in response to violent student protests, I describe the limited progress in improving the infrastructure of disinvested communities that some institutions made in response to those protests. I summarize current student and faculty demands that the university be more community-engaged and socially just and less racist and exploitative. I end by suggesting how the pedagogy described herein might help achieve those demands. But first, my synthesis of academia's engagement with democracy.

According to historians, higher education's obligation to serve society began with the founding of Harvard College before the American Revolutionary War and intensified after the Civil War when colleges and universities became the engines for building a new nation literally from the ground up. They also note that, early in the twentieth century, Dewey established enduring principles for education's social purpose.[2] Historians say as well that higher education witnessed a reawakened social purpose after World War I and again during World War II, when the experience of fighting authoritarianism overseas heightened American consciousness of the university's essential role in a free and democratic society. They note that, in 1946, after World War II's end, President Harry S. Truman appointed a commission to investigate academia's discriminatory practices, which set in motion a halting trajectory toward educational equity, including civil rights legislation and the establishment of a network of community colleges.[3] Historians point to explicit mandates in the Truman Commission Report and the G.I. Bill calling for an alignment between higher education and the federal government that would most effectively further American democracy, which led to unprecedented investment in both public and private institutions.[4]

Critics of higher education say that these halting notions of academia's social purpose began to erode in 1950 when the federal government established the National Science Foundation to support the scientific research that could drive the nation's economy, enhance its security, and sustain its global leadership.[5] Emphasizing that the government "put its immense weight behind the siting of scientific research in the university," critics say that in 1963 higher education made a decisive pivot toward a corporate structure. They claim that it was no longer a tool of democracy but rather became a "knowledge industry" devoted to sponsored research, innovation, and productivity. Since then, critics argue, higher education has moved further and further away from building a shared understanding of democracy and citizenship to offering individual benefits to those who qualify, transforming students from learners into customers whose consumer needs must be met.[6] They complain that its measures of success mirror those of commercial enterprises and include the volume of degrees earned by different demographic groups, the cost per customer in relation to the employment that different degrees yield, and the accountability of employees in a top-down reporting system.[7]

Having spent forty-eight years in academia, I agree wholeheartedly that the university has increasingly adopted a corporate model that emphasizes central administration over shared governance; externally funded research over scholarship, teaching, and public service; and job training over and above all else.[8] However, when considering the rhetoric about its higher ideals, I cannot resist pointing out that, from the get-go, higher education has magnified and normalized the inequity that exists in the larger society, offering the rewards of its credentialing system to an ever more select few within a strictly regulated social hierarchy. Skipping over the fact that the transatlantic slave trade financed its growth,[9] I would point out that, in its historic and current practices, the university has consistently run counter to democratic ideals. For example, at the time of its supposed democratic zenith, most privileged white males received a decidedly more prestigious education than most middle- or working-class ones or Jews, who received a decidedly more prestigious education than most African Americans or women (if they received any education at all), and the nation's first people were not even in the picture.

At the time of its supposed downfall at the hands of the marketplace, the university had made some progress through civil rights statutes that prohibit discrimination against historically marginalized populations, but its current lack of equity is breathtaking, encompassing overpaid presidents, ever-proliferating administrators, and athletic coaches and their assistants; underpaid custodians and other low-end employees who commute long hours because they cannot afford in-town housing; expanding numbers of contingent faculty many of whom do not receive a living wage but do the lion's share of work to meet the university's teaching mission;[10] and students—some of them homeless or without money for food, others on the brink of suicide as a result of the stress of competing for success with peers from high-earning families who have oodles of support in applying for admission and completing coursework.[11]

This well-documented lack of equity notwithstanding, my concern is with the university's deficiencies as a commons, the core topic in this book, and the struggle to remedy those deficiencies among activist students and their faculty supporters. In the model of democratic education that I elaborated herein,

community-based organizations and the youth they served first secured participatory parity and a strong infrastructure internally; then, using an array of
political, intellectual, manual, and artistic means, they took collective action
to bring about those conditions within the surrounding neighborhood, making sure to include residents as co-beneficiaries of the wealth they generated.
The university measures up poorly against this community-based model of
democratic education. Though it has long touted faculty governance as evidence of its democratic structure and though unions have formed to demand
equal rights for teaching assistants and contingent faculty, true participatory
citizenship remains out of reach, thwarted by economic inequalities that mirror those of the larger society, with teaching staff receiving a small fraction of
the compensation that managerial staff and executive leaders receive and many
teachers lacking health insurance and job security. Though nationally contingent faculty average about 50 percent of the teaching staff—and almost
90 percent at my small private institution in the world's most expensive city—
universities shave the cost of paying for this army of instructors while raising
tuition and investing in heavily glitzy facilities.[12] True participatory citizenship is
also thwarted by academia's system of rewards, including student grades, faculty
promotion and tenure procedures, rules that limit governance to full-time faculty, and staff evaluations, among other mechanisms to stifle the voice that the
organizations described herein so valued.

Campuses with their libraries, classrooms, cafeterias, dormitories, and other
facilities—often with gated entries, I.D. cards, and special security forces—offer
students the tangible infrastructure to support their learning, but even pre-
Covid some students had less access to this infrastructure because of something called "distributed learning," which allows universities to use technology to
free education from locality (and the cost of real estate). In this emerging era,
the tangible infrastructure of education will likely be that afforded by students'
private realms, some of them more commodious than others. Even if the university's tangible infrastructure continues as its primary benefit, its intangible
infrastructure is seriously compromised as a result of its fundamentally individualistic, competitive nature. The organizations described herein prepared
young people for the work of democracy by creating family-like, intergenerational settings where they could experience the love that would allow them to
go forth as an empathic, responsible collective. Higher education, and all of
education, is predicated upon individual success. Even in situations that incorporate teamwork among students or faculty, rewards are individual and
highly suspect if they are otherwise. Thus, the internal functioning of the
university leaves it ill-prepared to go forth and liberate its host communities,
as the youth-serving organizations aspired to do. Historically, the university's

internal power imbalance has moved outward and blighted its relationship with nearby residents and too often resulted in the callous destruction of the community's infrastructure in order to accommodate the university's.

In the 1960s, students, especially African American students, called the university to task over such failings. Demanding revolutionary change on their campuses, they called for participatory democracy, self-determination, and respect for all individuals.[13] African American student protests began at HBCUs but quickly spread to white colleges and the Ivy League as the tone of protest transitioned from nonviolent resistance to calls for Black Power and solidarity with oppressed people throughout the world.[14] White, Asian, and Hispanic students joined African Americans to disrupt nearly one thousand campuses in every state except Alaska, demanding an end to the war in Vietnam, increased recruitment of African American faculty and students, a relevant non-Eurocentric curriculum, and an end to exploitative relationships with nearby low-income neighborhoods, among other calls for justice. My recruitment to Columbia University School of Architecture in 1968 grew out of just such demands, so virulent that classes were suspended for five months.

For a short while, universities undertook a number of transformations in response to the 1960s student activism, including eliminating grades in favor of written evaluations, opening faculty meetings to students and staff, adopting student-generated curricula, recruiting more diverse faculty and students, and creating departments specializing in the study of marginalized populations, among other efforts to create an academic commons. Some institutions, including Columbia, also focused outward to address the poverty that surrounded them through service-learning courses and storefront studios. However, these transformative initiatives soon vanished as multiple dynamics in the larger society—the Vietnam War, urban unrest, white backlash, forced busing, escalating energy costs, a newly affluent middle class unwilling to support social programs—impeded academia's thrust toward democracy.[15] Nevertheless, outreach to disinvested communities persisted as a result of the commitment of some faculty who used the tools of scholarship and design "to teach students how to participate effectively in the democratic community."[16] University-community partnerships evolved from individual faculty initiatives and university-affiliated community design centers increased after one was initiated in 1963, both arrangements offering student interns an opportunity to work alongside licensed professionals in "communities traditionally underserved by public- and private-sector planning and design."[17] To help you see how these efforts connect to those undertaken by the exemplar organizations featured in this book, I refer you to the model of activism illustrated in Figure 7 of Conclusions. As was true for the youth featured in this book, students in the community development fields who participate in outreach projects typically create plans and designs for community clients that contain ideas for transforming a particular place, thereby provoking a change in how their clients envision existing conditions, which amounts to place-based activism in the commons.

Place-based activism occurs in university centers and institutes that balance learning with advancing the common good by engaging students in volunteerism, community and national service, service learning, and paid and unpaid political and environmental activism. University-community partnerships, once one-way offerings of the university's noblesse oblige to poor people, have progressed to two-way exchanges that facilitate a more active and engaged democracy. Some scholars even claim that a "civic engagement movement" has coalesced within higher education, but they also see it as a "rather conventional, even timid, civic engagement—one that rests easily within the status quo and the prevailing norms, customs, and structures of the academy," more intent upon gaining acceptance and legitimacy than upon advancing social change.[18] According to noted educator Ernest L. Boyer, community engagement is often "more concerned with credentialing students and faculty than with addressing the nation's pressing urban problems." He noted that most initiatives "were poorly supported and lacked a larger sense of purpose in elevating civic discourse between academics and the public."[19] Certainly, given academia's undisputed power, its aspirations for social change seem rather timid in comparison to the ones embraced by the miniscule organizations presented herein—for example, using philanthropic funds to secure really expensive real estate so families can eat healthier food, parading sweating and covered in soil for several miles in order to reclaim privatized public space, or hanging a huge banner out of a window of a long-abandoned building with a telephone number to call to demand action.

Nevertheless, there are students and faculty who are willing to use their privilege as activists and scholars to push the university toward riskier community engagement activities. In addition, in the wake of George Floyd's murder, another group has coalesced within the community development fields, consisting of mostly students and recent alumni but also a few faculty and staff who have demanded that their universities adopt nonracist practices. During summer 2020, the group wrote letters to school and college administrators (beginning in the Ivy League but spreading throughout the country) demanding changes in the curriculum, in the makeup of lecture series and review panels, in the recruitment of students and faculty, in the methods of adjudicating complaints about racism, and in the methods of doling out awards. In addition, most letters demanded that institutions create a diversity strategic plan

and report progress in achieving the plan. Only a few letters demanded improved town-gown relationships or community-engaged learning, and just one
letter demanded that students be included in governance[20]—these three less
cited concerns being major ones for the 1960s student revolutionaries. The
group pursuing nonracist practices coexists with another group that has organized against unfair labor practices, demanding that institutions remove the
mask of hypocrisy and model the values that won them a social contract with
special privileges. This groups wants a fair distribution of rights, responsibilities, and resources, which is the essence of participatory democracy.

I would argue that the community engagement and the nonracist/labor activists are on parallel, but separate tracks: parallel because they all want to
transform their institutions' exclusionary practices, separate because one group
looks outward, seeking to improve the community's tangible infrastructure and
the other looks inward, seeking to improve the institution's intangible infrastructure, but neither seems to recognize the interdependence of their respective goals. I believe that both groups have much to learn from the youth-serving
organizations in this book about the connection between individual and community transformation. Building upon what I learned during the six years
that it took me to unravel the story in this book, I propose that the university
needs to disrupt the inequity in its own house—it needs to create a just, politically engaged commons within the campus. At the same time, the university
needs to put community empowerment at the center of its teaching and research agenda so that outcomes "belong" to the common good and contribute
to its revitalization. To paraphrase one of the study participants, universities
need to help the community inside their campuses first, and then they can
help the community all around.

Thinking back to the quote that introduced this Epilogue, I suggest that
the architecture of a beloved community, found at the end of Conclusions,
offers an ideal structure for housing academia's highest ideals. It specifies:
learning across age, race, class, and culture; learning through the whole person
in order to improve conditions in local communities; learning to love, honor,
and respect each other and the earth; investing its resources in a communal,
rather than a capitalistic, way; and—importantly—learning to engage in the
struggle of making the democracy. Once this architecture is in place, I suggest that, as faculty and student activists, you work across groups with diverg-
ing viewpoints to develop critical understandings (plural) of your institution's
historical social justice record, considering the degree to which it has progressed toward democracy internally and in the local community. Bring
alumni and community members of all ages and origins (especially first people)
into the discussion so you can collectively figure out what reparations are

needed to mend your relationships with each other and with the earth's eco-systems. Be willing to struggle to exorcise neoliberalism's ruthless competitive-ness by constructing a spiritual framework for those relationships that offers love, loyalty, and listening as tools of coexistence. Then think broadly about the skills and habits of mind that you will need to call forth your full humanity—heart, body, and mind—and reimagine a participative, socially just commons both within and outside the academy.

## Notes

1. The epigraph is from John C. Burkhardt and Jessica Joslin, "If This Is a Movement, Why Don't We Feel Anything Moving?," *Michigan Journal of Community Service Learning* (Spring 2012): 1; review essay.

Henry A. Giroux, "Introduction," in *On Critical Pedagogy* (London and New York: Bloomsbury Publishing, 2020), 1–15, http://ebookcentral.proquest.com/lib/washington/detail.action?docID=5997010.

2. Maria J. D'Agostino, "Fostering a Civically Engaged Society: The University and Service Learning," *Journal of Public Affairs Education* 14, no. 2 (Summer 2008): 191–204.

3. Claire Gilbert and Donald Heller, "The Truman Commission and Its Impact on Federal Higher Education Policy from 1947 to 2010," Working Paper no. 9 (University Park: Pennsylvania State University, Center for the Study of Higher Education, November 2010), 1–21.

4. Burkhardt and Joslin, "If This is a Movement, Why Don't We Feel Anything Moving?"

5. See "At a Glance," National Science Foundation, https://www.nsf.gov/about/glance.jsp.

6. Geoffrey Galt Harpham, "From Eternity to Here: Shrinkage in American Thinking about Higher Education," *Representations* 116, no. 1 (Fall 2011): 46.

7. Colleen Lye, Christopher Newfield, and James Vernon, "Humanists and the Public University," *Representations* 116, no. 1 (Fall 2011): 1–18.

8. See Wendy Brown, "The End of Educated Democracy," *Representations* 116, no. 1 (Fall 2011): 19–41; and Harpham, "From Eternity to Here," 42–61.

9. Craig Steven Wilder, *Ebony and Ivy: Race, Slavery, and the Troubled History of America's Universities*, Kindle ed. (London and New York: Bloomsbury Publishing, 2013).

10. Harpham, "From Eternity to Here."

11. Sharon Egretta Sutton, "Afterword," in *Teaching and Designing in Detroit: Ten Women on Pedagogy and Practice*, ed. Stephen Vogel and Libby Balter Blume (New York and London: Routledge, 2019), 183–88.

12. Kimiko de Freytas-Tamura, "New School Adjuncts' Push for Better Pay Drives Acrimonious Strike," *New York Times* (December 6, 2022).

13. Laura Kalman, *Yale Law School and the Sixties* (Chapel Hill: University of North Carolina Press, 2005), 6.

14. Benjamin P. Bowser, *The Black Middle Class: Social Mobility—and Vulnerability* (Boulder, Colo.: Lynne Rienner Publishers, 2007).

15. Matthew Dallek, "The Conservative 1960s," *Atlantic Monthly* 276, no. 6 (December 1995): 130–35.

16. Jeremy Cohen, "A Laboratory for Public Scholarship and Democracy," *New Directions in Teaching and Learning*, no. 105 (Spring 2006): 9.

17. Donovan Finn and Jason Brody, "The State of Community Design: An Analysis of Community Design Center Services," *Journal of Architectural and Planning Research* 31, no. 3 (Autumn 2014): 184, https://www.jstor.org/stable/44114603.

18. Burkhardt and Joslin, "If This is a Movement, Why Don't We Feel Anything Moving?," citing John Saltmarsh and Matthew Hartley, eds., *To Serve a Larger Purpose: Engagement for Democracy and the Transformation of Higher Education* (Philadelphia: Temple University Press, 2011), 290.

19. Sutton, "Afterword," 179.

20. Student demands did not include being involved in school governance, but they did include being compensated for time spent developing transformational interventions.

# Bibliography

Alexander, Michelle. *The New Jim Crow: Mass Incarceration in the Age of Color-blindness.* Kindle ed. New York: New Press, 2010, 2012.

Antonio, Robert J. "Plundering the Commons: The Growth Imperative in Neo-liberal Times." *Sociological Review* 61, S2 (2013): 18–42.

Aronowitz, Stanley. "Preface to the Morningside Edition." In *Learning to Labor: How Working-Class Kids Get Working-Class Jobs,* by Paul Willis, ix–xiii. New York: Columbia University Press, 1977.

Banner, Stuart. "Preparing to Be Colonized: Land Tenure and Legal Strategy in Nineteenth-Century Hawai'i." *Law and Society Review* 39, no. 2 (June 2005): 273–314. https://www.jstor.org/stable/3557617.

Bannister, Jon, and Ade Kearns. "The Function and Foundations of Urban Tolerance: Encountering and Engaging with Difference in the City." *Urban Studies* 50, no. 13 (October 2013): 2,700–2,717. https://www.jstor.org/stable/10.2307/26145612.

Benner, Chris, and Manuel Pastor. *Equity, Growth, and Community: What the Nation Can Learn from America's Metro Areas.* Los Angeles: University of California Press, 2015.

Billies, Michelle. "PAR Method: Journey to a Participatory Conscientization." *International Review of Qualitative Research* 3, no. 3 (Fall 2010): 355–75. https://www.jstor.org/stable/10.1525/irqr.2010.3.3.355.

Binkley, Collin. "U.S. Students Stage Massive Walkout to Protest Gun Violence. *AP News,* March 14, 2018. https://apnews.com/c183323b5e6546419ae08b8c469b065a.

Boggs, Grace Lee. "A Question of Place." *Monthly Review* 52, no. 2 (June 2000): unnumbered, https://monthlyreview.org/2000/06/01/a-question-of-place/.

Boggs, Grace Lee, with Scott Kurashige. *The Next American Revolution: Sustainable Activism for the Twenty-First Century.* Foreword by Danny Glover; Afterword with Immanuel Wallerstein. Kindle ed. Berkeley, Los Angeles, and London: University of California Press, 2011.

Bowles, Samuel, and Herbert Gintis. *Schooling in Capitalist America: Educational Reform and the Contradictions of Economic Life.* New York: Basic Books, 1977.

Bowser, Benjamin P. *The Black Middle Class: Social Mobility—and Vulnerability.* Boulder, Colo.: Lynne Rienner Publishers, 2007

Boydston, Jo Ann, ed. *John Dewey, the Later Works, 1925–1953.* Vol. 6, *1931–1932.* Carbondale: Southern Illinois University Press, 1985. Originally published in 1932.

Bremer, Sidney H. "Home in Harlem, New York: Lessons from the Harlem Renaissance Writers." *PMLA* 105, no. 1 (January 1990): 47–56. http://www.jstor.org/stable/462342.

Brown, Wendy. "The End of Educated Democracy." *Representations* 116, no. 1 (Fall 2011): 19–41.

Burkhardt, John C., and Jessica Joslin. "If This Is a Movement, Why Don't We Feel Anything Moving?" *Michigan Journal of Community Service Learning* (Spring 2012): 1–4. Review essay.

Bynum, Cornelius L. "The New Negro and Social Democracy during the Harlem Renaissance, 1917–37." *Journal of the Gilded Age and Progressive Era* 10, no. 1 (January 2011): 89–112. http://www.jstor.org/stable/23046624.

Cammarota, Julio. "A Map for Social Change: Latino Students Engage a Praxis of Ethnography." *Children, Youth, and Environments* 17, no. 2 (2007): 341–53.

Campana, Alina. "Agents of Possibility: Examining the Intersections of Art/ Education, and Activism in Communities." *Studies in Art Education* 52, no. 4 (Summer 2011): 278–91. https://www.jstor.org/stable/41407910.

Chappell, Sharon Verner, and Melisa Cahnmann-Taylor. "No Child Left with Crayons: The Imperative of Arts-Based Education and Research with Language 'Minority' and Other Minoritized Communities." *Review of Research in Education* 37 (2013): 243–68. https://www.jstor.org/stable/24641963.

Charmaraman, Linda. "Congregating to Create for Social Change: Urban Youth Media Production and the Sense of Community." *Learning, Media, and Technology* 38, no. 1 (2013): 102–15.

Chatterton, Paul. *Unlocking Sustainable Cities: A Manifesto for Real Change.* London: Pluto Press, 2019.

Christens, Brian D., Lawrence T. Winn, and Adrienne M. Duke. "Empowerment and Critical Consciousness: A Conceptual Cross-Fertilization." *Adolescent Res Rev* 1 (2016): 15–27.

Chronopoulos, Themis. "Race, Class, and Gentrification." In *Race Capital? Harlem as Setting and Symbol,* edited by Andrew M. Fearnley and Daniel Matlinn, 213–66. New York: Columbia University Press, 2018. http://www.jstor.com/stable /10.7312/fear18322.16.

Clark, Tara. "Detroit's Empowerment Zone: Evaluation of Success." *Virginia Policy Review* (Fall/Winter 2013): 44–60. https://pages.shanti.virginia.edu/VPR_Journal _Team/files/2013/02/Lynch.Benjamin_VPRFallWinter.ClarkResearchFINAL CDC.44-60.pdf.

Coddou, Marion. "An Institutional Approach to Collective Action: Evidence from Faith-Based Latino Mobilization in the 2006 Immigrant Rights Protests." *Social Problems* 63, no. 1 (February 2016): 127–50, https://www.jstor.org/stable/44014898.

Cohen, Jeremy. "A Laboratory for Public Scholarship and Democracy." *New Directions in Teaching and Learning*, no. 105 (Spring 2006): 7–15.

Cohen-Cruz, Jan. "A Hyphenated Field: Community-Based Theatre in the USA." *New Theatre Quarterly* 15, no. 4 (November 2000): 364–78.

———. *Local Acts: Community-Based Performance in the United States.* New Brunswick, N.J.: Rutgers University Press, 2003.

Correa, Prabhir. "Surviving a Leadership Transition. *Times of India*, Business, December 8, 2020. https://timesofindia.indiatimes.com/blogs/developing -contemporary-india/surviving-a-leadership-transition/.

Cruz, Lynette Hi'ilam. *From Resistance to Affirmation, We Are Who We Were: Reclaiming National Identity in the Hawaiian Sovereignty Movement, 1990–2003.* Ann Arbor, Mich.: ProQuest Dissertations Publishing, 2003. http://search .proquest.com/docview/305327402/.

Cuba, Lee, and David M. Hummon. "A Place to Call Home: Identification with Dwelling, Community, and Region." *Sociological Quarterly* 34, no. 1 (Spring 1993): 111–31. https://www.jstor.org/stable/4121561.

D'Agostino, Maria J. "Fostering a Civically Engaged Society: The University and Service Learning." *Journal of Public Affairs Education* 14, no. 2 (Summer 2008): 191–204.

Dallek, Matthew. "The Conservative 1960s." *Atlantic Monthly* 276, no. 6 (December 1995): 130–35.

Davies, Tom Adam. "Black Power in Action: The Bedford-Stuyvesant Restoration Corporation, Robert F. Kennedy, and the Politics of the Urban Crisis." *Journal of American History* (December 2013): 736–60.

Delgado, Melvin. *Music, Song, Dance, and Theatre: Broadway Meets Social Justice Youth Community Practice.* New York: Oxford University Press, 2018.

Department of Justice. "Crime in the United States: Uniform Crime Report." Washington, D.C.: Federal Bureau of Investigation, 2004. https://www2.fbi.gov /ucr/cius_04/summary/index.html.

Derr, Victoria, Louise Chawla, and Mara Mintzer. *Placemaking with Children and Youth: Participatory Practices for Planning Sustainable Communities.* New York: New Village Press, 2018.

Dewey, John. *Experience as Education.* New York: Collier Books, 1938.

———. *John Dewey, the Later Works, 1925–1953.* Vol. 6, *1931–1932*, edited by Jo Ann Boydston (1932). Carbondale: Southern Illinois University Press, 1985.

Diemer, Matthew A., and Cheng-Hsien Li. "Critical Consciousness Development and Political Participation among Marginalized Youth." *Child Development* 82, no. 6 (November/December 2011): 1,815–33. https://www.jstor.org/stable/41289885.

Dirlik, Arif. "Place-Based Imagination: Globalism and the Politics of Place." *Review* 22, no. 2 (1999): 151–87. https://www.jstor.org/stable/40241454.

Doyle, Dennis A. *Psychiatry and Racial Liberalism in Harlem, 1936–1968*. Rochester, N.Y.: University of Rochester Press, 2016. http://www.jstor.org/stable/10.7722/j .ctt1wx918z.11.

DuBois, W. E. B. *The Souls of Black Folk*. Original Classic Edition. Kindle ed. Gildan Media LLC, 2019. Originally published in 1903.

Duncan, Arne. "Back to School: Enhancing U.S. Education and Competitiveness." *Foreign Affairs* (November/December 2010): 65–74. http://www.foreignaffairs .com/articles/66776/arne-duncan/back-to-school.

Dunn, Julie, and Madonna Stinson. "Learning through Emotion: Moving the Affective in from the Margins." *Springer* (June 29, 2012): 203–18.

Dworkin, Martin S., ed. *Dewey on Education*. New York: Teachers College, 1959.

Edwards, Ditra, Nicole Johnson, and Kim McGillicuddy. *An Emerging Model for Working with Youth: Community Organizing + Youth Development = Youth Organizing*. New York: Funders' Collaborative on Youth Organizing, 2003.

England, Christopher. "John Dewey and Henry George: The Socialization of Land as a Prerequisite for a Democratic Public." *American Journal of Economics and Sociology* 77, no. 1 (January 2018): 169–200.

Fairley, Nan, and Mark Wilson. Chapter One, "From Service to Something Else." In *Living Democracy: Communities as Classrooms, Students as Citizens*, edited by Mindy LaBreck. Dayton, Ohio: Kettering Foundation, 2017. http://ebook central.proquest.com/lib/washington/detail.action?docID=5214874.

Farley, Reynolds, Mick Couper, and Maria Krysan. "Race and Revitalization in the Rust Belt: A Motor City Story." *Michigan Sociological Review* 20 (Fall 2006): 1–67. https://www.jstor.org/stable/40969161.

Finn, Donovan, and Jason Brody. "The State of Community Design: An Analysis of Community Design Center Services." *Journal of Architectural and Planning Research* 31, no. 3 (Autumn 2014): 181–200. https://www.jstor.org/stable/44114603.

Fisher, Teresa A. "If Obesity Is So Bad, Why Are So Many People Fat? Interrogating, Exploring, and Understanding Obesity through Theatre." Unpublished dissertation topic proposal. New York: NYU Steinhardt School of Culture, Education, and Human Development, 2009.

Fitsimmons, Emma G. "In a Crowded New York City, Should Newcomers 'Go Back to Iowa'?" *New York Times*, January 21, 2020.

Frank, Annalise. "Mexicantown Avenue to be Remade as Shared Street." *Crain's Detroit Business* 34, no. 21 (May 28, 2018).

Franklin, Sekou. "Black Youth Activism and the Reconstruction of America: Leaders, Organizations, and Tactics in the Twentieth Century and Beyond." *Black History Bulletin* 79, no. 1 (Spring 2016): 5–14. http://www.jstor.org/stable/10 .5323/blachistbull.79.1.0005.

Freire, Paolo. *Pedagogy of the Oppressed*. Translated by Myra Bergman Ramos. New York: Seabury Press, 1970. Other editions cited include:

———. *Pedagogy of the Oppressed*. New York: Continuum, 1993. https://www.jstor .org/stable/10.7721/chilyoutenvi.17.2.0341;

——. *Pedagogy of the Oppressed.* New York: Continuum, 1994.

——. *Pedagogy of the Oppressed.* New York: Continuum Press, 1996.

——. *Pedagogy of the Oppressed.* New York: Continuum Press, 2000.

——. *Pedagogy of the Oppressed.* 30th anniversary ed. New York: Continuum Press, 2003.

Gieryn, Thomas F. "A Space for Place in Sociology." *Annual Review of Sociology* 26 (2000): 463–96. http://links.jstor.org/sici?sici=0360-0572%282000%2926%3C463%3 AASFPIS%3E2.0.CO%3B2-S.

Gilbert, Claire, and Donald Heller. "The Truman Commission and Its Impact on Federal Higher Education Policy from 1947 to 2010." *Working Paper no. 9.* University Park: Pennsylvania State University, Center for the Study of Higher Education, November 2010.

Ginwright, Shawn A. "Peace Out to Revolution! Activism among African American Youth: An Argument for Radical Healing." *Young* 18, no. 1 (2010): 77–96.

Ginwright, Shawn, and Julio Cammarota. "Youth Activism in the Urban Community: Learning Critical Civic Praxis within Community Organizations." *International Journal of Qualitative Studies in Education* 20, no. 6 (2007): 693–710.

Ginwright, Shawn, Pedro Noguera, and Julio Cammarota, eds. *Beyond Resistance! Youth Activism and Community Change.* Kindle ed. New York: Routledge, 2006.

Giroux, Henry A. *America on the Edge: Henry Giroux on Politics, Culture, and Education.* New York: Palgrave Macmillan, 2006.

——. *On Critical Pedagogy.* New York: Bloomsbury Publishing, 2020. http://ebook central.proquest.com/lib/washington/detail.action?docID=5997010.

Glassman, Michael. "Dewey and Vygotsky: Society, Experience, and Inquiry in Educational Practice." *Educational Researcher* 30, no. 4 (May 2001): 3–14. http://www.jstor.com/stable/3594354.

Goldsmith, William W. "From the Metropolis to Globalization: The Dialectics of Race and Urban Form." In *Globalizing Cities: A New Spatial Order,* edited by Peter Marcuse and Ronald van Kempen, 37–55. Oxford: Blackwell Publishers, 2000.

Goldstein, Brian D. *The Roots of Urban Renaissance: Gentrification and the Struggle Over Harlem.* Cambridge, Mass.: Harvard University Press, 2017.

Guevara, Ariel. "Mirror News: A Solution for Southwest Detroit." *ULOOP Inc.* (February 1, 2016).

Gutiérrez, Kris D., Bryce L. C. Becker, Manuel L. Espinoza, Krista L. Cortes, Arturo Cortez, José Ramón Lizárraga, Edward Rivero, Karen Villegas, and Peng Yin. "Youth as Historical Actors in the Production of Possible Futures." *Mind, Culture, and Activity* 26, no. 4 (2019): 291–308. https://doi.org/10.1080/10749039 .2019.1652327.

Hansen, Gail. "When Students Design Learning Landscapes: Designing for Experiential Learning through Experiential Learning." *NACTA Journal* 56, no. 4 (December 2012): 30–35. https://www.jstor.org/stable/10.2307/nactajournal.56.4.30.

Hardin, Garrett. "The Tragedy of the Commons." *Science* 162, no. 3,859 (December 13, 1968): 1,243–1,248. https://www.jstor.org/stable/1724745.

Harding, Vincent. "Introduction." In Martin Luther King, Jr., *Where Do We Go from Here: Chaos or Community?* Location 19–179. Kindle ed. Boston: Beacon Press, 2010. Originally published in 1968.

Harpham, Geoffrey Galt. "From Eternity to Here: Shrinkage in American Thinking about Higher Education." *Representations* 116, no. 1 (Fall 2011): 42–61.

Harvey, David. Chapter 3, "The Creation of the Urban Commons." In *Rebel Cities: From the Right to the City to the Urban Revolution*, 67–88. London and New York: Verso, 2013.

Heathcote, Dorothy. "Drama as a Process for Change." In *The Applied Theatre Reader*, edited by Tim Prentki and Sheila Preston, 9–15. New York and London: Routledge, 2009.

Heinrich, William F., Geoffrey B. Habron, Heather L. Johnson, and Lissy Goralnik. "Critical Thinking Assess across Four Sustainability-Related Experiential Learning Settings." *Journal of Experiential Education* 38, no. 4 (2015): 373–93.

hooks, bell. *Black Looks: Race and Representation.* Boston: South End Press, 1990.

———. *Killing Rage.* New York: Owl Books, 1995.

———. *Teaching Community: A Pedagogy of Hope.* New York: Routledge, 2003.

———. *Teaching to Transgress: Education as the Practice of Freedom.* New York and London: Routledge, 1994.

Immerwahr, Daniel. "The Death of America's Political Imagination." *New York Times*, Opinion, 4.

Inda, Christy, Anuenue Washburn, Sheila Beckham, Bryan Talisayan, and Desiree Hikuroa. "Home Grown: The Trials and Triumphs of Starting up a Farmers' Market in Wai'anae, Hawai'i." *Community Development* 42, no. 2 (April 1, 2011): 181–92.

Inwood, Joshua F. J. "Searching for the Promised Land: Examining Dr Martin Luther King's Concept of the Beloved Community." *Antipode* 41, no. 3 (2009): 487–508.

Illich, Ivan. *In the Mirror of the Past.* New York: Marion Bayers, 1984.

Jackson, Kenneth T., Lisa Keller, and Nancy V. Flood, eds. "Harlem." In *The Encyclopedia of New York City*, 2nd ed., 573–75. New Haven, Conn.: Yale University Press, 2010. http://www.jstor.org/stable/j.ctt5vm1cb.13.

Jackson, Tambra O., and Tyrone C. Howard. "The Continuing Legacy of Freedom Schools as Sites of Possibility for Equity and Social Justice for Black Students." *Western Journal of Black Studies* 38, no. 3 (2014): 155–62.

Jacobs, Jane. *Systems of Survival: A Dialogue on the Moral Foundations of Commerce and Politics.* New York: Vintage Books, 1994.

Jemal, Alexis. "Critical Consciousness: A Critique and Critical Analysis of the Literature." *Urban Rev* 49 (2017): 602–26.

Jenkins-Dale, Lizabeth. "Soo Theatre Project Announces Ken Miller as Executive Director." *Sault News* Online (March 26, 2016): B2.

Johnson, Kimberley. "Community Development Corporations, Participation, and Accountability: The Harlem Urban Development Corporation and the Bedford-Stuyvesant Restoration Corporation." *Annals of the American Academy of Political and Social Science* 594 (July 2004): 109–24. https://www.jstor.org/stable/4127697.

Joint Center for Housing Studies of Harvard University. "The State of the Nation's Housing 2020." Cambridge, Mass.: Harvard Graduate School of Design / Harvard Kennedy School, 2020. https://www.jchs.harvard.edu/sites/default/files/reports /files/Harvard_JCHS_The_State_of_the_Nations_Housing_2020_Report _Revised_120720.pdf.

Jones, Kenneth R. "Influences of Youth Leadership within a Community-Based Context." *Journal of Leadership Education* 7, no. 3 (Winter 2009): 246–64.

Joseph, Peniel E. "Black Liberation without Apology: Reconceptualizing the Black Power Movement." *Black Scholar* 31, no. 3/4 (Fall/Winter 2001): 2–19. https://www .jstor.org/stable/41069810.

Kaiser, Charles. *1968 in America: Music, Politics, Chaos, Counterculture, and the Shaping of a Generation.* Kindle ed. New York: Weidenfeld & Nicolson, 1988.

Kalman, Laura. *Yale Law School and the Sixties.* Chapel Hill: University of North Carolina Press, 2005.

Keck, Markus, and Patrick Sakdapolrak. "What Is Social Resilience: Lessons Learned and Ways Forward." *Erdkunde* 67, no. 1 (January–March 2013): 5–19. http://www.jstor.org/stable/23595352.

Kauanui, J. Kēhaulani. *Paradoxes of Hawaiian Sovereignty: Land, Sex, and the Colonial Politics of State Nationalism.* Durham, N.C.: Duke University Press, 2018.

Kelley, Robin D. G., and Jeffrey J. Williams. "History and Hope: An Interview with Robin D. G. Kelley." *Minnesota Review*, nos. 58–60 (Spring/Fall 2002–Spring 2003): 93–109.

Kemp, Susan P. "Leaders of Today, Builders of Tomorrow." In *The Paradox of Urban Space: Inequality and Transformation in Marginalized Communities*, edited by Sharon E. Sutton and Susan P. Kemp, 135–56. New York: Palgrave Macmillan, 2011.

Kennedy, Merrit. "Controversial Emergency Manager of Detroit's Public Schools Resigns." *The Two Way*, February 2, 2016. https://www.npr.org/sections/thetwo -way/2016/02/02/465279038/controversial-emergency-manager-of-detroits-public -schools-resigns.

Kilohana, Ke. "Hana Lima: Decolonial Projects and Representations." In *Detours: A Decolonial Guide to Hawai'i*, edited by Hokulani K. Aikau and Vernadette Vicuna Gonzalez, 119–22. Durham, N.C.: Duke University Press, 2019.

King, Martin Luther Jr. *Where Do We Go from Here: Chaos or Community?* Kindle ed. Boston: Beacon Press, 2010. Originally published in 1968.

Kirshner, Ben. *Youth Activism in an Era of Education Inequality.* Kindle ed. New York and London: New York University Press, 2015.

Kolb, David A. *Experiential Learning: Experience as the Source of Learning and Development.* Upper Saddle River, N.J.: Prentice Hall, 1984.

Kruse, Kevin M., and Julian E. Zelizer. *Fault Lines: A History of the United States Since 1974*. New York: W. W. Norton, 2019.

Kwon, Soo Ah. "Moving from Complaints to Action: Oppositional Consciousness and Collective Action in a Political Community." *Anthropology and Education Quarterly* 39, no. 1 (March 2008): 59–76. https://www.jstor.org/stable/25166648.

———. *Uncivil Youth: Race, Activism, and Affirmative Governmentality*. Durham, N.C.: Duke University Press, 2013.

Lappé, Frances Moore, and Paul Martin Du Bois. *The Quickening of America: Rebuilding Our Nation, Remaking Our Lives*. San Francisco: Jossey-Bass Publishers, 1994.

Leis, Anna, M. Susie Whittington, Mark Bennett, and Matthew Kleinhenz. "Student Farms at United States Colleges and Universities: Insights Gained from a Survey of the Farm Managers." *NACTA Journal* 55, no. 1 (March 2011): 9–15. https://www.jstor.org/stable/10.2307/nactajournal.55.1.9.

London, Rebecca A., Manuel Pastor, Lisa J. Servon, Rachel Rosner, and Antwuan Wallace. "The Role of Community Technology Centers in Promoting Youth Development." *Youth & Society* 42, no. 2 (2010): 199–228.

Lye, Colleen, Christopher Newfield, and James Vernon. "Humanists and the Public University." *Representations* 116, no. 1 (Fall 2011): 1–18.

Mansbridge, Jane. "The Making of Oppositional Consciousness." In *Oppositional Consciousness: The Subjective Roots of Social Protest*, edited by Jane Mansbridge and Aldon Morris. Chicago: University of Chicago Press, 2001.

Mansbridge, Jane, and Aldon Morris, eds. *Oppositional Consciousness: The Subjective Roots of Social Protest*. Chicago: University of Chicago Press, 2001.

Marsh, Tyson E. J. "Critical Pedagogy for Black Youth Resistance." *Black History Bulletin* 79, no. 1 (Spring 2016): 14–23. https://www.jstor.org/stable/10.5323/blachistbull.79.1.0014.

Marshall, Wende Elizabeth. *Potent Mana: Lessons in Power and Healing*. Albany: State University of New York Press, 2011. muse.jhu.edu/book/1889.

Marwell, Nicole P. "Privatizing the Welfare State: Nonprofit Community-Based Organizations as Political Actors." *American Sociological Review* 69, no. 2 (April 2004): 265–91. https://www.jstor.org/stable/3593087.

Matlin, Daniel. "Who Speaks for Harlem? Kenneth B. Clark, Albert Murray, and the Controversies of Black Urban Life." *Journal of American Studies* 46, no. 4 (November 2012): 875–94. http://www.jstor.org/.

Mattingly, Doreen. "Place, Teenagers, and Representations: Lessons from a Community Theatre Project." *Social & Cultural Geography* 2, no. 4 (2001): 445–59. https://doi.org/10.1080/14649360120092634.

McEvoy-Levy, Siobhan. "Youth Spaces in Haunted Places: Placemaking for Peacebuilding in Theory and Practice." *International Journal of Peace Studies* 17, no. 2 (Winter 2012): 1–32. http://www.jstor.com/stable/41853033.

McGraw, Bill. "Life in the Ruins of Detroit." *History Workshop Journal*, no. 63 (Spring 2007): 288–302. https://www.jstor.org/stable/25472916.

Mei-Singh, Laurel, and Vernadette Vicuña Gonzalez. "DeTours: Mapping Decolonial Genealogies in Hawai'i." *Critical Ethnic Studies* 3, no. 2 (Fall 2017): 173–92. https://www.jstor.org/stable/10.5749/jcritethnstud.3.2.0173.

Mendenhall, Ruby. "The Political Economy of Black Housing: From the Housing Crisis of the Great Migrations to the Subprime Mortgage Crisis." *Black Scholar* 40, no. 1 (Spring 2010): 20–37. https://www.jstor.org/stable/41163903.

Meyer, Manulani Aluli. "Our Own Liberation: Reflections on Hawaiian Epistemology." *Contemporary Pacific* (Spring 2001): 124–48.

Miller, Isaac Ginsberg. "Place-Branding Detroit: Beloved Community or Big Society?" *Berkeley Journal of Sociology* 60 (2016): 6–17. http://www.jstor.com/stable/44713555. Quoting Malik Yakini, lifelong Detroiter and cofounder of the Detroit Black Community Food Security Network. No source provided.

Montgomery, Alesia. "Reappearance of the Public: Placemaking, Minoritization, and Resistance in Detroit." *International Journal of Urban and Regional Research* (2016): 776–99.

Morton, Matthew H., Amy Dworsky, Jennifer L. Matjasko, Susanna R. Curry, David Schlueter, Raúl Chávez, and Anne F. Farrell. "Prevalence and Correlates of Youth Homelessness in the United States." *Journal of Adolescent Health* 62 (2018): 14–21. https://www.jahonline.org/action/showPdf?pii=S1054-139X%2817%2930503-7.

National Science Foundation. "At a Glance." Alexandria, Va.: National Science Foundation. https://www.nsf.gov/about/glance.jsp.

Nelson, Dana D. "The Enduring Appeal of the Commons." *Arizona Quarterly* 75, no. 2 (Summer 2019): 1–21.

Neumann, Richard. "American Democracy at Risk." *Phi Delta Kappan* 89, no. 5 (January 2008): 328–39. https://www.jstor.org/stable/20442493.

Norris, Fran H. "Behavioral Science Perspectives on Resilience." Unpublished Report Prepared for the Community and Regional Resilience Institute (CARRI). Washington, D.C.: Meridian Institute, June 2010.

Orr, David W. *Earth in Mind: On Education, Environment, and the Human Prospect.* Washington, D.C.: Island Press, 1994.

———. *Ecological Literacy.* Albany: State University of New York Press, 1992.

Ostrom, Elinor. *Governing the Commons: The Evolution of Institutions for Collective Action.* New York: Cambridge University Press, 1990.

"Out of Reach 2020." Washington, D.C.: National Low-Income Housing Coalition, 2020. https://reports.nlihc.org/oor.

Paddeu, Flaminia. "Legalizing Urban Agriculture in Detroit: A Contested Way of Planning for Decline." *Town Planning Review* 88, no. 1 (January–February 2017): 109–29.

Poncelet, Julie Anne Paul. *A Community-Based Grassroots Organization in the South Bronx as a Catalyst for Youth Organizing and Activism: Analyzing the Dynamics of a Transformative Youth Program.* Ann Arbor, Mich.: ProQuest Dissertations Publishing, 2013.

Pratt, Geraldine, and Caleb Johnston. "Turning Theatre into Law, and Other Spaces of Politics." *Cultural Geographies* 14, no. 1 (January 2007): 92–113. https://www.jstor.org/stable/44243683.

Prentki, Tim. "Citizen Artists and Human Becomings." *Journal of Aesthetic Education* 50, no. 2 (Summer 2016): 72–83. https://www.jstor.org/stable/10.5406/jaesteduc.50.2.0072.

Prentki, Tim, and Sheila Preston. "Introduction." In *The Applied Theatre Reader*, edited by Tim Prentki and Sheila Preston, 9–15. New York and London: Routledge, 2009.

Price, Jenny. "Resilience!" *Resilience: A Journal of the Environmental Humanities* 1, no. 1 (January 2, 2014): unnumbered. http://www.jstor.org/stable/10.5250/resilience.1.1.16.

"Read the Full Transcript of President Obama's Farewell Speech." *Los Angeles Times*, January 10, 2017. https://www.latimes.com/politics/la-pol-obama-farewell-speech-transcript-20170110-story.html.

Rhoades, Mindi. "LGBTQ Youth + Video Artivism: Arts-Based Critical Civic Praxis." *Studies in Art Education* 53, no. 4 (Summer 2012): 317–32. https://www.jstor.org/stable/24467920.

Robertson, Stephen, Shane White, Stephen Garton, and Graham White. "This Harlem Life: Black Families and Everyday Life in the 1920s and 1930s." *Journal of Social History* 44, no. 1 (Fall 2010): 97–122. http://www.jstor.org/stable/40802110.

Robinson, Martin. "Drama." In *What Should Schools Teach? Disciplines, Subjects and the Pursuit of Truth*, edited by Alka Sehgal Cuthbert and Alex Standish, 89–102. London: UCL Press, 2021. https://www.jstor.org/stable/j.ctv14t475s.

Rodriguez, Maria Elena. *Images of America: Detroit's Mexicantown*. Charleston, S.C.: Arcadia Publishing, 2011.

Rothstein, Richard. *The Color of Law: A Forgotten History of How Our Government Segregated America*. Kindle ed. New York and London: Liveright Publishing, 2017.

Rule, Sheila. "Some Ex-Residents Keep Coming Home to Harlem: Harlem Is an Attitude." *New York Times*. ProQuest Historical Newspapers: *New York Times*, December 7, 1980.

Saar, Maarja, and Hannes Palang. "The Dimensions of Place Meanings." *Living Review of Landscape Research* 3 (2009): 5–24. Online article: cited July 2021. http://www.livingreviews.org/lrlr-2009-3.

Saltmarsh, John, and Matthew Hartley, eds. *To Serve a Larger Purpose: Engagement for Democracy and the Transformation of Higher Education*. Philadelphia: Temple University Press, 2011.

Schachter, Judith. *The Legacies of a Hawaiian Generation*. New York and Oxford: Berghahn Books, 2013.

Schneekloth, Lynda H., and Robert G. Shibley. *Placemaking: The Art and Practice of Building Communities*. New York: Wiley, 1995.

Sengupta, Somini. "Climate Strike N.Y.C.: Young Crowds Demand Action, Welcome Greta Thunberg." *New York Times*, September 20, 2019. https://www.nytimes.com

/2019/09/20/nyregion/climate-strike-nyc.html?action=click&module=Related
Links&pgtype=Article.

Shiller, Jessica T. "Preparing for Democracy: How Community-Based Organizations
Build Civic Engagement among Urban Youth." *Urban Education* 48, no. 1 (2013):
69–91.

Steele, Fritz. *The Sense of Place.* Boston: CBI Publishing, 1981.

Stephens, Alexis. "Lessons on Collaborative Practice between Artists and Community Developers." *Community Development Innovation Review* (November 13,
2019), unnumbered. https://www.frbsf.org/community-development/publications
/community-development-investment-review/2019/november/lessons-on
-collaborative-practice-between-artists-and-community-developers/.

Stoneman, Dorothy. "The Role of Youth Programming in the Development of Civic
Engagement." *Applied Developmental Science* 6, no. 4 (2002): 221–26.

Sutton, Sharon Egretta. "Afterword." In *Teaching and Designing in Detroit: Ten
Women on Pedagogy and Practice,* edited by Stephen Vogel and Libby Balter
Blume, 183–88. New York and London: Routledge, 2019.

———. "Sharon Sutton: Envisioning a Communitarian World House." *Architect
Magazine,* June 5, 2020. https://www.architectmagazine.com/practice/sharon
-sutton-envisioning-a-communitarian-world-house_o.

Sutton, Sharon E., and Susan P. Kemp. "Children's Participation in Constructing a
Socially Just Public Sphere. In *Children and Their Environments: Learning,
Using, and Designing Spaces,* edited by Mark Blades and Christopher Spencer,
256–76. Cambridge: Cambridge University Press, 2005.

———. "Introduction: Place as Marginality and Possibility." In Sutton and Kemp,
*Paradox of Urban Space,* 1–10.

———. "Place: A Site of Individual and Collective Transformation." In Sutton and
Kemp, *Paradox of Urban Space,* 121–22.

———, eds. *The Paradox of Urban Space: Inequality and Transformation in Marginalized Communities.* New York: Palgrave Macmillan, 2011.

Sutton, Sharon E., Susan P. Kemp, Lorraine Gutiérrez, and Susan Saegert.
*Urban Youth Programs in America: A Study of Youth, Community, and Social
Justice Conducted for the Ford Foundation.* Seattle: University of Washington,
2006.

Sturkey, William. "'I Want to Become a Part of History': Freedom Summer,
Freedom Schools, and the Freedom News." *Journal of African American History*
95, no. 3–4 (Summer–Fall 2010): 348–68. https://www.jstor.org/stable/10.5323
/jafriamerhist.95.3-4.0348.

———. "The 1964 Mississippi Freedom Schools." *Mississippi History Now.* Feature
Story, May 2016. Unnumbered. http://www.mshistorynow.mdah.ms.gov/articles
/403/The-1964-Mississippi-Freedom-Schools.

Thomas, June Manning. "Neighborhood Response to Redevelopment in Detroit."
*Community Development Journal* 20, no. 2 (April 1985): 89–98. https://www.jstor
.org/stable/44256327/.

Thomas, R. Elizabeth, and Julian Rappaport. "Art as Community Narrative: A Resource for Social Change." In *Myths about the Powerless: Contesting Social Inequality*, edited by M. Lykes Brinton, Ali Banuazizi, Ramsey Liem, and Michael Morris, 317–36. Philadelphia: Temple University Press, 1996.

Toolis, Erin E. "Theorizing Critical Placemaking as a Tool for Reclaiming Public Space." *American Journal of Community Psychology* 59 (2017): 184–99.

Trinidad, Alma M. O. "Sociopolitical Development through Critical Indigenous Pedagogy of Place: Preparing Native Hawaiian Young Adults to Become Change Agents." *Hūlili: Multidisciplinary Research on Hawaiian Well-Being* 7 (2011): 185–221.

Tyner-Mullings, Alia R. "Central Park East Secondary School: Teaching and Learning through Freire." *Schools: Studies in Education* 9, no. 2 (Fall 2012): 227–45. https://www.jstor.org/stable/10.1086/667919.

United States Census Bureau. "1990 Census of Population: Social and Economic Characteristics—Wyoming." Washington, D.C.: U.S. Department of Commerce, Economics and Statistics Administration. https://www2.census.gov/library /publications/decennial/1990/cp-2/cp-2-52.pdf.

United States Census Bureau. "Quick Facts: Detroit City, Michigan; Michigan," 1–3. Washington, D.C.: United States Census Bureau. https://www.census.gov /quickfacts/fact/table/detroitcitymichigan,MI/PST045219.

United States Department of Commerce. "Waiʻanae Ecological Characterization." Community Report, DZM Hawaiʻi and National Oceanic and Atmospheric Administration.

Villarosa, Linda. "'A Terrible Price': The Deadly Racial Disparities of Covid-19 in America." *New York Times*, April 29, 2020. https://www.nytimes.com/2020/04/29 /magazine/racial-disparities-covid-19.html.

Watson, Trisha Kehaulani. *Ho'i Hou iā Papahānaumoku: A History of Eco-Colonization in the Pu'uhonua of Wai'anae*. Ann Arbor, Mich.: ProQuest Dissertations and Theses, 2008.

Westheimer, Joel, and Joseph Kahne. "What Kind of Citizen? The Politics of Educating for Democracy." *American Educational Research Journal* 41, no. 2 (2004): 237–69.

Wilder, Craig Steven. *Ebony and Ivy: Race, Slavery, and the Troubled History of America's Universities*. Kindle ed. London and New York: BloomsburyPublishing, 2013.

Willis, Paul. *Learning to Labor: How Working-Class Kids Get Working-Class Jobs*. New York: Columbia University Press, 1977.

Woodson, Stephani Etheridge. "Performing Youth: Youth Agency and the Production of Knowledge in Community-Based Theater." In *Representing Youth: Methodological Issues in Critical Youth Studies*, edited by Amy L. Best, 284–303. New York and London: New York University Press, 2007. http://www.jstor.com /stable/j.ctt9qgopf.16.

# Index

Academe, 19–20, 21; collective action and, 144–147, 156–160, 167; collective agency and, 140–144, 154–156, 166; collectivity and, 142; commons and, 20, 21, 135, 164, 165, 168, 170–171, 182; community revitalization and, 178–179; critical awareness and, 136–140, 151–154; critical placemaking and, 170–171; critical thinking and, 154–155; empowerment and, 134–135; future visions for, 160–162; historical context of, 129–135; mind-centric critical pedagogy and, 163–167, 164; organizational stability and, 187–188; place agency and, 169–170; place awareness and, 168; place-based activism and, 167–168, 172; self-worth and, 136–137; social justice and, 139–140; staff, 133–134; strengths sand shortcomings of, 149–151; worldview and, 137–139
activism: capitalism and, 12; democracy and, 7; dwelling and, 14; emotional realm of, 18, 21; intellectual realm of, 19–20, 21; physical realm of, 18–19, 21; youth, 5–6. *See also* place-based activism
aesthetic vision, 35–36
African Americans: education and, 163–165; in Harlem, 129; homelessness among, 3; intelligentsia, 168; segregation of, 129–130. *See also* racism
agency: creation of, through knowledge, 155–156; critical awareness and, 155–156; place, 12, 13, 66–67, 72n7, 115, 164; revealing opportunities for, 104–105. *See also* collective agency
agriculture: urban, 69–70. *See also* Hoʻoulu ʻŌpio Farms
aloha ʻāina, 19, 77, 84, 98, 102, 111–113, 118, 119, 122, 182
Americorp, vii
attitudinal dimension, 10, 11, 12, 18, 21

Baldwin, James, 165
behavioral dimension, 10–11, 11, 12, 19, 63, 122, 185
Black Lives Matter, ix, 5–6
Black Power Movement, 165
Boal, Augusto, 62, 64
Boggs Center, 68–69
Boggs, Grace Lee, 5, 11–12, 117, 118
Brazil, 61–62
Bush, George W., vii

capitalism, 71, 153; global, 12, 121,169, 189; neoliberal, 68, 71, 121–122
Capitol insurrection, x
CBOs. *See* community-based organizations (CBOs)
CDCs. *See* community development corporations (CDCs)
celebration(s), 13, 52–53, 69, 99
Cisneros, Sandra, 34–35
Civil Rights movement, 6, 12, 60
cognitive, 10; 61, 184; abilities, 66; dimension, 10, 11, 12, 20, 62, 171, 185; skills, 42

Sʜᴀʀᴏɴ Eɢʀᴇᴛᴛᴀ Sᴜᴛᴛᴏɴ is an educator, licensed architect, and outspoken champion for improving disinvested communities. An early pioneer in moving the field of architecture toward equity and inclusion, she is currently Distinguished Visiting Professor of Architecture at Parsons School of Design. Sutton has written several books; her most recent publication is *When Ivory Towers Were Black: A Story about Race in America's Cities and Universities* (Fordham, 2017).

www.ingramcontent.com/pod-product-compliance
Lightning Source LLC
Chambersburg PA
CBHW020250030426
42336CB00010B/704